Northwest

TOP 10

GARDEN GUIDE

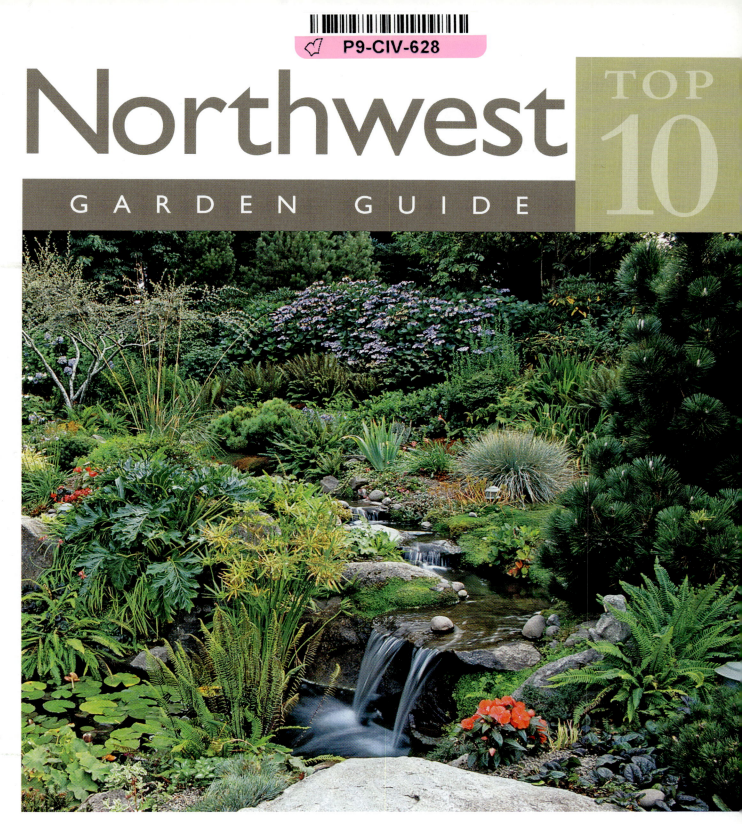

Edited by Fiona Gilsenan and the Editors of Sunset Books

Principal Photography by Robin Bachtler Cushman

MENLO PARK · CALIFORNIA

SUNSET BOOKS, INC.

VICE PRESIDENT, GENERAL MANAGER: Richard A. Smeby
VICE PRESIDENT, EDITORIAL DIRECTOR: Bob Doyle
PRODUCTION DIRECTOR: Lory Day
OPERATIONS DIRECTOR: Rosann Sutherland
RETAIL SALES DEVELOPMENT MANAGER: Linda Barker
EXECUTIVE EDITOR: Bridget Biscotti Bradley
ART DIRECTOR: Vasken Guiragossian
SPECIAL SALES: Brad Moses

STAFF FOR THIS BOOK

MANAGING EDITOR: Fiona Gilsenan
SENIOR EDITOR: Tom Wilhite
SUNSET BOOKS SENIOR EDITOR: Marianne Lipanovich
COPY EDITORS: Julie Harris, Rebecca LaBrum
ASSOCIATE EDITOR: Carrie Dodson Davis
DESIGN & PRODUCTION: Maureen Spuhler
ADDITIONAL PAGE PRODUCTION: Linda M. Bouchard
PREPRESS COORDINATOR: Danielle Javier
PROOFREADER: Pam Cornelison
INDEXER: Erin Hartshorn
ILLUSTRATORS: Lois Lovejoy, Erin O'Toole, and Jane Shasky
MAP ILLUSTRATOR: Jane Shasky

COVER: Photograph by Robin Bachtler Cushman.
Design by Vasken Guiragossian.

10 9 8 7 6 5 4 3 2 1

First printing January 2005
Copyright © 2005 Sunset Publishing Corporation,
Menlo Park, CA 94025.

Library of Congress Control Number: 2004109879.
ISBN 0-376-03531-5.

Printed in the United States.

For additional copies of *Northwest Top 10 Garden Guide*
or any other Sunset book, call 1-800-526-5111 or visit
our web site at www.sunsetbooks.com.

CONSULTANTS

BARBARA BLOSSOM ASHMUN (*Ground Covers*) is a garden journalist
and author in Portland, OR.

SAM BENOWITZ (*Edibles*) has been for 32 years the owner of
Raintree Nursery in Morton, WA.

JIM BROCKMEYER (*Ornamental Grasses*) is the owner of Bluestem
Nursery in Christina Lake, B.C.

ED CHAVEZ (*Roses*) is a rose specialist for Minter's Earlington
Greenhouse Nursery in Seattle, WA.

VALERIE EASTON (*Vines*) is a garden columnist, journalist, and author
based on Whidbey Island, WA.

SEAN HOGAN (*Shrubs*) is an author and editor and the owner of the
nursery and design firm, Cistus Design, in Sauvie Island, OR.

PATRICIA HOLLOWAY (*Annuals*) is a horticulture professor at the University
of Alaska in Fairbanks, and director of the Georgeson Botanical Garden.

ED HUME (*Perennials*) is an author, lecturer, and radio and television
personality. He is the owner of Ed Hume Seeds in Kent, WA.

ARTHUR LEE JACOBSON (*Trees*) is an author, lecturer, educator, and
plant expert in Seattle, WA.

STEVE LORTON is Northwest bureau chief for *Sunset* magazine.

JIM MCCAUSLAND (*Bulbs*) is a longtime writer for *Sunset* magazine
and Sunset Books. He lives in Port Orchard, WA.

VALERIE MURRAY (*Evergreen Trees*) is Head Gardener at the Abkhazi
Garden in Victoria, B.C.

PHOTOGRAPHERS

*UNLESS OTHERWISE NOTED, ALL PHOTOGRAPHS ARE BY ROBIN BACHTLER
CUSHMAN.* COURTESY OF DAVID AUSTIN ROSES: 187 B; DAVID
CAVAGNARO: 140 TL, 147 ALL; LAURA DUNKIN-HUBBY: 3 BL, 44 C, 55 BL,
55 BR, 171 B, 191 B; FIONA GILSENAN: 35 B, 37 B R, 50, 51 ALL, 54, 55 B C,
81 T, 85 B, 92 BL, 100, 112, 113 B, 134, 135 T, 145 B, 148, 149 ALL, 183 BL,
203 B, 223 B, 229 BL, 229 R, 232, 235 BL, 235 TR, 235 BR, 243 B, 263;
DAVID GOLDBERG: 5; LYNNE HARRISON: 36, 37 BL, 37 T, 91 T, 101 B, 111
ALL, 119 B, 135 C, 135 B, 146, 153 B, 157 B, 192 BC, 192 BR, 193 T, 194 L,
195 T, 196 BL, 196 R, 197, 198 B R, 203 TL, 208, 209 TR, 209 B, 211 C, 211
B, 216, 217 TR, 217 B, 218, 219 TR, 219 B, 224, 225 TR, 225 B, 233 TC, 233
BC, 233 B, 247, 251, 256; JERRY PAVIA: 242, 243 C; NORMAN A. PLATE: 3 BR,
68 C, 234, 244 TL; SUSAN A. ROTH: 3 LBC, 108, 109 BR, 238 ALL, 239 B,
262; THOMAS J. STORY: 73 L, 257 T; PADDY WALES: 37 BC, 101 T, 118; TOM
WOODWARD: 22 T L, 46 TL, 70 TL, 92 C, 94 TL, 116 TL, 138 C, 162 TL, 184 C,
200 TL, 222 TL.

GARDEN DESIGN

ALSEA RIVER GARDENS: 1, 143 B, 155; BALTZER'S SPECIALIZED NURSERY:
214 B, 223 T; LIZ DECK: 46; CINDEE EICHENGREEN: 185 T; FAIRIE
PERENNIAL & HERB GARDEN: 38, 130; RACHEL FOSTER: 9, 22, 23 L, 57 L,
66, 95, 138 B, 150, 158, 165 ALL, 187; GARDEN ARTSCAPES: 44 T, 114,
139 B, 141 T; GOSSLER FARMS NURSERY: 3 TC, 58 B, 125 BC, 179 ALL, 220;
GREER GARDENS: 8; JOSEF HALDA: 237 TC; LADY BUG FARM: 107 T; LOG
HOUSE PLANTS: 28, 71, 92 T, 107 B, 145 T; ANN LOVEJOY: 144, 153 T;
MARY-KATE MACKEY: 210; CHRISTIANE MALO: 30; NORTHWEST GARDEN
NURSERY: 7, 29 B, 68 T, 124, 140, 228; BRAD STANGELAND: 32, 139 T;
ULUM & BARRETT: 160, 227 B.

SPECIAL THANKS TO: Edward Buyarski, American Primrose Society.
Harry Landers, Portland Rose Gardens. Don Julien, Seattle Rose Society.
Dr. Robert Norton, Professor Emeritus, Washington State University.

TOP 10

Contents

Northwest Gardening

Chances are, if you've got this book in your hands, you already garden in the Pacific Northwest. If you don't realize how blessed that makes you, pause now to thank fate.

This is a rich corner of the planet for gardening. From the banana belt down on the southern Oregon coast all the way up through the mossy, fern-carpeted forests of Washington, over the Cascade Mountains to the arid Inland Empire, and on to frosty Alaska, nature gives us the inspiration to garden in a variety of styles and settings. And to our great good fortune, the Northwest also abounds with talented and dedicated experts who travel the world looking for new and exciting plants and scour our own wild lands for undiscovered treasures. Universities in places as diverse as Seattle, Fairbanks, and Vancouver conduct trials to find the absolute best plant choices for each region, while plant breeders work to develop new varieties of old favorites. And creative gardeners open the gates of their gardens—both private and public—so that visitors can marvel at their labors of love.

OPPOSITE PAGE: *A beautiful blend of cool tones, this peaceful garden scene includes lavender and sage in the foreground, a rhododendron and coreopsis behind, and an arching spray of Rosa glauca.*

WHERE TO START?

For gardeners just starting out, all this abundance can be overwhelming. The latest version of Sunset's *Western Garden Book,* for instance, describes more than 8,000 plants. How on earth can you narrow it down to the one you need to fill that bare spot by the back door?

I know about this feeling of bewilderment firsthand. I grew up in the farm country of western Ohio, and I can't remember a time when almost everyone around me wasn't growing something: beans, corn, or wheat as cash crops; vegetables for the dinner table; petunias and zinnias for window boxes;

geraniums and roses for garden urns; and periwinkle for summer porches and ancestral graves. So I thought I knew a thing or two about plants. But when I arrived in Seattle (more years ago than I care to admit), I was dumbfounded by the number of species I saw around me—ten times more than I knew from my youth. I had looked forward to gardening under towering evergreens and the delicate filigree of vine maples, but palm trees? Indeed, windmill palm *(Trachycarpus fortunei)* was thriving. And what was that beautiful low shrub with tiny, bell-shaped flowers and fruits like glowing red jewels? I learned it was kinnikinnick *(Arctostaphylos uva-ursi),* and since that time my garden has never been without one.

COMMON GROUND

But what, you might ask, does a gardener in Yakima or Bend have in common with somebody in Portland or Seattle? East of the mountains, one might spend a weekend cultivating a rock garden, pruning sage, or amending alkaline soil. On the west side, one might tend sweeps of perennials or plant rhododendrons and azaleas in soil so acidic it smells like overripe strawberries. What is the connection? The

answer lies in two facets of the Northwest gardener's spirit. First, both are responding to a natural environment so beautiful that they can't resist taking part in it—whether mimicking it, modifying it, or just bringing it a little closer to home. And second, both gardeners have adopted a pioneering attitude that says, "I got all the way out (or up) here, and I'm going to put down roots and surround myself with lasting beauty." Given all that we have to work with, it's hardly a mystery that so many people spend a lifetime gardening so beautifully.

This book is a good place to start your own Northwest gardening journey. We've made it easy for you by dividing the book into sections covering all categories of garden plants, from tiny bulbs to tall trees, from climbing vines to spreading ground covers. Then we've selected the Top 10 plants for each category. What makes them the Top 10? They are the easiest to grow, the hardiest, and the most disease-resistant plants for the Northwest—plus they're good-looking and widely available. Finally, we tell you all you need to know about successfully growing these favorites in your garden.

A GARDENER'S EDUCATION

At this point in life, I have two very different gardens—both quintessentially northwestern. My city garden includes a floriferous third-floor deck that overlooks a bustling, tree-lined marketplace in Seattle. And I have a house with 10 garden-filled acres in the Upper Skagit Valley. Both of my gardens are so crowded with plants that my more erudite horticultural pals always try to edit them—but I won't let

LEFT: Many of our Top 10 plants hail from diverse and far-flung places. Here a Japanese maple is paired with an English-bred 'Exbury Orange' azalea. ABOVE: This pretty sweep of lawn is bordered with many of our Top 10 plants, including giant feather grass (left), balls of boxwood, clematis vines, and hardy geraniums.

them remove a single seedling! On the other hand, when they fuss at me, I do listen. Gardening is, after all, an adventure in learning. And thanks to my job as Northwest bureau chief of *Sunset* magazine, I've been able to learn from many remarkable gardeners. With the great English gardener Rosemary Verey, I trudged up into the woods to collect our native sword fern *Polystichum munitum,* which she said she loved as much as any plant. Nancy Davidson, who hired me at *Sunset,* instilled in me the joys of generosity and an aversion to plant snobbery, saying, "Any plant worth growing is worth sharing." The overriding message

from innovators like Valerie Easton and Sean Hogan, both of whom have contributed to this book, is that eclecticism and good garden bones are not mutually exclusive. And the wonderful Ed Hume shares his endless enthusiasm for plants with me—and in these pages— with the same knowledge and style he's always shown. The list of gardening friends and mentors goes on and on.

All these people and experiences have taught me that gardening is really nothing more than choosing a few favored plants and putting them where they'll thrive. But these simple steps can lead to something almost too magical to describe. Along with being colorful, fragrant, leafy, sculptural, and full of bloom—all the interesting and beautiful things that gardens are supposed to be—a garden is a stage upon which some of the most important scenes in life are played out. I remember the time when, just as guests were arriving for one of our first dinner parties, my wife, Anna Lou, realized to her horror that we didn't have enough plates, and so we would have to wash dishes between courses. But husband and gardener came to the rescue by rushing out and plucking half a dozen big, flat, glossy leaves from a *Fatsia japonica* to make elegant green plates for her bright salad of raisins and shredded carrots. I recall the awe I felt when a rare great gray owl landed on our burn pile one winter afternoon, and the joy I experienced as friends from China gleefully picked apples and berries. I remember my son's godfather, Poppo, harvesting tomatoes and biting into the warm, red fruit right there in the garden. I can't forget the scent of sweet bay *(Magnolia virginiana)* on a summer night when the Washington sky was a blaze of brilliant stars. And I think of my wife pointing to an old orange tiger lily and saying, "That makes me think of Mother."

Northwest gardens cast a spell. They really do. Use this book to start creating your own garden magic, an adventure that will provide you with pictures and feelings that are forever recalled by the sight or scent or feel of a particular plant. Perhaps someday you'll come to my garden or invite me to yours. We'll create a shared memory—and perhaps we'll pause to thank fate for bringing us here to the gardening paradise that is the Northwest. —STEVE LORTON

Seasonal Chores

Thanks to the Northwest's mild climate, there's nearly always something to do or enjoy in the garden—whether in your own yard, or on a visit to a nursery or public garden nearby. Even when it's snowy or rainy outside, you can plan for future floral extravaganzas. This season-by-season guide will help you keep everything in peak condition.

Spring

BULBS Plant summer-flowering bulbs like crocosmia and lily.

VINES Set out vines like akebia and late-blooming clematis.

ORNAMENTAL GRASSES In dry parts of the garden, plant blue oat grass and feather grass; for wetter areas, plant Japanese forest grass and sedges.

BERRIES AND FRUIT In zones 4–7 and 17, plant trees and canes from nursery containers.

SHRUBS AND TREES After the last frost, plant deciduous and evergreen types. In cold zones, plant lilac and rhododendron in midspring.

ANNUALS Look for pansies and poppies at the nursery. After the last frost, plant summer annuals like cornflower, flowering tobacco, and impatiens.

VEGETABLES In zones 4–7 and 17, plant cool-season crops like lettuce in early spring. Elsewhere, wait for midspring.

BARE-ROOT ROSES As soon as the soil can be worked, plant bare-root roses, but wait until after the last frost to plant container-grown roses.

PERENNIALS In zones 4–7 and 17, plant and divide perennials and groundcovers. Elsewhere,

LEFT: *Spring brings forth the blossoms of flowering tree and bulbs.* ABOVE: *Cheerful crocus are one of the season's first delights.*

wait until growth starts. Divide spring-bloomers just after flowering.

SHRUBS Sprinkle a controlled-release fertilizer or organic compost around shrubs.

HOW TO DIVIDE PERENNIALS

If you noticed during the growing season that some of your perennials were dying out at the center, flowering less, or tending to flop over, they are probably overcrowded and need to be divided.

1 Choose a cool, overcast day and, working with one clump at a time, dig up the entire root ball.

2 Remove excess soil from the root ball so you can see what you're doing. Use your fingers for small, delicate plants. For larger ones, shake or hose off as much of the soil as possible.

3 For most perennials you'll need a knife or sharp spade to cut off divisions. For plants like hostas that form big clumps, use the two-fork method: shove the garden forks back to back into the top of the root ball and pry the clump apart.

4 Replant the divisions immediately and water them well.

VEGETABLES While soil is still cool, feed growing vegetables with a liquid fertilizer.

BULBS After daffodils and other spring bulbs finish blooming, fertilize them lightly and keep watering until leaves die back.

HERBS Cut back perennial herbs such as sage and thyme to encourage new growth.

HEDGES Shear them so that the bottom is slightly wider than the top, which allows light to reach the whole plant.

ROSES In early spring, cut out any dead or crossing canes, then prune hybrid teas and old roses back by about a third. Remove old, unproductive canes of climbing roses. Feed all rose types now with a commercial rose food.

LILACS After bloom, remove spent flowers, damaged growth, and any suckers. Cut back a few of the oldest stems on mature plants to encourage more flowers.

PESTS Bait for slugs as they emerge from hiding in spring, and keep up with the job. Spray aphids off of tender new growth with a jet of water from the hose; treat more severe infestations with insecticidal soap.

MULCH Renew mulch in all areas. For plants that thrive on fertile soil, enrich the mulch with some compost.

GARDENS TO VISIT Rock-garden enthusiasts will want to make a springtime visit to Ohme Gardens in Wenatchee, WA; Berry Botanic Garden in Portland, OR; and Siskiyou Rare Plant Nursery in Medford, OR.

To see vast fields of daffodils and tulips in bloom (and order a few for yourself), take a trip to Roosengaarde in Mt. Vernon, WA; Van Lierop Bulb Farm in Puyallup, WA; or Wooden Shoe Tulip Farm in Mt. Angel, OR.

If rhododendrons are your thing, don't miss the spring shows at Washington's Meerkerk Gardens (Whidbey Island), Whitney Gardens and Nursery (Brinnon), or the Washington Park Arboretum (Seattle). In Oregon, visit the Shore Acres State Park (Newport) and Crystal Springs Rhododendron Garden (Portland). A springtime visit to Victoria, B. C., wouldn't be complete without touring the newly restored Abkhazi Garden and the colorful Butchart Gardens.

Spring in the Northwest brings an explosion of iris blooms around a pond.

Summer

PERENNIALS Plant late-summer bloomers like coreopsis.

BULBS In zones 4–7 and 17, plant cyclamen bulbs.

BEARDED IRIS Stop watering overcrowded plants early in summer; at the end of July, trim back leaves into fans, then divide the rhizomes.

Let them heal in the shade for a day, then replant.

ANNUALS Plant seedlings of coleus, impatiens, marigolds, petunias, and zinnias.

EDIBLES Set out seedlings of squash and tomato in early summer, once soil has warmed. For a fall harvest, plant bush

beans, peas, and lettuce and other salad greens.

PERENNIALS Pick or deadhead flowers every few days to stimulate continued bloom. Stake tall or floppy plants. After bloom stops on peonies and penstemons, cut the flowering stems all the way back.

LOBELIA Cut back these annuals by half when the blossoms fade; feed plants with a balanced fertilizer for a second flush of bloom.

VINES Keep an eye out for wayward or tangled growth and trim it out.

TREES Thin and shape spring-blooming trees, if needed.

EVERGREENS Trim spruces to improve their shape in mid-summer; yew trees are best clipped in late summer.

BERRIES AND VEGETABLES Keep up production by harvesting every second or third day.

HERBS Snip leaves and stems early in the morning, just after the dew has dried.

LAVENDER After bloom, shear back plants by one half.

COMPOST Combine non-meat kitchen waste and garden debris and add to the pile (except for diseased plant parts, and weeds with seed heads or persistent bulbs). Turn and moisten the pile each week to help it break down into rich compost for your vegetable beds.

SLUGS AND SNAILS Apply a little bait in the cool, shaded parts of the garden, or hand-pick the pests in the evening or after a rainfall.

IRRIGATE Water early in the morning to minimize evap-

LEFT: Summer is when roses are in full, glorious bloom. This casual shrub rose border features favorites like 'Gertrude Jekyll' and 'Reine Victoria'. RIGHT: Hot summer zinnias.

oration. Soak moisture-loving shrubs like rhododendrons and camellias every 7 to 10 days, and spray their foliage to wash off dust and help them better absorb water.

GARDENS TO VISIT See the year's first heavy flush of roses in June at Minter Gardens in Chilliwack, B.C.; The Oregon Garden in Silverton, OR; or Manito Park in Spokane, WA.

Stroll through the Japanese Garden in Portland, OR; the Yashiro Japanese Garden in Olympia, WA; or the Kubota Gardens in Seattle, WA. Enjoy Chinese style in Vancouver, B.C., at the Dr. Sun Yat Sen Classical Chinese Garden or in Oregon, at the Portland Classical Chinese Garden.

HOW TO STAKE VARIOUS PLANTS

Support thin-stemmed, bushy perennials with a grid-style stake (upper left) or stakes and string (bottom left). Tie tall plants to a bamboo stake (right).

Autumn

GROUNDCOVERS Plant cotoneaster, bishop's hat, kinnikinnick, knotweed, and lily turf.

TREES Shop for trees with colorful fall foliage, such as maples, ginkgo, katsura tree, and sourwood.

SHRUBS Plant now so winter rains help settle them in, especially Northwest native shrubs, many of which resent too much summer water.

EVERGREENS It's a good time to plant false cypress, hemlock, holly, Japanese cryptomeria, pine, spruce, and yew.

VEGETABLES In early September in zones 4–7 and 17, set out cool-season types from nursery cell-packs, such as lettuce and other salad greens.

PERENNIALS Set out perennial ferns and grasses, as well as flowering plants like daylily, euphorbia, hellebore, penstemon, and bare-root peonies. Right after bloom, divide fall-flowering perennials, or wait until spring to do it.

SEDGES In mild areas, cut back evergreen types for a new flush of leaves; elsewhere, do it in spring.

CARPET BUGLE Renew spent plants by trimming with a mower at its highest setting.

BULBS Plant spring-flowering bulbs, such as allium, camass, daffodil, fritillary, and tulip.

CLARKIA Sow seeds in mild-winter areas; wait until spring in colder zones.

ANNUALS Set out colorful pansies, poppies, and violas. When frost nips annuals, just pull them up, shake the soil off the roots, and toss them in the compost. In warmer zones, shear off spent flowers and fertilize plants one last time to keep blooms coming until frost.

VINES Plant container-grown vines such as akebia, winter jasmine, and ornamental kiwi.

LILACS In colder zones, prepare lilacs for winter by reducing water from early fall.

ROSES Stop feeding roses when the weather cools. After fall bloom, leave some spent blossoms in place to form hips.

JAPANESE MAPLES Prune them in early fall in mild-winter areas, or from summer to the end of January where temperatures remain below freezing.

CANE BERRIES Prune June-bearing raspberries to the ground when they've finished fruiting and start to look withered. For everbearing berry

HOW TO PLANT A TREE OR SHRUB SOLD IN A CONTAINER

1 Remove the plant from its container by placing the container on its side and rolling it on the ground while tapping it to loosen the roots from the insides. Upend the container and slide the plant out. Spray the soil with a strong jet of water to loosen any roots that may be matted or coiled, then untangle them with your fingers. You may have to cut badly coiled roots.

2 Dig a planting hole twice as wide as but no deeper than the root ball. The plant should sit an inch or so above the surrounding soil. Spread the roots wide so they are pointing outward as much as possible. Backfill the hole with the original garden soil. (Amending the soil will only encourage the roots to circle around the plant instead of probing outward for nutrients, and slow down the process of adapting to the new site.)

3 Mound soil to create a ridge around the plant to direct water to the roots. The trunk should not be directly exposed to water or it may rot.

plants, cut back the top half of the canes that have fruited this year.

COVER CROP Enrich your vegetable beds by sowing crimson clover or vetch. Till them under in spring, about a month before planting time.

IRRIGATION Keep watering your garden until fall rains take over the job. Deeply irrigate even well-established trees and shrubs.

GARDENS TO VISIT Experience the delight of dahlias in September by visiting Swan Island Dahlias in Canby, OR; Connell's Dahlias in Tacoma, WA; or the Horticulture Centre of the Pacific in Victoria, B.C. September is also the best month to view the world-famous giant vegetables at the Georgeson Botanical Garden in Fairbanks, AK. October is a great time to visit the many first-class wineries located throughout the Northwest. Want to see fiery leaves on a lush green carpet? You can see both fall foliage color and incomparable moss gardens at the Bloedel Reserve (Bainbridge Island, WA) and the Alaska Botanical Garden in Anchorage, AK. Visit county fairs, agricultural shows, and fall harvest celebrations in rural communities everywhere.

HOW TO PLANT A BARE-ROOT SHRUB

1 Make a firm cone of soil in the planting hole. Spread the roots over the cone, positioning the plant at the same depth as (or slightly higher than) it was in the growing field. Use a shovel handle or yardstick to check the depth.

2 Hold the plant upright as you firm soil around its roots. When backfilling is almost complete, add water. This settles the soil around the roots, eliminating any air pockets. If the plant settles below the level of the surrounding soil, pump it up and down while the soil is saturated to raise it to the proper level.

3 Finish filling the hole with soil, then water again. Take care not to overwater while the plant is still dormant, since soggy soil may inhibit the formation of new roots. When the growing season begins, build up a ridge of soil around the planting site to form a basin that will keep water from running off; water the plant whenever the top 2 inches of soil is dry.

Winter

HARDY ANNUALS In February, sow godetia, pansy, and poppy directly into the garden in mild areas, or wait until March to plant seedlings.

VINES Prune akebia, summer- and fall-blooming clematis, grape, honeysuckle, and ornamental kiwi vine.

ORNAMENTAL GRASSES Cut back feather grass, feather reed grass, Japanese forest grass, and maiden grass in late winter.

WINTER-BLOOMING SHRUBS Shop for sasanqua camellias and witch hazels in flower.

DECIDUOUS TREES AND SHRUBS Plant from containers in zones 4–7 and 17 during December; wait until January to plant bare-root stock.

SMOKE BUSH Cut this shrub nearly to the ground in late winter if you want a smaller plant with fresh new foliage.

ROSES Protect them in cold-winter areas by mounding a foot of soil dug from another part of the garden over the base of the bushes, being sure to cover the bud union.

Once the mound freezes, cover it with straw or evergreen boughs. In zones 4–7 and 17 in January or February, cut back hybrid tea roses to the most vigorous three to five canes, then cut those back by about a third. Trim landscape roses to shape. In cold zones, wait until April to prune roses.

TREES Prune fruit trees, sourwood, and Southern magnolia in late winter. In cold-winter areas, wait until the weather turns mild.

HOLLIES Remove dead or damaged branches, and collect a few berry-studded branches for holiday decorations.

LIVING CHRISTMAS TREES Douglas fir, noble fir, or white fir are good choices. Try to limit their time indoors to 10 days, and keep them well watered (empty a tray of ice cubes on top of the soil each day). Store potted trees in a cool, bright place where the root ball won't freeze, and plant the tree in the garden when the soil is workable.

There's plenty of color in the Northwest even when snow is on the ground. 'Robert Chapman' scotch heather glows hot orange in winter.

FRUIT TREES Plant bare-root fruit trees and prune existing ones to create a vase shape and remove crossing branches.

DORMANT OIL On a mild, dry day in January, spray leafless fruit trees and roses with horticultural oils.

GARDENS TO VISIT See holiday displays at the Northwest's major conservatories in Wright Park (Tacoma, WA); Volunteer Park (Seattle, WA), and Queen Elizabeth Park (Vancouver, B.C.).

In February, Seattle's Northwest Flower and Garden Show is a must-see.

Perennials

Exquisite flowers that span the color spectrum, intriguing leaf shapes and textures, and a wide range of heights and blooming times make perennials a must for use in the Northwest landscape. No matter the season, you can depend on the abundance of perennials for color and diversity.

From my own experience as a nurseryman and gardener, I know just how beautiful and cost effective perennials can be. The reason I call them cost effective is because they are so long lived. Plant them once and they'll come back year after year, increasing in size and beauty. Many also reseed or grow by division, giving you more plants for the garden or to trade with your gardening friends.

others sway beautifully in summer breezes.

Some perennials die back to the ground in fall; others remain green year-round. This can be confusing to the first-time gardener, because some plants seem to disappear completely. I was so proud of my first hosta—a gorgeous, big, green-and-white thing—and then it suddenly disappeared in late summer. I just couldn't imagine how I had lost it. When I looked closer, however, I could see it was still there, waiting for next spring to arrive.

HOW THEY GROW

Some perennials grow in the sun, others in the shade, and yet others prefer a dappled mix of both. Some are sturdy, others need staking, and

Because perennials tend to be spreading or shrubby, different leaf shapes or textures blend into each other. That means you can mix and

match them almost anywhere, whether in the ground or in containers. In my own garden, I add variety to my shrub plantings by tucking perennials in between, behind, and in front of them and then complement them during the summer with the addition of a few annual flowers. Rather than planting perennials singly, I prefer to use them in groups of three, which creates more eye-catching splashes of color.

Most perennials thrive on a certain amount of neglect, requiring only occasional feeding, seasonal watering, and occasional dividing.

With limited care you can have a beautiful perennial garden. Now that's practical!

Once you have become acquainted with the Top 10 choices on the following pages, try some of my other favorites, including bellflowers *(Campanula),* chrysanthemums, columbines *(Aquilegia),* delphiniums, and coneflowers *(Echinacea).*   —ED HUME

Black-eyed Susan
Rudbeckia

These descendants of North American meadow natives seem at home in drifts among wildflowers and ornamental grasses—but you can also use black-eyed Susans effectively in more orderly borders and cutting gardens. Whether displaying their charms in the garden or in a vase, they evoke the casual charm of the countryside.

The plants come in a range of sizes, from the stately *Rudbeckia laciniata* 'Golden Glow', which grows to 7 feet tall and is capable of spreading widely, to the charming *R. hirta* 'Toto', which grows to only 10 inches tall, perfect for containers or the front of the border. All types first form loose mounds of dark green leaves; then, from midsummer into fall, they produce an abundance of yellow or orange daisies, each centered with a prominent black, brown, or green cone.

Black-eyed Susans are dependable and easy to grow. Birds, butterflies, and bees all find them irresistible. The sturdy flowers also last for a long time in arrangements—so fill up an old crockery pitcher or mason jar with their warm, bright blooms.

LEFT: *A river of bold black-eyed Susans flows through a mixed border of equally bright summer blooms.*

PEAK SEASON

Black-eyed Susans bloom from summer into fall. The dark seed heads are attractive if left in place in winter.

OUR FAVORITES

Rudbeckia fulgida sullivantii 'Goldsturm' grows 2 to 2½ feet tall, sporting 3- to 4-inch, bright yellow flowers with black cones.

R. hirta 'Indian Summer' reaches 3½ feet tall, with black-eyed yellow flowers up to 9 inches across.

R. laciniata 'Goldquelle' grows about 3 feet tall, with double flowers in lemon yellow. The green cones fade to yellow with age.

R. nitida 'Herbstsonne' ('Autumn Sun') grows 6 to 7 feet tall, with bright yellow elegantly drooping petals around green cones. Its stems may need some light staking or support.

GARDEN COMPANIONS

Plant black-eyed Susans with other late-summer and fall performers like ornamental grasses, asters, phlox, sedum, Japanese anemones, and zinnias.

When Black-eyed Susans in nursery containers are best planted in spring.

Where Choose a site in full sun with well-drained, average to rich soil.

How Amend the soil with organic matter before planting. Plant in groups of three, five, or more, spacing plants 1½ to 2 feet apart, depending on the variety. (Overcrowding encourages leaf spots and powdery mildew.) Water thoroughly and keep the soil moist until plants are established. A 1- to 2-inch layer of mulch around (but not touching) the base of each plant will keep moisture in and weeds out.

ABOVE: Rudbeckia hirta *'Indian Summer'.* BELOW: *An exuberant clump of black-eyed Susans rises behind a more sedate pink-flowering heather.*

TLC Black-eyed Susans do best with regular water. The tallest types may need staking. If you want shorter, bushier plants, pinch back tips in June. Remove spent flowers early in the season, but you can leave the last flush of blooms in place for winter interest. Divide clumps in spring every three years or so.

*2–7, 17 for R. nitida 'Herbstsonne'

Daylily
Hemerocallis

With more than 50,000 named varieties on the market, you might think these are so-named because a new one is introduced each day. Hybridizers have now moved beyond the classic yellows and oranges to produce a rainbow of flowers—even some with stripes or banding in contrasting colors or iridescent dots called diamond dust. Blooms may be spider shaped, star shaped, triangular, rounded, or fully double.

All daylilies start off as a fountain of narrow, arching leaves. Plant size varies from 1 to 6 feet, with most modern hybrids reaching 2 to 4 feet tall and not quite as wide. Deciduous types are a better choice for colder regions, as their dormancy allows them to survive even Alaska's bitter lows. Evergreen varieties are fine additions to flower gardens in mild to moderate climates.

Daylilies are truly tough customers. Your only chore is to remove faded blooms and the occasional yellowed leaf. And, yes, the real reason they're called daylilies is because each flower lasts only a day.

Sprays of daylilies soften the edge of a lively mixed border and echo the massed golden blooms of a neighboring tickseed (Coreopsis grandiflora).

PEAK SEASON

The main bloom time is midspring to early summer, but some types give a second show in late summer or fall.

OUR FAVORITES

Lemon daylily (*H. lilioasphodelus*, also sold as *H. flava*) is an old-fashioned species with 3-foot-tall stalks of lushly fragrant, pure yellow flowers.

Among the most widely sold daylilies are long-blooming dwarf hybrids, which reach no more than 2 feet tall. Try 'Happy Returns', with canary yellow flowers; 'Pardon Me', with red blooms; and 'Stella de Oro', an old favorite with bright yellow flowers.

For the coldest zones choose grass-leaf daylily (*H. minor*). It reaches 2 feet tall and has fragrant, golden flowers.

Impress all your friends with fancy varieties like 2-foot-tall 'Strawberry Candy', which has coral pink petals with ruffled edges and a strawberry red center; 1½-foot-tall 'Moonlit Masquerade', which has nearly white flowers with a rich purple center; and 2½-foot-tall 'Ed Brown', with pale pink petals with ruffled yellow edges.

GARDEN COMPANIONS

Bold clumps of daylilies contrast nicely with mounding or spreading perennials like geranium, euphorbia, peony, and yarrow. Deciduous types can disguise the fading foliage of spring-blooming bulbs like daffodils (*Narcissus*) and camass (*Camassia*).

When In mild-winter climates, plant from containers at any time of year; in fall and winter, you can also put in bare-root plants. In colder areas, plant container-grown daylilies from midspring to early autumn and bare-root plants in spring or summer.

Where Daylilies can thrive in full sun to light shade, but the more sun they get the more flowers they'll produce. The blooms will turn to face the sun, so keep that in mind when deciding where to plant them. Smaller types are ideal for containers.

ABOVE: *Soft yellow blooms and darker buds create a two-tone look.*
BELOW: *Daylilies and penstemons of confectionary pink.*

How Space daylilies 1½ to 3 feet apart, depending on the variety. The plants spread, so give them plenty of room. Dig each planting hole the same depth as the container and about twice as wide, and amend the dug soil with organic matter. Place the root ball in the center of the hole and refill with amended soil; press the soil lightly in place with your fingers. Water thoroughly, then apply a 2-inch layer of mulch around the plants, but keep it away from their bases. Keep the soil moist until plants are established.

TLC Water regularly, about once a week. Every year in early spring, dig in compost or a controlled-release fertilizer; apply it again four weeks later. Watch out for slugs. To keep

plants looking neat after blooms fade, snap off the entire flower, not just the petals. You can cut back the whole flowering stem to the ground when its blooms are finished. Divide every four to six years.

*Grass-leaf daylily also grows in zones A1–A3.

Euphorbia

Euphorbia

Euphorbias come in all shapes and sizes, from delicate leafy annuals to treelike species that resemble giant cacti. The genus even includes the familiar poinsettia. But the most popular euphorbias for Northwest gardens form dense, leafy mounds that are topped in late winter or early spring by curious flower heads. The true flowers are tiny and intricate (fascinating on close inspection), but the real show comes from the bracts that surround the flowers. These cup-shaped structures are a fresh, vibrant chartreuse, which combines nicely with a range of other hues.

Two tough but exuberant perennials: Euphorbia characias wulfenii *and the wallflower,* Erysimum *'Bowles Mauve'.*

As the season progresses and the bracts fade, check the plant's base for the small shoots that will form next year's stems. Their appearance is the signal to cut off the older stems to make way for the new. Be careful when handling euphorbias, though—the milky white sap that drips from broken stems and leaves can irritate skin and eyes.

ABOVE: *Striking color contrast in the individual bracts of E. × martinii. BELOW: E. griffithii 'Fireglow' lives up to its moniker with flaming orange-and-red bracts.*

PEAK SEASON

Euphorbias bloom in late winter or early spring.

OUR FAVORITES

Euphorbia characias wulfenii (zones 4–7, 17) forms an attractive evergreen mound about 4 feet tall and wide that blooms over a long season. *E. × martinii* (zones 3–7, 17) is similar but reaches only 2 to 3 feet tall and wide and has leaves that are tinged reddish purple when young.

E. myrsinites (zones 2–7, 17), only 6 inches tall and 1 foot wide, looks almost like a low-growing sedum, with sprawling stems closely set with blue-gray leaves. Chartreuse flower heads grace the upheld stem tips.

The hardiest euphorbia listed here is *E. polychroma* (zones A2; 1–7, 17), sometimes sold as *E. epithymoides* or cushion spurge; it disappears completely in winter but returns in spring to form a neat, low hummock about 1½ feet tall and 2 feet wide. Leaves of dark green are topped by chartreuse bracts and yellow flowers; the fall color is orange to red.

GARDEN COMPANIONS

Euphorbias combine well with equally striking plants, such as New Zealand flax *(Phormium)* and red-hot pokers *(Kniphofia),* as well as lavender, spring bulbs, and shrubs, particularly those with dark green or burgundy foliage.

When Plant from nursery containers in spring or fall.

Where Choose a spot in full sun for the euphorbias listed here. They'll take just about any soil as long as it is well drained. *E. characias wulfenii* gets quite large, so give it plenty of room to grow. *E. myrsinites* makes an excellent edging or a ground cover puncutated with spring-blooming bulbs.

How Make the planting hole about twice the width of the plant's container and slightly shallower than the root ball. Take the plant out of its container and lightly loosen the roots if they are compacted. Set the root ball into the hole so that it is just a bit higher than the level of the surrounding soil, then fill in with soil, firming it with your fingers. Water well. Apply a 2-inch layer of mulch to keep the soil moist and the weeds down, but keep it away from the plant's base.

TLC Most euphorbias need only moderate water during dry periods, though *E. myrsinites* is especially drought tolerant. In spring, after the floral heads have turned brown, cut the stems all the way back to the plant's base, being careful not to damage the next year's emerging stems.

Hellebore

Helleborus

Hellebores don't scream for attention with towering stems or flashy blooms. They beckon softly with small, bowl-shaped flowers held in clusters above finger-like leaves that reach down as if to touch the earth. Depending on which type you plant, expect branched stems of single or double blooms in white or creamy green, soft yellow, pink, or purple in late winter or early spring. All gradually fade to a pleasant light green.

In the summer shade of an old apple tree, a sprawling hellebore consorts with other low-growing plants, including hardy geranium and sweet woodruff.

The plants do best in semishady areas; a single specimen makes a nice accent among ferns and hostas. Since most types have flowers that hang down or face outward, consider siting plants in a raised bed or where they'll billow over a wall with a path below. Another ideal spot would be alongside steps, where you can look up into the intricately constructed blooms as you climb. Hellebores also look splendid massed as a ground cover and will naturalize under favorable conditions.

These long-lived, sturdy perennials are never eaten by deer or rodents, which seem to know something you should, too: all parts of the hellebore are quite poisonous.

PEAK SEASON

Hellebores bloom in late winter or early spring.

OUR FAVORITES

Bear's-foot hellebore *(Helleborus foetidus)* has evergreen leaves divided into very narrow leaflets; flowers are light green with purplish red edges. It grows to 2½ feet tall and wide.

Corsican hellebore *(H. argutifolius,* also sold as *H. corsicus)* is more sun and drought tolerant than other species. It forms a bushy, evergreen clump 2 to 3 feet tall and wide, with bold, blue-green, toothed leaves and pale green flowers.

Lenten rose *(H. orientalis)* grows about 1½ feet tall and wide, with white or creamy green flowers.

Christmas rose *(H. niger)* is deciduous and reaches 1 foot by 1½ feet, with deep green, smooth, foliage and large white flowers. It requires shade and moist, alkaline soil.

GARDEN COMPANIONS

Plant hellebores in partly shaded gardens with bleeding hearts *(Dicentra),* lily turf *(Liriope),* hostas, primroses *(Primula),* and ferns—or group with bulbs like bluebell *(Scilla),* cyclamen, crocus, or snowdrops *(Galanthus).* Hellebores are wonderful beneath deciduous trees and shrubs such as dogwoods, maples, witch hazels, and viburnums.

When Plant hellebores in spring or fall.

Where Grow in partial shade in well-drained soil that is neutral to slightly alkaline. (Christmas rose must have alkaline soil; if necessary, add lime to the planting hole and sprinkle it around the base of the plant yearly.) If possible, site hellebores where you can look up into the pendent flowers. They also look good massed beneath deciduous trees and shrubs; they thrive in winter sun and summer shade.

How Dig a planting hole the same depth as the container and about twice as wide, and amend the dug soil with plenty of organic matter. Place the root ball in the center of the hole. Refill with the amended soil and press it lightly into place with your fingers. Water thoroughly, then apply a 2-inch layer of mulch, keeping it away from the base of the plants. Water thoroughly and keep the soil moist until the plant is established.

TLC Feed in spring with an all-purpose plant food or sprinkle mushroom compost around the plant's base. Add a sprinkling of lime each year if the soil is acid. Watch for snails and slugs, which may damage the young foliage. Remove old flowering stems to the base when they begin to look ratty. Division is usually not needed, as plants grow slowly and resent being moved.

TOP: *A Lenten rose spattered with crimson.* MIDDLE: *The curious blooms of bear's-foot hellebore.* BOTTOM: *Lacy dark foliage sets off lighter hellebore flowers.*

*Christmas rose grows in zones 1–7, 17; Corsican hellebore in zones 3b–7, 17.

Hosta

Hosta

Some may think that hostas are a little too prevalent in Northwest gardens, but there are plenty of good reasons for their popularity. They're exceedingly easy to grow in rich soil and partial shade. They have only two serious enemies: deer and the accursed slug. They come in a wide variety of leaf sizes, shapes, and colors. (The flowers are rarely showy.) And they're useful in so many situations, from breaking up a monotonous expanse of shrubs to edging a woodland path or covering the ground with a tapestry of leaves.

Most hostas aren't at their best in deepest shade; an ideal spot would receive morning sun and afternoon shade or dappled shade for most of the day. Gold-leafed types tolerate more sun; those with white variegation need more shade. If slugs are a problem in your garden, choose heavier textured or puckered types, which the mollusks seem to disdain. Another method of foiling the pests is to grow hostas in pots with copper tape around the rims, as snails and slugs won't cross that barrier. Although hostas maintain their good looks over a long season, they all die down in winter; it's a good idea to mark their locations with stakes or labels so you don't accidentally dig them up.

Hostas combine well with a variety of plant shapes, from shrubby hydrangeas to low-growing lady's-mantle (Alchemilla).

PEAK SEASON

Hosta foliage looks good from late spring into fall.

OUR FAVORITES

Hosta 'Frances Williams', to 2 feet by 3 feet, sports heavily corrugated, heart-shaped blue leaves bordered with yellow.

H. 'June' forms clumps about 2 feet tall and wide of heart-shaped leaves with yellow-gold spring color fading in summer to chartreuse with blue-green margins.

H. 'Sum and Substance' is a chartreuse giant to 6 feet across with deeply veined, heart-shaped leaves.

H. fortunei varieties, available in a wide range of colors, are perhaps the hardiest of all hostas; they'll thrive in any part of the Northwest.

H. sieboldiana 'Elegans' is nice for a big blue accent, growing 3 feet tall and 4 feet wide, with heavily veined, puckered leaves.

GARDEN COMPANIONS

Grow larger types among smaller shade lovers such as epimedium, lily turf (*Liriope*), Japanese forest grass (*Hakonechloa macra* 'Aureola'), sedges (*Carex*), coleus, impatiens, and pansies. To keep a garden bed interesting until hostas emerge in spring, plant early-spring bulbs and primroses.

TOP: *Blue hosta blooms rise up to meet a tiled birdbath.* BOTTOM: *Many varieties of hosta have blue or gray leaves that look great against a background of conifers.*

When In temperate areas of the Northwest, hostas can be planted any time the soil is workable, whether the plant is growing or in its dormant stage. In colder regions, plant in early spring.

Where Choose a partly shady spot that does not get hot afternoon sun.

How Check the mature size of your hosta and make sure you allow plenty of room for it to spread. Dig a planting hole the same depth as the container and about twice as wide, and amend the dug soil with plenty of organic matter like compost or well-rotted manure. Place the root ball in the center of the hole and refill with amended soil; press soil lightly in place with your fingers. Water thoroughly, then apply a 2-inch layer of mulch around the plants to retain moisture and keep down weeds, keeping it away from the base of the plants.

TLC All hostas grow best with regular water, but they will get by on less once they become established. Fertilize with a high-nitrogen, controlled-release plant food in early spring, or feed with manure or another organic fertilizer in early spring and again in midsummer. Remove flower stalks after they've faded or, if you don't care for the look of the blooms, snip them off as they emerge. When left undisturbed, hostas will grow for many years, but if you want to divide them, just remove plantlets from a clump's perimeter and replant them. This is best done in dormancy or just as the leaves are emerging. Start to control slugs and snails in early spring, before they become a real problem.

*Hosta fortunei will grow in zones A1–A3; 1–7, 17.

Penstemon
Penstemon

Border penstemon 'Garnet', gray-leafed crown-pink (Lychnis coronaria), and the climbing rose 'Blaze' bring sizzle to a curving garden path.

You can't buy hummingbirds or butterflies at the local nursery, but if you plant penstemons, those winged visitors will surely be drawn to your garden. They can't resist the narrowly bell-shaped flowers of white, light pink, rose pink, yellow, or purple. The blooms range along erect stems that rise like crowds of exclamation points. Most penstemons have bushy clumps of narrow, pointed leaves at the base.

Nearly all penstemons are native to western North America, and many hail from mountainous areas, making them ideal for dry mountainside gardens. Fast drainage is a must for these plants, so consider planting them on a slope, along the edge of a gravel path, or atop a stone wall. In a casual mixed border or cottage garden almost anywhere in the Northwest, penstemons will look right at home.

ABOVE: *The pink border penstemon 'Apple Blossom' is accompanied by a silver dusty miller.* BELOW: *Border penstemon 'Burgundy' has reddish purple flowers.*

PEAK SEASON

Penstemons bloom from late spring through summer.

OUR FAVORITES

Penstemon barbatus reaches 3 feet tall and half as wide, with bright green leaves and red flowers.

P. digitalis 'Husker Red' grows 2½ to 3 feet tall by 1 foot wide, with maroon leaves that set off the pinkish white flowers.

Border penstemon (*P. × gloxinioides*) is perennial in temperate areas and annual elsewhere. It forms a bushy plant 3 feet tall and wide. Try pale lilac 'Alice Hindley', soft pink 'Apple Blossom', and maroon 'Blackbird'. The Kissed series has white-throated, brightly colored blooms.

P. pinifolius is an adaptable plant that appreciates good drainage. It grows to 1½ feet tall and 2 feet wide, with leaves like tiny pine needles and red-orange flowers. 'Mersea Yellow' is a bit smaller, with soft yellow flowers.

Rock penstemon (*P. rupicola*) is native to the Cascades and Siskiyou Mountains. It grows to only 4 inches tall and 1½ feet wide, with long-lasting, bright rose flowers.

GARDEN COMPANIONS

Combine penstemons with informal-looking daylilies, yarrow (*Achillea*), salvia, and gaura.

When Plant penstemons in spring or fall.

Where Choose a well-drained spot in full sun for best bloom. Where summers are hot and dry, penstemons appreciate a bit of afternoon shade.

How Dig a planting hole the same depth and about twice as wide as the plant's container. Unless your soil is very well drained, it's a good idea to dig an inch or two deeper and add a layer of dug soil mixed with gravel, sand, or organic matter to the bottom of the hole. Mulch around the plant with gravel; organic mulches hold too much moisture for penstemons.

TLC Most penstemons are quite drought tolerant, but some, such as the border penstemons and 'Husker Red', do best with regular water. Penstemons don't need feeding. Like other plants with tall flower spikes, they may need support, such as twiggy branches inserted near the base. Also, you can pinch the growing tips when plants are about 1 foot tall to encourage bushy growth. After the first period of bloom is over, cut back stems to side growth for a second flush.

P. barbatus and *P. digitalis* 'Husker Red' will also grow in zone 1.

Peony
Paeonia

Herbaceous peonies require more work at planting time than the other Top 10 perennials—and it can take them a couple of years to really hit their stride. But the work and the waiting pay off once they open up their first spectacular blooms. The bowl-shaped flowers—some up to 10 inches across—may be white, cream, yellow, pink, red, or purple, many with radiant golden centers. They make great cut flowers, often with a light, clean fragrance.

The carmine blooms of this brilliant red peony are enhanced by its maroon-tinged leaves and stems.

Knockout flowers aren't the only reason to grow peonies; the stems and foliage provide months of interest. In early spring, the bright carmine shoots coil up out of the soil like snakes being charmed by the sun. These develop into shrubby plants 2 to 4 feet tall and wide with rich green leaves that remain attractive right into fall.

Peonies are useful in a host of garden situations, from concealing a fading drift of daffodils to supporting the thin stems of lilies—they even make a nice path edging or low hedge. And as an added bonus, peonies are extremely long lived.

When Plant from containers in spring, as bare-root plants in fall.

Where Choose a site with full sun and good air circulation, but avoid windy spots. Space peonies 3 to 4 feet from each other and from other plants. This may seem like a lot of room at first, but the plants will fill in, and they need good air circulation to avoid foliar diseases.

How Dig a planting hole 1½ feet deep and 2 feet wide, then amend the dug soil with plenty of organic matter (such as compost or well-rotted manure) along with some high-phosphate fertilizer. Add a little lime if the soil is acidic. Sprinkle the area lightly with water and let it settle for a few days before planting. Planting depth is very important: When planting bare-root peonies, make sure the buds or eyes on the tubers are 1 inch below the soil in warmer areas, 2 inches deep in colder regions. When planting from containers, plant peonies at the same level they were growing in the pot. Firm the soil with your fingers, and water the area well.

TLC Mulch peonies in spring with well-rotted manure or compost and feed with a balanced fertilizer. Peonies often need staking with link stakes or peony rings, available at garden centers. Cut flowers for bouquets just as the buds are starting to open, leaving three large leaves on every cut stem. Remove no more than half the buds from each plant. Cut back flower stems after bloom. Ants often appear on flower buds, but they do no harm. To prevent fungal diseases, especially in cool, humid areas, dispose of all stems each fall and apply copper fungicide to new leaves in spring. To get new plants, divide peonies in fall by digging clumps and separating them into sections, each one with at least three eyes.

ABOVE: *'Magic Melody'*. BELOW, LEFT TO RIGHT: *'Coral Charm'*, buff pink *'Sarah Bernhardt'*, and deep crimson red *'Rubra Plena'*.

PEAK SEASON

Peonies flower in spring and early summer.

OUR FAVORITES

'Bowl of Beauty' has fragrant pink flowers with creamy white centers.

'Coral Charm' is tall, with exotic, pale salmon-colored blooms.

'Félix Crousse' (sometimes 'Krousse') has fragrant, deep pink blooms.

Fernleaf peony (*Paeonia tenuifolia*) grows 1½ to 2½ feet tall and wide, with ferny, dark green foliage and deep red flowers.

'Festiva Maxima' boasts fragrant white flowers with crimson flecks.

'Karl Rosenfield' is disease resistant, with brilliant red double flowers.

'Sarah Bernhardt' has fragrant blooms of apple-blossom pink.

GARDEN COMPANIONS

Put peonies at the front of beds of irises, roses, geraniums, and delphiniums or pair them with spring bulbs like bluebells (*Scilla*), grape hyacinth (*Muscari*), and crocus.

Primrose

Primula

Gardeners outside the Pacific Northwest may well turn green with envy when it comes to our primroses. These dainty perennials thrive in the cool summers, chilly winters, and high humidity of the coastal Northwest—but several types also succeed in the warmer, drier environs east of the Cascades. Since most are cold hardy, even gardeners as far north as southeast Alaska can enjoy primroses. No matter where you garden, give these plants the rich soil and regular irrigation of their native woodlands, and you'll be rewarded with perky spring blooms in a wide array of colors.

All primroses form a low tuft of attractive oval leaves, often puckered or quilted, from which rise solitary stems with single flowers or flower clusters at the top, or tiers of clusters along the stems. Some primroses are evergreen; others go dormant in winter. Tuck a few of these little garden jewels into partly shady nooks of your garden (or in sunnier spots where summers are cool or foggy), or plant a large drift of a few selected colors. Over time, the plants will naturalize and spread.

The edge of a lushly planted pond is a natural location for Japanese primroses. They need ample water to thrive, and will gradually spread.

PEAK SEASON

Most primroses are spring blooming, but some start in mid- to late winter in mild climates, and a few bloom in early summer.

OUR FAVORITES

For cold-winter areas, try Japanese primrose (Primula japonica), which has tiered blossoms in purple, pink, or white, or drumstick primrose (P. denticulata), with ball-shaped clusters. Common primrose (P. vulgaris) has single flowers of white, yellow, red, blue, brown, bronze, or wine. Cowslip (P. veris) has clusters of cheery yellow, fragrant flowers.

Juliana hybrids, such as the pale yellow 'Dorothy', take slightly drier conditions than other primroses. Other colors include white, blue, orange-red, pink, and purple.

Polyanthus hybrids are sturdy plants with flower clusters in a rainbow of bright colors.

Gardeners in warmer regions can try the lovely P. vialii, an unusual primrose topped with narrow spikes of lavender blooms opening from bright crimson buds.

GARDEN COMPANIONS

Plant primroses with dwarf daffodils, lungwort (Pulmonaria), tulips, sedges (Carex), ferns, hostas, azaleas, and Japanese iris.

When Plant from nursery containers or sow seed directly in place in early spring.

CLOCKWISE FROM LEFT: *Three common primroses: 'Miss Indigo', 'Sue Jervis', and 'Marianne Davey'.*

Where Generally, primroses do best in partial shade, though they can take more sun in cool-summer or foggy areas along the coast.

How Dig a hole the same depth as the nursery container and about twice as wide. Tip the root ball from the container and place it in the middle of the hole. Backfill with dug soil amended with organic matter such as compost. Water well. Add a layer of mulch to keep roots cool, but don't crowd the base of the plant.

TLC All primroses do best with consistent moisture, so be sure they don't dry out. Pull off yellow leaves in fall. After some years, if flowering begins to decline, divide clumps right after bloom or (in mild areas) in autumn; amend the soil and replant the divisions. Control snails and slugs.

Drumstick primrose grows in zones A2, A3; 1–6; polyanthus hybrids thrive in 1–7, 17; and P. vialii is suited to 4–6, 17.

Tickseed
Coreopsis

How better to liven up the garden than with plants that happily churn out hundreds of little yellow daisies all summer long? That's exactly what these members of the sunflower family do. Requiring only a sunny spot and occasional water, tickseed grows into leafy mats or bushy tufts topped with blooms in various shades of gold and yellow. To keep the blooms coming, shear off the spent flowers regularly; while you're at it, snip some fresh blossoms for long-lasting indoor arrangements.

Coreopsis grandiflora adds a sweep of sunny warmth to a composition of cooler tones, including lavender, purple sage, ornamental alliums, roses, and foxgloves.

These are informal-looking plants that work well in a variety of situations. They're ideal along a driveway or sidewalk—the reflected heat won't faze them, and their casual form will soften the harsh edge. Try tickseed in a meadow planting or in sunny, exposed parts of the garden where more finicky plants have failed. They even grow well in containers, so you can move a little pot of sunshine wherever you like.

PEAK SEASON

Some start blooming in spring and others continue through fall, but the main bloom season is summer.

OUR FAVORITES

Coreopsis auriculata 'Nana' is a low grower—to 6 inches tall and about 2 feet wide—good for the edge of a border or path. The long-lasting blooms are bright orange-yellow.

C. grandiflora is upright, reaching 2 feet and spreading a bit wider. Bright yellow flowers are held on long, slender stems. 'Early Sunrise' is a popular, long-blooming variety.

Threadleaf coreopsis *(C. verticillata)* grows 2½ to 3 feet tall and half as wide, forming a bushy mound of ferny leaves and bright yellow blossoms from summer through fall. 'Moonbeam', 1½ to 2 feet tall and wide, has pale yellow flowers that blend beautifully with many colors. 'Zagreb' reaches only 1 foot tall, with golden yellow flowers.

GARDEN COMPANIONS

The soft foliage of tickseed contrasts well with the grassy leaves of red-hot poker *(Kniphofia)*, and the yellow or golden flowers are lovely with blue- and purple-blooming plants like many salvias, purple coneflower *(Echinacea purpurea)*, and lavender. They also pair handsomely with blue oat grass *(Helictotrichon sempervirens)* and ornamental onions *(Allium)*.

When Plant tickseed from nursery containers in spring.

Where These plants will flower best in the sunniest parts of your garden. Good drainage is a must, so slopes and hillsides are particularly good spots.

How Dig a hole the same depth as the container and a bit wider. Gently tip the root ball from the container and loosen the roots. Set the plant in the center of the hole, making sure that the top of the root ball is level with the surrounding soil. Refill the hole and firm the soil around the plant with your fingers. Water thoroughly and keep the soil moist until the plant is well established.

TLC Though they will survive drought, plants do best with moderate water. Snip off spent flowers regularly to prolong bloom. Or you can wait until a wave of bloom is over and shear the whole plant back. Every couple of years, you'll want to divide the plants in early spring by digging them up, separating the clumps into several pieces, and replanting. Bait for slugs and snails if they're a problem in your garden.

ABOVE: Coreopsis grandiflora *'Early Sunrise'*. RIGHT: *Canary yellow* C. auriculata *'Nana' in an eye-catching combination with scarlet African daisy (Osteospermum).*

Upright Sedum
Sedum

The way these succulent perennials change from season to season, it's like getting four plants for the price of one. Starting in early spring, new shoots first appear like crowded clumps of little cabbages. As the stems lengthen, each plant is transformed into an upright, rounded mass of fresh-looking succulent leaves that makes a textural contrast to busy spring flowers.

The third act begins in summer with clusters of tiny, pale green buds that gradually transform to a slightly different color each day until the blazing pink high point in late summer. In fall, the flower heads darken further, to a rusty red. Finally, even in winter, sedums are still not ready to take their bow, holding onto their dark brown seed heads for a final scene that is especially effective against a backdrop of snow. Early the next spring, when it's time to clip off the previous year's stems, you'll see the new shoots already preparing for a repeat performance.

In the height of summer, the blazing flowers of Sedum 'Autumn Joy' are displayed to maximum effect in front of dark green spruce foliage.

PEAK SEASON

Flowering starts in mid- to late summer and continues into fall.

OUR FAVORITES

Sedum 'Autumn Joy' is a very popular hybrid that grows to 2 feet tall and wide, with blue-green leaves and pink flowers. 'Autumn Fire' is an improved form with thicker blooms.

S. 'Frosty Morn' is similar in form to 'Autumn Joy' but sports blue-green leaves boldly outlined in creamy white. Flowers are white or pale pink.

S. 'Vera Jameson', to 9 inches tall and 1½ feet wide, has gorgeous pinkish purple leaves and rose pink flowers.

S. spectabile varieties grow to 1½ feet tall and wide, with blue-green leaves and red or white flowers.

S. telephium reaches about 2 feet tall and wide, with gray-green leaves and purplish pink flowers over a long period. 'Mohrchen' has purple new growth and rosy pink flowers. 'Matrona' has pink-edged gray-green leaves and pink blooms on wine red stems. *S. t. maximum* 'Atropurpureum' has burgundy foliage and dusty pink flowers.

GARDEN COMPANIONS

Flowering grasses such as blue oat grass (*Helictotrichon sempervirens*) and fountain grass (*Pennisetum*) make wonderful contrasts.

When Plant sedums in spring or late summer.

Where Choose a spot with full sun and well-drained soil. These plants look best when planted in groups of three or more, or among boulders or in gravel beds. Space the plants 1½ to 2 feet apart, depending on their mature width.

How Water the plants in their nursery containers. Dig planting holes the same depth as the containers and about twice as wide. Gently tip each root ball from its container and loosen the roots. Place the plant in the center of the hole, making sure the top of the root ball is level with the surrounding soil. Refill the hole, and firm the soil around the plant with your fingers. Water thoroughly and keep soil moist until plants are established. A 2-inch layer of mulch will keep the roots moist and the weeds down.

TLC Give sedums moderate to regular water. If you don't like the look of the faded seed heads, cut the stems down to ground level in late fall. Otherwise let them stand through winter and remove them in early spring. After a few years, flowering may decrease due to crowding. At that point, dig up clumps in early spring, divide them into sections no larger than your fist, and replant.

TOP: Sedum *'Autumn Joy'*. MIDDLE: *A variegated form of* S. spectabile, *shown with the plain green form.* BOTTOM: *The soft pink blooms of* S. s. *'Carmen'.*

Ferns

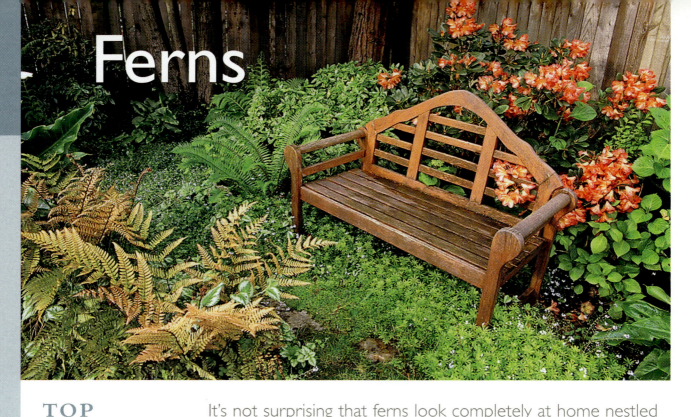

TOP 10 PLUS

It's not surprising that ferns look completely at home nestled among glistening, damp boulders; those two ancient elements are all you need for a handsome garden. And because they look so fresh and cool, ferns brighten any spot that possesses a bit of shade and moisture.

Want to turn a damp backyard into a tropical-looking garden? Use five-finger ferns to carpet the ground beneath the giant leaves of *Gunnera*, and you're well on your way. Do you want to transform a shady wilderness into a woodland garden? Plant drifts of lady fern here and there to give continuity to your design.

For maximum visual impact, how about a single emerald-green royal fern erupting from a sea of orange daylilies?

Ferns' delicate fronds contrast beautifully with other plant forms, which makes them easy to combine with fellow shade lovers such as bleeding heart *(Dicentra)*, hosta, hellebores, and bishop's hat.

Our Favorites

Deer fern (*Blechnum spicant;* zones 2b–7, 17) is a formal-looking North-west native evergreen that grows 3 feet tall and wide. Each plant has deep green fronds of two types: ster-ile ones that spread luxuriously, and fertile ones that stand stiffly upright.

Five-finger or Western maidenhair fern (*Adiantum aleuticum;* zones 1–7, 17) has wiry stems holding fans of airy fronds in a fingerlike pattern. It stands 1 to 2½ feet tall and wide and looks great in containers. This fern is evergreen in mild areas.

Japanese painted fern (*Athyrium nipponicum* 'Pictum'; zones 1–7, 17) is the most colorful of all ferns, with fronds that are purple at the base, then lavender shading to silvery green toward the tips. It is deciduous, and grows 1½ feet tall and wide.

Lady fern (*Athyrium filix-femina;* all zones) can reach 4 feet tall and 3 feet wide but still looks graceful thanks to its fountain of lacy, delicate fronds. Lady fern is deciduous, and grows vigorously in all parts of the Northwest, tolerating quite a bit of sun if kept well watered.

Royal fern (*Osmunda regalis;* zones 1–7, 17) is the thirstiest and most sun-loving fern in our list. Give it plenty of water and light and you'll be rewarded with majestic fronds to 6 feet tall and half as wide. The upright fertile fronds resemble light brown flower heads.

Sword fern (*Polystichum munitum;* A3, 2–7, 17) is an old standby in Northwestern gardens because it is easy to grow and always looks lovely. This native fern forms a sturdy ever-green clump of shiny, dark green fronds 2 to 4 feet tall and wide.

Planting and Care

Ferns grow best in a moist site with bright or dappled shade or morning-only sun; most won't thrive in deep-est shade. Place them some distance from paths so that their delicate fronds aren't crushed underfoot. Water the ferns in their containers and keep them in shade until plant-ing time. Dig a hole the same depth as the container and twice as wide. Carefully slip the ferns from their pots into the hole, then refill with soil gen-erously amended with organic matter such as rotted leaves, peat moss, or aged compost. Water deeply, then spread a 3-inch-deep layer of mulch around the fern; you can add a little compost or rotted leaves to enrich the mulch. Keep plants well watered at all times. Each spring, sprinkle com-post around your ferns and replenish the mulch. The fronds of deciduous ferns die back after a few hard frosts; you can clip them off or leave them in place for winter protection.

TOP: *Rhododendrons, ferns, and mosses are perfect companions.* RIGHT: *Western sword fern.* OPPOSITE PAGE, TOP: *This shady mixture around a stone bench includes rust colored autumn fern* (Dryopteris ery-throsora). OPPOSITE PAGE, BOTTOM: *A fern fiddlehead; maidenhair fern.*

Bulbs

I love blue. So when I read Meriwether Lewis's comment that the camass on Idaho's Weippe Prairie looked like a "lake of fine clear water," I bought some camass bulbs and made my own lake—well, puddle. It might not quite compare to the vast tracts that Lewis wrote of, but it's still very satisfying.

I also love white. So when I saw avalanche lilies growing by the acre on the flanks of Mount Rainier, I decided to grow a few of those as well. Then wild irises caught my eye on a road trip through Oregon, followed by a sprinkling of native lilies in the Cascades, and I had an epiphany: Long before commercial growers got into the act, the North-west was already world-class bulb territory.

These days, most of the country's Easter lilies (*Lilium longiflorum*) are grown on a narrow strip of coast in southern Oregon and northern California. The fields between Silverton and Salem, Oregon, are the epicenter of American iris production. And millions of daffodils and tulips are grown around Puyallup, Mount

Vernon, and Woodland, Washington, as well as in Oregon's lush Willamette Valley.

SEASONAL BULBS

Once the scales fell from my eyes, I starting seeing bulbs everywhere and in every season. Oddly, the little ones seem the toughest, braving the coldest months without missing a beat. Winter aconites (*Eranthis hyemalis*) awaken the garden in January, while crocuses pop up through the turf in February (see how they carpet the lawns at the Bishop's Close in Portland). Violet-scented *Iris reticulata* comes later in the same month, completely unfazed by wind and rain. Tiny, deep crimson *Cyclamen coum* also carpets the forest floor in winter. Daffodils, grape hyacinths (*Muscari*),

ABOVE: *Tulips, pansies, and daffodils.* OPPOSITE PAGE AND BELOW: *Asiactic lilies showing off their colors.*

and tulips greet spring with a shout, accompanied by a chorus of bluebells *(Scilla),* hyacinths, snowdrops *(Galanthus),* and fritillaries.

In many ways, summer bloomers are the most impressive. Dahlias and tuberous begonias bloom for months without ceasing. Lilies grace early and midsummer with the most aristocratic flowers imaginable; I grow Asiatics for color and Orientals for size and fragrance.

And as summer wanes, the cycle swings back to cyclamens. This time it's *C. hederifolium,* whose pink or white flowers peak in late summer and fall, followed by intricately marbled deciduous winter foliage.

After you've gardened for a while, you notice that some of these (like hybrid tulips and hyacinths) seem to be short lived in the Northwest, while others (like daffodils, grape hyacinths, crocuses, and bluebells) go on and on. So plant the naturalizers in the landscape, and the short-lived bulbs in containers, where they're easy to replace.

My own journey started with the notion that "I love blue," but it's become clear that I simply love bulbs. In the garden world, there aren't many plants that offer as much, over as long a season, as bulbs do.

—JIM McCAUSLAND

Camass
Camassia

A generous drift of great camass sends up its bold blooms along a low-maintenance streetside planting.

Most of our Top 10 bulbs hail from faraway places, but camass is a homegrown beauty. The most common species, *Camassia quamash,* is widespread in the moist meadows and damp hillsides of the Northwest on both sides of the Cascades. Its bulbs were an important food for native peoples, who steamed them and enjoyed the sweet flavor.

All camass species send up long, narrow, green or gray-green leaves with a distinctive ridge running down their length like the keel of a boat. A sturdy spike rises above the leaves, holding loosely spaced stars of blue, violet, or white. Blooms last a long time, whether on the plant or in a vase.

Camass is a must-have for the meadow garden; strong growing and trouble free, it naturalizes beautifully among tall grasses and other wildflowers. It's also a good choice along the edge of a pond or in a low-lying area that gets plenty of sunshine but no summer irrigation. You can grow camass in a flower border, provided you let the soil dry out after bloom. It even grows contentedly in a container.

PEAK SEASON

Camass blooms in late spring.

OUR FAVORITES

Camassia cusickii, from the Blue and Wallowa mountains of eastern Oregon, grows 3 feet tall and bears dense clusters of pale blue flowers sporting prominent yellow stamens.

Great camass *(C. leichtlinii),* native to western Oregon, has creamy white flowers on 3- to 4-foot-tall stems. *C. l. suksdorfii* (often sold as *C. l.* 'Caerulea') and *C. l.* 'Blue Danube' have deep blue blooms.

Indian hyacinth *(C. quamash,* also sold as *C. esculenta)* carries loose clusters of white, blue, or purple flowers on 1- to 2-foot stems. 'San Juan Form' has very deep blue blooms.

GARDEN COMPANIONS

Plant these bulbs among daffodils (Narcissus) and early-blooming tulips to provide a second wave of color. The soft tones of camass combine beautifully with similarly hued cornflowers (Centaurea cyanus) or delicate pink clarkias. Ornamental grasses do a great job of hiding the bulbs' fading foliage.

When Plant in fall, after weather cools.

Where Camass species need full sun or light shade and fertile, moisture-retentive soil. They adapt to heavy soils but will not thrive in waterlogged areas. Choose a spot that will remain undisturbed for many years, as the plants resent being moved.

How Dig individual holes 3 to 4 inches deep (or excavate a patch of soil to that depth); set bulbs at least 6 to 8 inches apart. Amend the dug soil with organic matter; fill in the holes, then water well.

TLC Provide plenty of water during growth and bloom, but let plants dry out after flowering has finished. They disappear completely during dormancy, so be sure to mark the planting spot.

ABOVE, LEFT: *Camassia leichtlinii.* ABOVE, RIGHT: *Indian hyacinth (C. quamash).* BELOW: *Indian hyacinth mingles with other woodland wildflowers.*

Crocosmia

Crocosmia

This hot border shows the brilliant colors of midsummer. It contains burgundy Japanese barberry, orange daylilies, and blazing scarlet 'Lucifer' crocosmia.

If sizzling hot colors are your thing, you'll love crocosmias. Starting from unassuming little corms, they thrust up fans of sword-shaped foliage in spring. The leaves are often pleated or ribbed and can reach 3 feet long. As summer heats up, wiry stems appear, holding rows of small, funnel-shaped flowers in fiery hues: bright reds, golden yellows, and blazing oranges. These make long-lasting cut flowers that virtually arrange themselves in the vase, due to their arching stems. If left on the plant, blooms mature into long-lasting seed capsules resembling peas lined up along the stem; these, too, can be cut for fresh or dried bouquets.

Plant crocosmias en masse for best effect, as single plants look a bit spindly. Rugged and carefree, they're great for naturalizing at the garden's edge or among shrubs—but also sparkle in a more formal flower border, offering a spiky, upright contrast to plants with a mounded form or rounded leaves. By the time crocosmias have flamed out, the first hints of fall color may have already begun to flicker elsewhere.

PEAK SEASON

Crocosmias bloom in mid- to late summer.

OUR FAVORITES

Crocosmia masoniorum, to 3 feet tall, displays double rows of flaming orange to orange-scarlet flowers on arching stems. Leaves are broader than those of other types.

Hybrid crocosmias come in various colors and heights. Some of the best are 'Emberglow' (2½ feet tall, with burnt orange-red, yellow-throated flowers); 'Emily McKenzie' (2 feet tall, with red-throated orange flowers); 'Jenny Bloom' (2 to 3 feet tall, with golden yellow blooms); and the vigorous, popular 'Lucifer' (to 4 feet tall, with bright red flowers).

Montbretia (*C. × crocosmiiflora*) is an old-fashioned favorite, with orange-crimson flowers on 3- to 4-foot stems. It's especially good for naturalizing on slopes or in fringe areas.

GARDEN COMPANIONS

Mix crocosmias with other spiky-leafed plants like New Zealand flax (*Phormium*) or daylily (*Hemerocallis*); or use them to provide contrast to the mounded forms of sedum, tickseed, or hardy geranium. For a blazing composition, plant with California poppy (*Eschscholzia californica*) and smoke tree (*Cotinus*).

When Plant corms in spring.

Where Crocosmias grow best in full sun. Soil should be well drained and fairly rich.

ABOVE: *The brilliant red blooms of* Crocosmia *'Lucifer'.* BELOW: *The long, straplike leaves of montbretia arch up in stiff clumps, giving the plant a handsome overall shape.*

How Plant corms in groups of at least seven, setting them 2 inches deep and about 3 inches apart. You can dig individual holes or excavate a suitably deep patch of soil and distribute the corms at the proper spacing. Amend the dug soil with organic matter; then refill the holes and water thoroughly.

TLC Water regularly during growth and bloom, then just moderately during dormancy. After a few years, when flowering begins to decline, it's time to divide the clumps: dig them in early spring, separate, and replant.

*Most hybrids will also grow in zone 4.

Daffodil
Narcissus

Daffodils are probably the most familiar of all garden bulbs, and they are certainly the easiest to grow. Planted in a suitable spot, they'll appear faithfully year after year, enduring extremes of heat and cold and increasing their numbers without any help from the gardener. They need water only during growth and bloom, which happens to be during the rainy season in most of the Northwest—and gophers and deer, who relish the taste of many bulbs, don't care for daffodils in the least.

Narrow, straplike leaves emerge in late winter or early spring and are followed by blossoms held just above the foliage. Yellow and white flowers are the most common, but you can also find daffodils in shades of orange, red, apricot, pink, and cream. In many varieties, the central cup is a different color than the outer petals. Some daffodils are fragrant, and all make fine cut flowers—though you should give them a vase of their own, as the freshly cut stems release a substance that causes other cut flowers to wilt.

A happy mix of daffodils and ferns spills into a casual hillside garden.

PEAK SEASON

Daffodils bloom in late winter or early spring.

OUR FAVORITES

Among the scores of outstanding daffodils with bold flowers are deep yellow 'Arctic Gold' and 'King Alfred'; white 'Mount Hood'; and bicolors like 'Ice Follies' (pale yellow cup, white petals), 'Salome' (apricot cup, creamy petals), 'Fortissimo' (orange-red cup, yellow petals), and fragrant 'Actaea' (red-edged yellow cup, white petals). All grow 16 to 18 inches tall.

For a subtle effect, plant smaller-flowered types that bear clusters of blooms. *Narcissus bulbocodium* 'Golden Bells' and *N.* 'Tête-à-tête', both with yellow blossoms, reach only 6 inches tall. *N.* 'Silver Chimes', to 1 foot tall, has a pale yellow cup and silvery white petals. Jonquil (*N. jonquilla*), to about 1 foot tall, bears golden yellow, very fragrant blossoms.

GARDEN COMPANIONS

Plant daffodils beneath flowering trees, around shrubs, and in mixed borders. They combine well with other bulbs such as tulips, Greek windflowers (*Anemone blanda*), and glory-of-the-snow (*Chionodoxa luciliae*). To hide the fading foliage, plant daffodils among perennials like hardy geraniums (*Geranium*) and *Coreopsis* 'Moonbeam' or summer-blooming annuals like cosmos or zinnias.

When Purchase and plant daffodils as soon as they become available in garden centers (usually in early fall); buy the largest, firmest bulbs you can find. In mild-winter regions where temperatures stay warm deep into fall, delay planting until the weather cools.

Where Choose a location where plants will be in sun from the time growth begins until after bloom; thereafter, partial shade is best. Daffodils aren't fussy about soil, as long as it is well drained. If your soil is heavy, you can put them on slopes.

How Set bulbs approximately twice as deep as they are tall. Dig individual holes or excavate a patch of soil to the proper depth; space bulbs 6 inches apart. If soil is poorly drained, amend the dug soil with organic matter. Cover bulbs with soil and water thoroughly. Continue to water until autumn rains take over the job for you.

TLC After daffodils bloom, continue watering until foliage starts to turn yellow. You can snip off any stems that start to form seedpods, but let the

TOP: *The flaming blooms of 'Jetfire' daffodils.* BOTTOM: *'Thalia' has two milky white blossoms atop each stem.*

leaves fade and dry naturally before cutting them back. Daffodils don't need water in summer, but they can tolerate a moderate amount if drainage is good. When a decline in bloom signals overcrowding, dig the clumps just after foliage has yellowed completely. Knock off loose soil, then store the bulbs in a dark, dry, well-ventilated area until planting time.

Dahlia

Dahlia

Dahlias are remarkably diverse plants, ranging in height from 1 to 7 feet and bearing flowers in every color save blue and green. The blooms—which may be as small as a ping-pong ball or as large as a dinner plate—are described with names that hint at their variety: pompon, cactus, waterlily, peony, orchid. Even the handsome foliage varies: most dahlias have dark green, oval leaflets, but some sport foliage that's fernlike or the deepest purplish red. 'Bishop of Llandaff', for instance, presents its bright red, yellow-centered blossoms against a backdrop of black-red foliage. How's that for garden drama?

All dahlias grow quickly from tuberous roots into dense, bushy plants; tall varieties make lively summer hedges and do a good job as screening plants or seasonal fillers among shrubs. Smaller types bring zest to flower borders and grow beautifully in containers. Dahlias are prized as cut flowers. Just snip when the blooms are fully open and immediately place them in 3 inches of hot water to seal the stems; then arrange in cold water.

LEFT: *Quilled florets around a central disk are hallmarks of many hybrid dahlias. They add drama to any garden.*

PEAK SEASON

Dahlias bloom midsummer into fall.

OUR FAVORITES

Dahlia specialists offer an amazing assortment in a wide range of colors, patterns, and flower sizes and styles. Retail nurseries sell a more limited selection, but still in a wide range of colors, sizes, and styles. Varieties are often identified by color only, usually accompanied by a color photo of the flower. Choose according to your taste—all are desirable plants.

GARDEN COMPANIONS

Plant low-growing dahlias with colorful summer-flowering perennials like penstemon, daylilies, and black-eyed Susans or among annuals such as nasturtium (*Tropaeolum*), lobelia, and coleus. Taller dahlias provide a great contrast with ornamental grasses such as feather reed grass (*Calamagrostis* × *acutiflora*), maiden grass (*Miscanthus*), and pennisetums.

When Plant dahlias in spring after the soil has warmed.

Where Plants grow and bloom best in full sun and rich, well-drained soil. Keep in mind that flowers will face the sun.

How Space tuberous roots of smaller varieties 1 to 2 feet apart, those of larger varieties 4 to 5 feet apart. A week or two before planting, dig a planting hole for each root; make it 1 foot deep, 1 to 1½ feet wide. Add organic matter to the dug soil and refill the holes. At planting time, redig holes to 1 foot deep and incorporate about ¼ cup of granular low-nitrogen fertilizer into the soil at the bottom. Return 4 inches of soil to each hole, then place the root horizontally in the hole with the growth bud facing up. For tall varieties, insert a 6-foot stake 2 inches from the root, with the growth bud pointing toward it. Cover with 3 inches of soil. As shoots grow, gradually fill the holes with soil and begin watering. Bait for slugs, which are attracted to the new shoots. When shoots reach ground level, apply a 2-inch layer of mulch around the base of the plants, keeping it a few inches away from the stems.

TLC Dahlias need deep, regular watering. When shoots have three pairs of leaves, pinch out the growing tip. When the first flower buds form, apply a low-nitrogen fertilizer. After plants die down, protect through winter with a deep layer of straw or mulch. If your soil freezes, lift the clumps: After the tops have been blackened by frost, cut stalks to 4 inches above ground, then pry up the entire clump with a spading fork. Shake off loose soil, let the clumps dry, then place them in a box of dry sand, sawdust, or peat moss. Store them over winter in a cool, dark, dry place. About two weeks before planting, separate clumps with a sharp knife, leaving 1 inch of stalk and a growth bud attached to each section. Place roots in moist sand to plump them up and encourage sprouting before planting time.

BELOW, LEFT TO RIGHT: *Dahlia shapes look like little explosions, whether pompons, cactus, or semicactus types.*

Fritillary

Fritillaria

Fritillaries are the eccentric aunts of the lily family, bedecked in odd-shaped blooms of uncommon colors. The flowers of smaller types look like little flared bells or hats, each dangling from its own stalk among the slender leaves. And though a few species offer bright, clear oranges and yellows, the majority come in muted purples and brownish reds, often intricately mottled or even checkered (no paisley-patterned species have been identified to date).

Fritillaries grow best where there is definite winter chill, so they're suited to all but the hottest parts of the Northwest. Small species are great for naturalizing among grasses or at the edge of a woodland planting; they also do well in pots. Larger fritillaries make stunning accents in mixed planting schemes. Individual bulbs sometimes rest for a year after blooming, so plant them in groups for an annual display.

The bulbs and foliage of crown imperial *(F. imperialis)* have a musky perfume that is not to everyone's taste; in fact, the scent is said to be strong enough to repel rodents. One of the largest and most recognizable fritillaries, this species has been popular in gardens since Elizabethan times.

Fritillaria affinis is a Northwest native with blooms charmingly checkered in brownish purple and gleaming yellow.

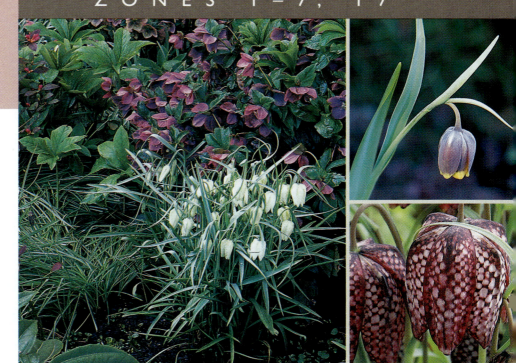

CLOCKWISE FROM LEFT: *Fritillaria pallidiflora, F. michailovskyi, and F. meleagris demonstrate the variety of colors and patterns of fritillaries.*

PEAK SEASON

Fritillaries bloom in spring.

OUR FAVORITES

Native black lily or chocolate lily (*Fritillaria camschatcensis*) grows to 1½ feet tall with nearly black blooms.

Crown imperial (*F. imperialis*) reaches 3 to 4 feet tall, with glossy leaves and a circular crown of large blossoms in red, orange, or yellow; a tuft of leaves tops the flowers and gives the plant the look of a startled tropical bird.

Checkered lily (*F. meleagris*) is a little charmer about 15 inches tall, with blooms checkered and veined in reddish brown and purple; leaves are gray green. *F. m. alba* has white flowers.

F. persica 'Adiyaman' sends up a leafy, 2- to 3-foot stalk loaded with small flowers in deep plum purple. The grayish green leaves contrast beautifully with the blooms.

GARDEN COMPANIONS

The small fritillaries combine well with other bulbs like camass and daffodil. Bishop's hat (*Epimedium*) and shade-tolerant *Geranium phaeum* are fine choices for hiding the fading foliage. Cool down the strong tones of crown imperial with *Geranium* 'Johnson's Blue' or ornamental alliums. Surround *F. persica* 'Adiyaman' with the soft gray of lamb's ears or silvery artemisia.

When Plant fritillaries in fall.

Where Most fritillaries prefer light shade, but both crown imperial and *F. persica* 'Adiyaman' grow best in full sun. All need porous, nutrient-rich soil.

How These bulbs are fragile and perishable, so handle them carefully and plant them as soon as you get them home. Dig holes to a depth of 1 foot and sprinkle a bulb fertilizer or bonemeal in the bottom. Mix a generous amount of organic matter such as rotted leaves or compost into the dug soil and partially refill the holes. Plant the bulbs root end down, setting smaller fritillaries 3 to 4 inches deep and 6 inches apart, larger types 5 to 6 inches deep and 8 to 12 inches apart. Cover with soil; keep well watered until winter rains take over.

TLC In areas where the ground freezes, cover the planting area with 6 inches of winter mulch; remove it in spring, before the bulb foliage comes up. Water regularly during growth and bloom, then cut back to moderate watering as foliage begins to die back. You can remove the spent blooms, but leave foliage in place until it is completely brown and withered. Water only occasionally during dormancy (checkered lily is an exception; it requires regular to moderate watering during summer).

*Black lily will also grow in zones A1–A3; F. persica 'Adiyaman' grows in zones 2–7, 17.

Iris

Iris

It's no mystery why the genus *Iris* is named for the Greek goddess of the rainbow: these flowers come in almost every color, often with several contrasting hues in a single bloom. The intricate blossoms of irises have three upright petals called standards and three drooping ones called falls; in some types, the falls are adorned with small, fuzzy, caterpillar-like structures known as beards. Both falls and standards may be lavishly ruffled or flared.

The tall bearded irises have fans of sturdy, gray-green leaves. These old-fashioned charmers are so easy to grow and divide that they get passed around from one gardener to another. Each year, breeders introduce new variations; the latest craze is for petals that are heavily striped, banded, or speckled.

Siberian irises have grassy leaves and beardless flowers in blue, purple, pink, yellow, or white. These are easy to work into a perennial border, and they're breathtaking in naturalistic drifts of a single color where the sun shines through their delicate petals.

LEFT, TOP: Siberian irises 'Miss Duluth' and 'Dewful' look like exotic birds taking flight. LEFT, BOTTOM: The large split seed capsules and orange seeds of Gladwin iris.

PEAK SEASON

Irises bloom in spring or early summer; "remontant" bearded types bloom again in fall.

OUR FAVORITES

Siberian irises grow 1 to 4 feet tall, depending on variety. Among the many lovely choices are 'Butter and Sugar' (white and yellow bicolor), 'Caesar's Brother' (deep blue, with distinctive markings), and 'Pink Haze' (lavender pink).

Tall bearded irises grow 2½ to 4 feet tall. There are thousands to choose from, including award-winning 'Beverly Sills' (coral pink and tangerine), 'Hello Darkness' (blackish purple), and 'Yaquina Blue' (true blue).

Gladwin iris (*I. foetidissima*) has glossy evergreen leaves and grows to about 1½ feet tall. After blooming it forms dramatic seed capsules.

GARDEN COMPANIONS

Irises combine well with mounding plants like coreopsis, euphorbia, hardy geraniums, peonies, and shrub roses. Siberian irises look great in a meadow setting among grasses and sedges.

When Plant irises in late summer or early fall.

Where Irises grow best in full sun and well-drained soil.

How Prepare the planting area a few days beforehand by incorporating organic matter such as compost or well-rotted leaves. Space plants 1 to 2 feet apart. Rhizomes of tall bearded irises need just the slightest covering of soil, while those of Siberian irises should be set 1 to 2 inches deep. Dig a hole deep enough to accommodate the roots, then set rhizomes at the appropriate depth. Fill in with soil around the roots; firm soil with your fingers, then water well. For bearded irises, water sparingly after planting until new growth appears.

ABOVE: *Showy seeds of Gladwin iris.* BELOW: *Tall bearded iris and Anthriscus sylvestris.*

TLC Once growth begins, water irises regularly until about six weeks after flowers fade; then cut back to moderate watering. Apply a balanced granular fertilizer when plants begin growth in late winter or early spring, then again right after the blooming season ends. Tall bearded irises need dividing every three or four years to keep blooming; Siberian irises can go much longer. In late summer or early fall, dig clumps and use a sharp knife to separate old, woody rhizomes from fresh new ones. Trim leaves to 6 to 8 inches and replant divisions in soil enriched with organic matter.

Lily
Lilium

Lilies are often extolled in regal terms—and rightly so, for they are the most stately and aristocratic of bulbs, with blossoms of generous proportions and, often, magnificent fragrance. The flowers are generally shaped like trumpets, though a few have petals that sweep back dramatically; all make excellent cut flowers. Asiatic and Oriental hybrids are the most popular and easiest to grow in the Northwest.

The flaming orange blooms of Asiatic lilies are complemented by the blue annual, Cerinthe 'Purpurascens', and a distant bench.

Asiatic hybrids shrug off winter lows of −30°/−34°C. They bloom in early summer, with flowers in vivid shades, often marked with dark spots or contrasting bands of color. Blooms rise from attractive clumps of narrow, dark green leaves. These midsize lilies are especially effective when planted in large drifts.

Oriental hybrids just may be the showiest of all flowers, sporting huge, extravagantly perfumed blooms in white, pink, or yellow. The petals may be spotted or banded with contrasting colors. They bloom later than Asiatic types and are a little less hardy (to about −20°F/−29°C). These lofty garden royals are ideal for crowning the back of a flower border, although—like some monarchies—they may need propping up.

PEAK SEASON

Asiatic hybrids bloom in early summer, Oriental types in midsummer and early fall.

OUR FAVORITES

Asiatic hybrids grow 1½ to 4½ feet tall, depending on variety; they are often sold in colorful mixes, including eye-popping bicolors. Smaller types, such as the Pixie series, are perfect for containers.

Among the many fragrant Oriental hybrids are 'Casablanca' (pure white), 'Magic Pink' (soft pink with a glowing golden center), and 'Stargazer' (deep pink petals edged in creamy white). The bulbs reach 3 to 6 feet tall.

GARDEN COMPANIONS

To hide their fading foliage, plant lilies in the middle or back of the flower border, among shrubby or mounding neighbors such as asters, bugbane (Cimicifuga), false spiraea (Astilbe), chrysanthemums, peonies, or roses.

When Plant lily bulbs in spring or fall, once they are available in nurseries. Or plant out from containers whenever the soil can be worked.

Where Lilies do best in well-drained soil in full sun or partial shade; ideally, the plants' bases should be shaded while the tops (the flowers) are in sun. Choose a site that has good air circulation but is protected from strong winds.

How Handle these fragile bulbs carefully. For each bulb, dig a hole 1 to 1½ feet deep, spacing the holes about 1 foot apart. Amend the dug soil with organic matter and refill the hole so that the top of the bulb will be 3 to 6 inches below ground level. Place each bulb with its fat end down, then fill in with amended soil, tamping it down firmly around the bulb to eliminate air pockets. If the variety you're planting needs staking, place supports now to avoid damaging the bulb later. Nursery-grown lilies should be planted at the same depth they were growing in their pots. Water regularly until plants are established.

TLC Water regularly during growth and bloom, and remove spent flowers promptly. Cut back to moderate watering once dormancy begins (when the leaves turn yellow), but never let the bulbs go completely dry. After foliage has died back, cut back the main stem to near ground level. In coldest climates, apply a thick layer of organic mulch to help the bulbs survive the winter; be sure to mark the spot so you can pull back the mulch in spring. If plants decline after a few years, carefully dig and divide them.

*Asiatic hybrids also thrive in zones A1–A3.

TOP AND MIDDLE: *Asiatic hybrids.* BOTTOM: *Oriental hybrid.* BELOW, LEFT: *Asiatic lilies with equally colorful snapdragons.*

Ornamental Allium
Allium

Although these bulbs are related to the edible onion (as well as to leek, garlic, chives, and shallot), their appeal is in their flowers, not their flavor. Tiny blooms form roundish clusters that look like solid balls or exploding fireworks in blue, purple, red, pink, yellow, or white, carried on leafless stems that rise anywhere from 6 inches to more than 5 feet high, depending on species. Ornamental alliums are peerless for bringing structural interest to the garden. The straplike leaves often begin to die back about the time the flowers are opening, but since the foliage is held close to the ground, it's easily masked with annuals or perennials that fill in by late spring.

Many ornamental alliums have a pleasant fragrance, and those that truly smell like onions have to be cut or bruised to give off the scent. Larger types make wonderful cut flowers, fresh or dried; the oniony aroma dissipates quickly when stems are placed in a vase of water. Butterflies are attracted to these bulbs, but rodents and deer seem to be of the "hold the onions" persuasion.

Giant allium is among the most dramatic flowers for mixed borders. The softball-size globes always attract attention.

PEAK SEASON

Most ornamental alliums bloom in late spring or summer, after spring bulbs have finished and before summer bloomers have emerged.

OUR FAVORITES

Blue allium (*Allium caeruleum*) grows to 1½ feet tall, with cornflower blue blossom clusters 2 inches across.

Giant allium (*A. giganteum*) holds softball-size, bright lilac flower heads on stems at least 5 feet tall in summer. *A. aflatunense* is similar but half as tall, with smaller blooms.

Golden garlic (*A. moly*) has bright yellow flowers in open, 2-inch-wide clusters on stems to 1½ feet tall.

Star of Persia (*A. christophii*), just 15 inches tall, has unusual starlike, pinkish purple flowers in loose clusters about 8 inches across.

GARDEN COMPANIONS

Group ornamental alliums with plants that will hide the bulbs' foliage as it yellows. Good candidates include artemisia, hardy geranium, daylily, knotweed (*Persicaria*), lady's-mantle (*Alchemilla*), ornamental grasses, sea holly (*Eryngium*), and upright sedums.

When Plant dormant bulbs in early fall, nursery-grown plants in spring.

Where Plant in full sun or partial shade in well-drained soil.

How Plant bulbs as deep as their height or width, whichever is greater. Dig individual holes or excavate a patch of soil to the proper depth; set bulbs 4 to 12 inches apart, depending on the eventual size of the plant. Amend the dug soil with organic matter and refill holes. Plant nursery-grown plants at the same depth they were growing in their pots. Water well.

ABOVE: *The flower heads of star of Persia resemble puffs of purple smoke.* BELOW: *A close-up of one "star."*

TLC Water regularly until bloom time is over, then give little or no water until new growth appears in spring. Remove the flower heads as they fade; or let them dry in place if you like the look. Let foliage wither and die back naturally.

*Blue allium, golden garlic, and star of Persia will also grow in zone 1.

Snowflake

Leucojum

The dainty flowers of these old-fashioned bulbs are like miniature lampshades, each crafted of six milky white petals touched at the tip with a dot of green. Dangling from curving, leafless stems, the fanciful blooms stand out dramatically, seeming to glow against the dark green, straplike foliage.

Snowflakes are easy to grow—and they make permanent additions to the garden, increasing each year to provide fuller clumps and more blooms. Because they prefer mostly sunny conditions during growth and bloom but require little light during their summer dormancy, these bulbs are perfect for naturalizing among deciduous shrubs and trees. Snowflakes are also charming at the front of a casual flower bed or tucked among stones at the edge of a woodland.

Summer snowflake *(Leucojum aestivum)* thrives in damp spots and will even grow well at the edge of a pond; despite its name, it blooms in early to midspring, somewhat later than spring snowflake *(L. vernum).* For a long season of attractive foliage and delicate blossoms, sprinkle both types of snowflakes here and there in your garden.

PEAK SEASON

All snowflakes bloom in early to late spring.

OUR FAVORITES

Spring snowflake (*Leucojum vernum*) will thrive only in areas with definite winter chill (below 20°F/–7°C). Foot-tall stems rise above a clump of attractive leaves, each holding one or two flowers.

Summer snowflake (*L. aestivum*) may reach 1½ feet tall and bears several flowers per stem; the blossoms have a faint chocolate scent. 'Gravetye Giant' is a larger, more robust grower with bigger blooms.

GARDEN COMPANIONS

Plant snowflakes with bluebells (*Scilla*) and pale yellow daffodils (*Narcissus*) for a colorful spring show. The spring sun and summer shade provided by deciduous shrubs and trees such as flowering quince (*Chaenomeles*) and maple (*Acer*) suit snowflakes perfectly.

LEFT: *Spring snowflakes snuggle up to a rhododendron, creating a simple but elegant composition of green and white.*

When Plant snowflakes in fall.

Where Choose a spot that receives full sun or light shade. Snowflakes bloom best if planted in well-drained, moist soil.

ABOVE AND BELOW: *Spring snowflake rises to 1 foot tall, with nodding blooms sporting dainty dots of pure green.*

How Set bulbs so that their tops are 3 to 4 inches deep, and space them about 4 inches apart. Dig individual holes to the proper depth and spacing or, if you're planting a sweep of bulbs, excavate a patch of soil to the correct depth. Amend the dug soil with organic matter. Cover bulbs with soil, then water thoroughly. Give newly planted bulbs regular water if autumn rains don't do the job for you.

TLC Water regularly until foliage dies down in late spring; give some water during summer dormancy. (If planted in shade, summer snowflake can get by with no summer water.) If clumps get too crowded to bloom well, dig them up after foliage dies down, then divide and replant.

*Summer snowflake also grows in zones 7 and 17.

Tulip
Tulipa

Pots of the stately, impressive 'White Triumphator' tulips can be moved front and center when in bloom.

Choosing tulips is like shopping in a candy store: there are so many delectable colors and enticing shapes to choose from, it's hard to know where to begin. These familiar bulbs have been divided into at least a dozen groups according to bloom time and flower appearance, but for the gardener, the main choice is between hybrid and species tulips.

Hybrids are large and fancy, with single or double blooms that may be solid colored, bicolored, or streaked with several contrasting hues. Most are shaped like goblets or bowls, though some look more like lilies and others have petals that are fantastically fringed or ruffled. Hybrid tulips are probably best treated as annuals, as they're unlikely to perform well after two or three glorious years.

Small, early-flowering species tulips are both more casual and more reliable than the hybrid types. They look like wildflowers and are more likely to return in successive years.

PEAK SEASON

Tulips bloom from early to late spring, depending on type.

OUR FAVORITES

Hybrid tulips come in so many shapes and colors that choosing is simply a matter of taste; sizes are mostly in the 1- to 2-foot range. Take note of the bloom time; package or catalog descriptions will specify early, midseason, or late.

Among species tulips, a few of the best for Northwest gardens are *T. batalinii,* with soft yellow flowers in midseason; *T. greigii,* with midseason blooms in many hues; *T. kaufmanniana,* with spectacular crimson flowers above burgundy-striped leaves; and *T. tarda,* a good choice for Alaska, with early blooms that look like gold-centered white stars.

GARDEN COMPANIONS

Plant tulips in groups among hardy geraniums, daylily, euphorbia, peonies, or larger types of primroses. They look great beneath flowering deciduous trees like dogwood, flowering cherry, and magnolia.

ABOVE: *Lipstick pink 'Barcelona' tulip.* BELOW, LEFT TO RIGHT: *T. gregii 'Authority'; Darwin hybrid tulips; the fringed tulip 'Aleppo'.*

When Plant bulbs in late fall, after soil has cooled.

Where Tulips need a sunny spot and good, fast-draining soil. It's best to plant hybrids in a different spot each year; if you want to replant in the same location, bring in fresh soil from elsewhere in the garden when you plant.

How Set bulbs three times as deep as they are wide; space them 4 to 8 inches apart. Dig individual holes to the proper depth and spacing or excavate a patch of soil to the proper depth. Amend the dug soil with plenty of organic matter. Cover bulbs with the amended soil, then water thoroughly. Tulips also grow well for a year in containers filled with rich potting soil; space bulbs closely and plant a little less deeply than you would in the garden.

TLC Give tulips regular water during growth and bloom. If you want to try growing them as perennials, feed with a balanced fertilizer just after leaves emerge from the soil; after bloom, remove the spent flowers but let the foliage wither completely before cutting it back.

*T. tarda *also grows in zones A1–A3.

Tiny Treasures

When you think about bulbs, you may picture a platter size dahlia or a beefy red tulip—the bigger, the better. But don't overlook the charms of smaller bulbs.

Standing less than a foot tall, these petite gems are perfect for sprinkling around the garden. Plant a handful here and there along a path, drive, or sidewalk—anywhere they'll catch your eye in very early spring, when most are in bloom. Let them spread into a carpet beneath a Japanese maple or a favorite old apple tree, or tuck a few into containers all around the garden.

Our Favorites

Bluebell or Siberian squill (*Scilla siberica;* zones A2, A3; 1–7) produces bell-shaped flowers on an upright stem that reaches 8 inches tall. Intensely violet blue forms are most popular, but there are varieties in white, lilac pink, and many shades of blue.

Cyclamen species (zones 2–7, 17) feature striking, often silver-patterned leaves and upswept blooms in shades from white to darkest pink. *C. coum* (to 6 inches tall) blooms from late fall into early spring, and *C. hederifolium* (about 4 inches tall and likely to spread by reseeding) blooms from summer into fall.

Dutch crocus *(Crocus vernus; zones 1–7, 17)* has grassy, silver-striped leaves and little gold-centered cups of white, yellow, and many shades of lavender and purple, often daintily streaked with other shades. Plants top out at 5 inches tall.

Glory-of-the-Snow *(Chionodoxa luciliae; zones 1–7, 17)* sports starlike blossoms in blue, white, or pink along stems that may reach 6 inches tall; leaves are narrow and midgreen. Plants spread by self-seeding.

Grape hyacinth *(Muscari armeniacum; zones A1–A3, 1–7, 17)* starts off early with masses of grassy, fleshy leaves that appear in fall and live through the cold months. In early spring, spikes about 8 inches tall hold tiny, urn-shaped blue flowers clustered like little bunches of grapes.

Greek windflower *(Anemone blanda; zones 2–7, 17)* forms a mat of soft foliage topped by open, shallowly cupped flowers in sky blue, pink, white, or purplish red; all have a woodland charm and stand just 2 to 8 inches tall.

Snowdrop *(Galanthus nivalis; zones 1–7, 17)* is like a miniature version (at 6 to 9 inches tall) of one of our

Top 10 bulbs, snowflake (*Leucojum*), with strap-shaped leaves and nodding, bell-like flowers. The outer petals are pure white, the inner ones marked with green.

Planting and Care

These little bulbs should be planted in fall (with the exception of cyclamen, which does best when planted during its summer dormancy).

Choose a well-drained site in bright light but not all-day baking sun; the dappled shade beneath deciduous trees is ideal for most of these plants. If you're going for a natural look, toss a handful of bulbs into the air and plant them where they fall; just make sure they are at least 3 to 4 inches apart. Dig each hole two to three times as deep as the bulb is tall and plant with the roots pointing down. If squirrels and other rodents are a problem in your area, you may want to enclose bulbs in a buried cage of wire mesh. Refill the hole with soil amended with a bit of sand to improve drainage. If you're planting in containers, use a commercial potting mix, which will provide adequate drainage without added sand. Water regularly during growth and bloom.

RIGHT, TOP TO BOTTOM: *Snowdrops; bluebells and 'Hawera' daffodils; Cyclamen* coum. OPPOSITE PAGE, TOP: *The lavender and white cups of Dutch crocus will multiply over the years as the bulbs naturalize.* OPPOSITE PAGE, BOTTOM: *'White Splendor' Greek windflower; grape hyacinth.*

Annuals

I'm sure I'm not the only person to have described annual flowers as brash, gaudy, exuberant, and too uniform. And yet that's exactly why I plant them. Like most Alaskans who enjoy seven months of snow, I find that color—any color, the brighter and more electric the better—makes summer come alive.

So each winter I follow a ritual along with many other gardeners all over the Northwest: perusing catalogs and searching greenhouses for the newest, most unusual annuals for my garden.

Our fondness for colorful annuals is evident all around us. Yes, it's true that they make up the precise (and predictable) patterns of floral clocks and theme displays in public gardens. But what about those piercing blue billows in the giant hanging baskets and planters along the streets of my hometown of Fairbanks? Annual lobelia. Those brilliant spots of season-long color in mixed borders? Starry cosmos. The pure white and sensational chartreuse plants that electrify my shade garden and make it glow against the framework of trees and shrubs? A mix of impatiens and coleus. The bright surprises that pop up here and there in my vegetable garden and along a stone path? Reseeding Johnny-jump-ups and poppies. And at the far northern edges of the Pacific Northwest, what garden would be complete without season-extending pansies and violas, those tough, hardy flowers that keep blooming long after the first fall frosts?

HOW THEY GROW

Annuals are plants whose life cycle occurs entirely in one growing season, from seed germination, through flowering, and finally to seed development. (But in my garden, this botanical definition mostly fits the weeds.) Only a handful of my annual flowers actually set seed; most exhaust their energies by naturally producing blankets of blooms, or I deadhead them to prevent seed formation and thus encourage more flowers. My garden is also full of plants that in milder climates are usually considered perennials, such as Shasta daisies (*Chrysanthemum maximum*) and black-eyed Susans. So I prefer to think of annuals as plants whose purpose has a definite time frame in the garden regardless of life span. They are single-season plants.

ANNUALS IN THE GARDEN

Annuals' fast growth from seed to full bloom is a necessity in cold climates, and their ease of cultivation makes them perfect candidates for a child's first garden as well as for the veteran landscaper searching for new combinations. I grow annuals for color. If I don't like a flower or a certain mix of blooms, I can try something new next season for relatively little cost.

ABOVE: *An exuberant blend of brilliant mixed zinnias surrounds a pillar of of orange and yellow sunflowers.*
OPPOSITE PAGE: *Introductions of annual vines such as this 'Alaska Mix' nasturtium feature stripes, stipples, and new color combinations.*

By far the most popular display at the University of Alaska Georgeson Botanical Garden is the trial fields where we test 300 or so annual flowers each year. The Top 10 annuals highlighted in this chapter show just how varied this group of plants can be. You're bound to find something irresistible for your own Northwest garden. —PAT HOLLOWAY

Clarkia
Clarkia

Clarkias are true northwesterners; the genus name, *Clarkia,* honors William Clark, who first collected the seeds during the Lewis and Clark expedition. Like many wildflowers, clarkias have a simple charm, with pretty, slightly fluted, upward-facing blooms. Planted in a mass, the overall effect is of a shimmery, rippling, silky sea.

Newer hybrids include types that are double flowered or have divided petals—some, like 'Pink Ribbons' and 'Passion for Purple', have petals so deeply divided they resemble geranium flowers. The color range has expanded beyond the flower's original pink to peach, coral, creamy yellow, white, mauve, and orange.

Like California poppies, clarkias look terrific in casual plantings, and make an impact when planted in drifts. Many of the new varieties, however, are well behaved in mixed borders and self-sow only enough to fill gaps in the planting scheme

A field of breezy godetia (Clarkia amoena) mixes happily with blue cornflowers. They'll look just as cheerful together if put into a pot or jug indoors.

in subsequent seasons. The taller-stemmed varieties also make excellent cut flowers.

There is a lot of confusion in the naming of *Clarkia* and *Godetia,* so you may find different species names at the nursery than those given here. Still, all types are easy to grow, as long as you don't spoil them with rich soil, fertilizer, or too much water.

PEAK SEASON

Clarkias bloom in spring and often again in fall.

OUR FAVORITES

Several hybrid series sold as *Clarkia amoena* or godetia make good candidates for borders or the cutting garden. The prolific dwarf Satin series grows 8 to 12 inches tall with flowers of deep rose, lavender, pink, red with white edges, salmon, white, or mixed colors. Bonita, also dwarf, comes in light pastel scarlet and cream. The Royal Bouquet and Grace series both grow to 2 feet tall. Royal Bouquet has double blooms in shades of scarlet, salmon, wine red, white, purple, and rose pink; Grace has simple rose, red, and purple flowers.

When Clarkias grow during the cooler temperatures of spring and early summer, and again in fall. In the mild-winter zones 4–7 and 17, sow in fall; in other zones, sow in spring.

Where Most clarkias are better off grown in the ground rather than in containers. They need sandy, well-drained soil and regular water.

How Seed plants in place, as clarkias do not transplant well. Keep the soil moist from seeding to flowering. Thin plants to 10 inches apart.

TLC Keep plants moist but don't overwater—these are tough wildflowers. Godetia (*C. amoena*) prefers a little more moisture than the other species. Clarkias need no fertilizer.

Newer varieties of clarkia and godetia often have watercolor-like markings on the petals. Many seed companies sell packages of mixed colors.

C. pulchella 'Passion for Purple' has deeply divided petals, as does pure white *C. p.* 'Snowflake'.

C. unguiculata (sometimes called *C. elegans*) 'Apple Blossom' and 'Salmon Queen' are old varieties that make good cut flowers.

Several varieties of *C. bottae* offer blue and purple hues, including 'Amethyst Glow', 'Lilac Blossom', and 'Lady in Blue'.

GARDEN COMPANIONS

Most clarkias look best with flowers of similar simplicity and open habit. You can mix them in with early- and late-summer bloomers such as columbines, poppies, annual phlox, penstemons, and bearded iris. *C. unguiculata* mixes well with poppies and cornflowers.

Coleus

Solenostemon scutellarioides (formerly *Coleus × hybridus*)

Coleus are about the most vibrantly colored foliage plants for the shady garden—variously spotted, striped, blotched, and edged in dazzling combinations of chartreuse, buff, orange, red, magenta, cinnamon, cerise, yellow, salmon, orange, purple, and brown (to name just a few). Got a summertime fern garden that needs a quick pick-me-up? Plant a coleus with lime green borders from the Dragon series. Want to punch up a north-facing border? Try deep cherry–and–pale green 'Pineapple Queen' and cranberry-and-lime 'Cranberry Salad'. Looking to create an outrageous group of container plants? Mix 'Copacetic Yellow' (lemon yellow spotted with lime) with 'Black Magic' (dark purple with avocado green margins) and 'Northern Lights' (a blend of lavender, rose, salmon, burgundy, and green)—or buy a cell-pack of a seed mix such as 'Dragon Sunset & Volcano Mixed'. Even the names generate sizzle.

Most coleus form bushy plants 10 inches to 3 feet in height. Though the plants do produce flower spikes, most gardeners pinch them off to focus attention on the foliage. Because coleus are cold-tender tropicals, you'll need to bid farewell to the plants in fall, but if you can't bear it bring them inside—they make fine houseplants.

Even black-eyed Susans can seem a little subdued beside a fiery, two-tone coleus. Darker varieties such as this one can tolerate more sun than other kinds.

PEAK SEASON

Coleus thrive in the garden from summer until frost.

OUR FAVORITES

New coleus seem to appear every day; this is just a sampling.

In the darker colors, 'Palisandra' has nearly black, velvety leaves; 'Inky Fingers' has chocolaty purple leaves with chartreuse edges; 'Black Magic' has black leaves bordered in green. Two of the most sun tolerant are 'Plum Parfait', with ruffled purplish leaves edged in pink, and 'Burgundy Sun', with heart-shaped leaves of deep burgundy.

Coleus in shades of red and copper include 'Black Dragon' (red with black edges), 'Rustic Orange' (salmon orange with yellow-green margins), 'El Brighto' (coral pink to molten burgundy and all colors in between), 'Kiwi Fern' (deeply cut red leaves edged with bright gold), and 'Aurora' (with pink and green, watercolor-like markings).

Light up the shade with pure chartreuse 'Amazon' or 'Golda'; creamy lemon 'Buttermint' or 'Wild Lime' (edged with green); green-and-cream-variegated 'Alligator' or 'Sparkler'; cranberry-and-cream 'Max Levering'; or pink-tinged 'Rose Blush' with forest green leaf margins.

When Plant in spring but not too early, as coleus simply won't grow until the weather warms up.

Where Plants need rich, loose, well-drained soil. Most types prefer shade, but darker types tolerate more sun. In general, the more red or purple pigment in the leaves, the greater the sun tolerance.

How Water the plants in their nursery containers. Dig planting holes larger than the root balls, no more than 1 foot apart. To remove the transplants, tip the containers on their sides and use your thumb to push the root balls up gently from the bottom. Loosen the roots, then set the plants in the holes, making sure the tops of the root balls are even with the surrounding soil surface. Firm soil around roots and water well.

TLC Water regularly and feed once monthly with high-nitrogen fertilizer. Pinch off flower spikes as they appear.

A kaleidoscope of colorful coleus. TOP TO BOTTOM: *'Kiwi Fern', 'Rustic Orange', 'Solar Sunrise', 'Red Ruffles'.*

GARDEN COMPANIONS

If you want to add some brio to your containers, match coleus with a variegated pelargonium such as 'Vancouver Centennial' or with lime green or burgundy sweet potato vine. If those combinations are too electric, show off your coleus in the border against a more restrained background of shade lovers such as ferns, hostas, and impatiens. Large-leafed coleus, such as those in the Wizard, Giant Leaf, and Giant Exhibition series, mix well with other exotic plants such as gingers, elephant's ear (*Colocasia esculenta*), New Zealand flax (*Phormium*), tree ferns, cannas, and hardy bananas.

Cornflower
Centaurea cyanus

No longer just "cornflower blue," varieties of this old favorite can now be found in hues of white, pink, purple, and maroon.

Cornflowers are like the teenagers of the garden: slightly gangly, with thistlelike flowers that seem too big for their slender, silvery stems. But these humble field flowers have qualities that some other annuals lack. First, cornflowers can boast a true, royal blue unmatched in blooms with this height. They also make everlasting cut flowers, which is why they are traditional favorites for boutonnieres. (Chances are your grandfather tucked one of these "bachelor's buttons" in his lapel on special occasions.) Finally, cornflowers will prosper in rocky or sandy soil, asking little in return for their happy-go-lucky blooms.

These plants may be too casual for the formal garden, but they're right at home in meadowlike settings mixed with other carefree flowers and grasses. Cornflowers range in height from about 10 inches to 2½ feet, depending on the variety. Newer types, such as the Florence series, have been bred for less height and more blooms, which makes them more suitable for the border—or for containers, where they can be mixed with other flowers and surrounded by spillers.

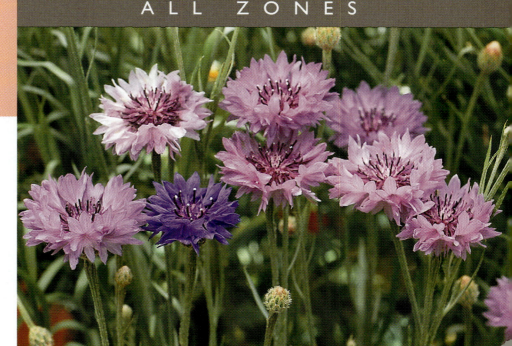

PEAK SEASON

Cornflowers bloom from late spring through summer.

OUR FAVORITES

The Boy series (to 2½ feet tall) makes good cut flowers in white, red, blue, and even a deep, sultry maroon.

The Florence series (to 13 inches tall) offers colors ranging from lavender to soft pink. These are bushy cornflowers with plenty of blooms per plant.

The Frosted Queen series (to 1 foot) has powder-puff blooms of red, burgundy, purple, and pink, each petal tipped with shimmery white.

GARDEN COMPANIONS

Cornflowers blend well with Mexican feather grass (Nassella tenuissima) and California or oriental poppies. Plant the tallest varieties with low spreaders such as hardy geraniums, licorice plant (Helichrysum petiolare), or nasturtiums, which will wind through the wiry cornflower stems without overwhelming them.

When Plant cornflowers in spring for summer bloom.

Where Cornflowers thrive in full or partial sun in moderately fertile soil.

ABOVE: *A mix of shades from the Florence series.* BELOW LEFT: *Cornflowers in not-quite-black shades of deep blue, maroon, and dark purple mix marvelously with orange and yellow flowers such as California poppies and tickseed.*

How Dwarf cornflowers are best started from seed sown in place after the last frost. Cover them with ⅛ to ¼ inch of soil or a layer of newspaper, as they germinate best in darkness. Taller types should be planted from nursery containers, so they'll have time to grow to their full height by summer. To transplant them, first water the plants in their containers. Dig planting holes just larger than the root balls, spacing them 1 to 2 feet apart (check the plant label). Tip containers on their sides and use your thumb to push the root balls up gently from the bottom. Loosen the roots, then set the plants in the holes, making sure the tops of the root balls are even with the surrounding soil surface. Firm soil around roots and water well.

TLC Cornflowers are drought tolerant and will flop over if given too much water. The tallest types may need support; if they start to collapse, tie them loosely with string to casual bamboo sticks, or store-bought plant stakes. After the first flush of bloom, shear the plants back to a few inches in height for another burst of color.

Cosmos

Cosmos

The name cosmos sounds almost celestial and, indeed, cosmos *are* stars in the garden—though they light up the border with more of a twinkle than a dazzle. Cosmos have a sweet simplicity, with daisylike petals in white, pink, or red surrounding a yellow buttonlike center, and ferny green foliage. The flowers come just in time to lift the garden out of the midsummer doldrums.

ABOVE: *Set against a cheery cottage wall, this glorious blaze of flowers includes sunflowers, pink and white* Cosmos bipinnatus *and golden* C. sulphureus. BELOW: C. sulphureus *'Ladybird Yellow'*.

Plant tall cosmos toward the back of a border, in front of a picket fence, or in a cottage garden. These 6-footers may need support, but a few casual sticks, a wall, or the fence should do the trick. Always err on the side of overplanting with these airy annuals; they look best in clumps or drifts. Dwarf types, which grow 1 to 2 feet tall, make a wonderful addition to a meadow planting, surrounded by low-growing grasses and perhaps a few English daisies. They'll generally pay you back for the original planting by reseeding themselves and emerging the following year.

When Plant cosmos from cell-packs or 4-inch pots in late spring, after all danger of frost has passed.

Where Cosmos produce the best flower show when planted in average or even poor soil. Richer soil will encourage the plants to grow more foliage than flowers.

ABOVE: *A garden visitor alights on a pure white cosmos bloom.* BELOW: *Cosmos from the Sonata series have large flowers on compact plants.*

How Water the plants in their nursery containers. Dig planting holes larger than the plants' root balls, spacing them about 8 inches apart. Tip the containers on their sides and use your thumb to push the root balls up gently from the bottom. Loosen the roots, then set the plants in the holes, making sure the tops of the root balls are even with the surrounding soil surface. Firm soil around roots and water well.

TLC Give cosmos moderate water, but forget the fertilizer—they don't need it. When flowers are spent and only the central disk remains, deadhead to prevent seed formation. You can leave a few seed heads in place at the end of the season and the plants will obligingly self-sow.

PEAK SEASON

Cosmos bloom summer through fall.

OUR FAVORITES

Several series of *Cosmos bipinnatus* in mixes are good for cutting, including Versailles (2 to 3 feet tall), Sensation (3 to 6 feet), Sonata (1½ to 2 feet), and Psyche (to 3½ feet).

The Seashell series (to 3 feet) has petals rolled into tubes, as does crimson 'Pied Piper Red' (to 2½ feet). 'Candy Stripe' (to 3 feet) has white flowers with crimson borders.

Yellow cosmos (*C. sulphureus*) can grow to 7 feet with fiery orange, scarlet, or gold flowers. The Bright Lights series grows to 4 feet with large (2½-inch), semi-double flowers in golden and orange shades. The dwarf Ladybird series grows to 1 foot with flowers that range from pale yellow to scarlet; those in the Sunny series top out at 15 inches in similar shades. 'Cosmic Orange' has semidouble incandescent orange flowers up to 1½ feet tall.

GARDEN COMPANIONS

Pair *C. bipinnatus* with other carefree plants, such as bearded iris, coneflowers (*Echinacea* and *Rudbeckia*), purple fountain grass (*Pennisetum*), lavender, , penstemon, gaura, and Santa Barbara daisy (*Erigeron*). *C. sulphureus* looks stunning with blue-flowered salvias, catmint (*Nepeta*), and *Scabiosa*.

Flowering Tobacco
Nicotiana

Relatives of the commercial tobacco plant they may be, but flowering tobaccos are much more ornamental—and fragrant—than their agricultural cousins. All form rosettes of sticky leaves, from which twiggy spikes of tubular flowers rise. And most have a sweet fragrance that is particularly intoxicating in the evening. Generally, the taller the plant, the headier the aroma.

The original flowering tobaccos had greenish blooms, but now there are many more colors available, including white, red, purple, pink, and salmon. Even that green has been refined to more elegant shades of lime and chartreuse.

Most flowering tobacco plants fully open their flowers only at night (but in coastal gardens, they may also open on overcast days). White varieties are best for the night garden, where they seem to gather up the moonlight and shoot it back out into the garden, especially the long, pendent trumpets of *Nicotiana sylvestris*.

Intermingling with foxgloves, mint, and zinnias, flowering tobacco growing around a birdhouse is a draw for birds seeking food and shelter.

ABOVE: Nicotiana sylvestris *produces a tangle of fragrant white trumpets.* BELOW: *The striking apple-green blooms of* N. langsdorfii.

PEAK SEASON

Flowering tobacco blooms from early summer to fall, depending on variety.

OUR FAVORITES

Nicotiana alata Havana series reaches 1½ feet tall and has large flowers in striking colors, including pale pink ('Havana Appleblossom') and deep red ('Havana Carmine Rose'). Nicki series blooms during the day in shades of lime, white, pink, and red. The shorter Domino series is best for containers, growing to 1 foot tall with upward-facing flowers.

The green flowers of *N. langsdorffii* resemble dainty bells swinging every which way on 3-foot-tall, wiry stems.

N. sylvestris is the aristocrat, growing to a majestic 7 feet tall with 3-inch, narrow tubular flowers that flare into pure white stars at the tip.

GARDEN COMPANIONS

Plant *N. sylvestris* with other airy annuals and perennials, such as *Verbena bonariensis,* spider flower *(Cleome),* or tall cosmos. To hide any ragged leaves, fill in around the base of the plants with phlox, cannas, or other late-summer growers.

Shorter varieties blend nicely with velvety-leafed scented geraniums, lamb's ears, and snow-in-summer *(Cerastium tomentosum).* Vegetable gardeners often plant *N. alata* to act as a decoy for pests such as tomato hornworm.

When Plant flowering tobacco outside after the last frost date for your area.

Where Flowering tobacco is a sun lover, and it appreciates good, organically enriched, well-drained soil. *N. sylvestris* can grow to 7 feet tall, so plant it where you want emphasis and height, yet where its sweet night fragrance can be appreciated. It is usually relegated to the back of the border, but don't be afraid to step it forward a bit, as the long stems and low cluster of leaves don't block the view of plants behind. Smaller types can be tucked into borders, or into window boxes or containers near seating areas, where their fragrance can be enjoyed.

How In areas with long summers, flowering tobacco can be planted from seed, but in most of the Northwest it's best to buy the plants in nursery containers. Before transplanting to the garden, water the plants in their containers. Dig planting holes just larger than the plants' root balls, spacing them 8 inches apart (1½ feet for *N. sylvestris).* Tip the containers on their sides and use your thumb to push the root balls gently up from the bottom. Loosen the roots, then set the plants in the holes, making sure the tops of the root balls are even with the surrounding soil surface. Firm soil around roots and water well.

TLC Keep the plants well watered, and mulch to retain moisture. Feed every two weeks with a balanced fertilizer. Removing spent flowers will keep the plant blooming, but it can be finicky work on the smaller varieties.

Impatiens
Impatiens

Probably the all-time favorite bedding plants for shady spots, impatiens deserve their popularity. Given a little soil and enough moisture, they reward the gardener with rapid growth followed by a long season of bloom. Nurseries stock many types, each with multiple subtle shades. What's more, impatiens are so undemanding that they make even a novice gardener feel accomplished.

In general, impatiens work best in simple designs. Use them to edge a shady bed, fill in between hostas and ferns in a woodland, or surround the base of a birdbath or sculpture. You can even plant them in and around fallen trees to make a natural vignette. In deepest shade, lighter colors show up better than darker hues.

Given sufficient water, impatiens also thrive in tubs, baskets, pots, window boxes, and stone troughs. Use such containers to display more unusual impatiens, such as double-flowered types or ones with unusual markings like those in the Swirl or Mosaic series, so their flower details can be seen close-up.

ABOVE: *Overlapping pink petals of a single impatiens flower.* RIGHT: *Snow white impatiens surround a gazing ball in a small, formal planting bordered with a neatly clipped square of boxwood.*

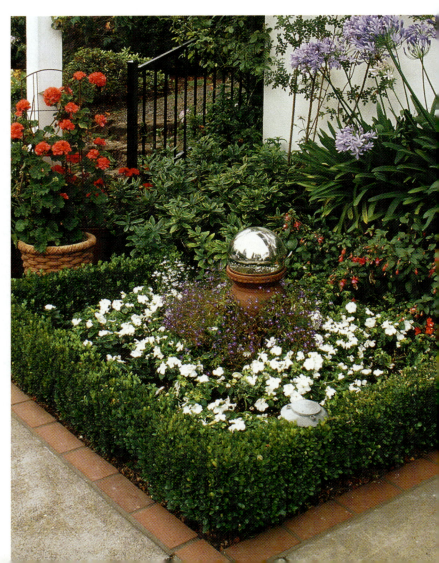

PEAK SEASON

Impatiens bloom from spring until the first frost.

OUR FAVORITES

Many series of *Impatiens walleriana* are available, most ranging from 8 to 12 inches tall. Flowers in the Mosaic series are lightly spotted with contrasting colors. Dazzler lives up to its name with blossoms up to 2 inches wide in numerous bright colors. Fanciful Mix impatiens resemble tiny roses in pastel shades. Showstopper blooms have attractive clear colors that hold up well in cold weather. Swirl series impatiens have a darker color outlining the petal edges.

New Guinea hybrids are a striking group of impatiens, some with multi-colored foliage; they stand taller (up to 2 feet) than *I. walleriana,* and tolerate more sun than other impatiens.

GARDEN COMPANIONS

Impatiens seem to prefer their own company, looking best in masses of mixed colors. In containers, however, you can combine them with other shade lovers such as variegated ivy, coleus, and Japanese forest grass (*Hakonechloa macra* 'Aureola').

When Plant impatiens from cell-packs after the last frost date for your area. Impatiens grow quickly, so there's no need to spend money on larger plants.

Impatiens will bloom for months in hanging baskets. This one is overflowing with blooms of rosy impatiens, deep blue lobelia, and two-tone fuchsias.

Where Impatiens do best in light shade, but coastal fog and overcast skies can provide the sun filter they like. New Guinea hybrids tolerate more sun. The soil should be fertile, moist, and well drained.

How Dig planting holes no more than 1 foot apart, as deep as the plants' root balls and twice as wide. Squeeze the cell-packs gently to remove the plants. Loosen the roots and set the plants in the holes. Fill in with soil so that the tops of the root balls are even with the surrouneding soil level. Firm the soil around the plants and water gently. In containers, plant impatiens in a moisture-retentive potting mix; add a teaspoon of controlled-release fertilizer pellets per cup of soil.

TLC Keep your impatiens wet but not soggy. Once a month, feed with a liquid fertilizer or sprinkle some controlled-release fertilizer on the soil around the plants. These truly low-maintenance plants require no deadheading or pinching, but if they become overgrown, cut them back as low as 6 inches above the ground. New growth will emerge almost immediately.

Lobelia
Lobelia erinus

Because lobelias are so often seen in pots, window boxes, and hanging baskets, their value as a border plant has been under-estimated. Not only do they offer every shade and tint of blue, as well as violet, lilac, pink, cherry, and white, but they start to do so during the summer, when these cool colors are a soothing antidote to the hot temperatures and tones of the season. Although each individual flower is tiny, resembling a miniature honeysuckle or salvia blossom, the blooms come in such abundance that the plant is literally smothered in color for six months or more.

The cool tones of 'Blue Eyes', 'Crystal Palace', and 'Riviera Blue Splash' lobelias in a complementary pot.

Lobelias are often divided into two categories: bushy (compact) types for borders and trailing types for containers. But there's nothing to prevent you from planting trailing types in the garden. With their wiry stems and free-flowering habit, trailing lobelias quickly ramble around in rock gardens, splash onto pathways, and drip over the edges of walls and containers.

PEAK SEASON

Lobelias flower from spring until first frost. During mild winters, plants can continue blooming through winter and live a second year.

OUR FAVORITES

Photographs do not always capture the true blue colors of lobelia; try to see some plants in bloom before making your choices.

Compact types (to 6 inches tall and 9 inches wide) include the lovely, pale sky-blue 'Cambridge Blue'; 'Crystal Palace', with cobalt flowers and bronzy foliage; and 'Rosamund', with deep crimson flowers each dotted with a white eye.

The Cascade series has trailing types (to 6 inches by 18 inches) in white, blue, crimson, lilac, and red. 'Sapphire' has deep blue flowers with a white eye. The Regatta series includes 'Blue Splash', which has white flowers splashed with blue.

GARDEN COMPANIONS

In containers, combine blue and white forms of lobelia with petunias in shades of lavender, lilac, and white—especially those from the Wave and Supertunia series. For a blue and yellow mix, combine blue lobelia with *Bidens ferulifolia* or signet marigolds *(Tagetes tenuifolia)*. Lobelias also make an effective cover-up for the bare ankles of roses and other shrubs.

When You'll find lobelias in cell-packs throughout the summer, but try to get plants in the ground as early as possible for a long period of bloom.

Where Lobelias prefer a sunny position and moist, well-drained soil. In the sunniest parts of the Northwest, place it where it will receive light afternoon shade.

How Dig planting holes 6 inches apart and carefully remove the plants from their containers. Loosen the root balls, especially if the roots are matted or compacted. Place the plants in the holes and fill in around them with soil. Firm down with your fingers and water gently. In containers, use a loose potting mix; add in controlled-release fertilizer pellets at the rate of 1 teaspoon per cup of soil.

TLC Lobelias take regular water and feeding. Give them a liquid fertilizer every four to six weeks or controlled-release pellets a month after planting. Trim back lobelia plants occasionally to encourage a new flush of bloom.

ABOVE: *'Crystal Palace' lobelia and 'Snowflake' bacopa.*
LEFT: *'Riviera Lilac' lobelia and 'Accent Rose' impatiens.*

Poppy

Papaver rhoeas, P. somniferum, Eschscholzia californica

Several annual poppies are easy to grow in Northwest gardens. Some have a country-lane quality to them. Others are exquisitely opulent, with dessert plate–size blooms that look as though they've been spun from the finest silk. Shirley poppies *(Papaver rhoeas)* and opium poppies *(P. somniferum)* are in the latter category. They have slender, 2- to 3-foot-tall, hairy stems topped with crinkly single or double flowers in a huge range of colors, from deep fire-engine red to the most gauzy pastel hues, centered with large disks. The petals have a slight shimmer that catches the sunlight as the delicate stems sway in the breeze. The blooms of opium poppy are followed by large, decorative seed capsules that can be used in dried arrangements.

California poppies *(Eschscholzia californica)* are rangy wildflowers native to California and Oregon. They grow to 10 inches tall with slender stems, finely divided blue-green leaves, and single flowers in yellow, pink, rose, flame orange, red, cream, or white. The petals close up in cool, overcast weather, so they aren't the best choices in areas with summer fog or rain. They are well suited to the natural garden, and ideal for sunny hillsides and other difficult planting areas.

The fringed petals of an opium poppy unfurl in spring. Many opium poppies have elaborate petal edges, ruffles, or markings.

When Some poppies start best in cool weather; others can be sown successively throughout the summer.

Where Plant in full sun to partial shade in fertile, well-drained soil.

How In the Northwest, poppies can be sown directly into the ground in early spring and then every few weeks after the last frost in spring. Mix the fine seed with sand to broadcast it evenly, and keep the seedbed moist until seedlings appear. Thin seedlings to 6 to 8 inches apart.

TLC Deadhead poppies to prolong bloom, but let some plants set seed for next year. (California poppies are tricky to deadhead, so leave them be.) Give average water. Shirley and opium poppies may wilt in extremely hot weather.

TOP TO BOTTOM: *California poppy 'Sunset Boulevard'; California poppies with a 'Flanders Field' bloom; opium poppy buds.*

PEAK SEASON

Poppies bloom in spring or summer, depending on type.

OUR FAVORITES

Papaver rhoeas 'Flanders Field' (also called 'American Legion') has a single scarlet flower with a black base. The Mother of Pearl series has a range of pastels, sometimes several blended together on a single bloom. The Angels' Choir series has similar muted colors, but with double flowers.

P. somniferum 'Black Cloud' and 'White Cloud' have large, double, ruffled flowers. Deep purple 'Lauren's Grape' is named for the Colorado gardener Lauren Springer. 'Applegreen' is an unusual pale green pom-pom. (Due to their narcotic properties, opium poppies are not as widely offered as other types.)

California poppies *(Eschscholzia californica)* have equally exquisite colors. Some of the best are in the Thai Silk series. 'Champagne and Roses' has heavily frilled flowers in rose or light pink; 'Ivory Castle' has glistening white blooms; 'Milky White' has a creamy cast.

Two perennial poppies, Iceland poppy *(P. nudicaule)* and oriental poppy *(P. orientale),* also grow well in most of the Northwest. In Alaska, Iceland poppy can be treated as an annual; with good snow cover, it self-seeds year after year.

GARDEN COMPANIONS

Shirley and opium poppies look wonderful with blue flowers such as love-in-a-mist *(Nigella damascena),* cornflowers, salvias, annual larkspur, borage, and cerinthe *(Cerinthe major* 'Purpurascens'). Because of their free-form habit, California poppies can blend well with low-growing grasses such as *Pennisetum alopecuroides* 'Little Bunny' or bronze sedges *(Carex),* and with red-flowered tickseed *(Coreopsis* 'Limerock Ruby') and zinnias.

Viola

Viola

Violas *(Viola cornuta)* are the most traditional of annuals, with delicate markings and a daintiness that is reminiscent of bone china. Pansies *(V. × wittrockiana)* are larger and more sprightly, with friendly "faces" adorned with whiskers and spectacles in various colors. Johnny-jump-ups *(V. tricolor)* are like wilder relatives from the other side of the hedgerow, spreading their cheerful charms around the garden.

All *Viola* species are low growers with a bushy habit. Despite the delicate appearance of their individual flowers, these are vigorous plants that can sometimes overwinter to perform a second season in the garden.

Any of the three species will add subtle charm to window boxes and small containers. Use Johnny-jump-ups to liven up rock and vegetable gardens as well. (There's no danger of them overrunning the strawberry bed.) You can even toss the edible flowers of these three species into a salad or use them as garnishes; they have a velvety mint flavor.

Avoid planting sweet violets *(V. odorata),* which are invasive in the Northwest.

'Copperfield' pansies in shades of apricot, bronze, yellow, and orange mix with 'Amber Waves' coral bells and red 'Helen' mums.

PEAK SEASON

Violas bloom during cool months.

OUR FAVORITES

There are so many lovely violas that your choices may boil down to personal preference. Confusion exists in the naming of *Viola* species but most are sold already in bloom, so you can choose the colors you like.

Pansies in the Imperial Antique Shades series come in finespun pastels. Both the Chalon Giant series and early-blooming 'Contessa' have ruffled petals. 'Purple Rain' is a cascading type for baskets and window boxes. Dramatic hybrids include ebony 'Accord Black Beauty', neon tangerine 'Padparadja', and the Joker series, with striking color combinations of orange, purple, and black. 'Tiger Eyes' has burnished petals scored with black lines.

Look for violas in the Sorbet series named after ice cream—'Sorbet Blueberry Cream', 'Sorbet French Vanilla', and the everchanging 'Sorbet Yesterday, Today, and Tomorrow'.

V. tricolor 'Helen Mount' is the traditional Johnny-jump-up. *V. t.* 'Molly Sanderson' is almost black.

GARDEN COMPANIONS

Tuck pansies and violas around the legs of tall spring-blooming bulbs. Mix large-flowered pansies with spring primroses and poppies.

When In the mild Northwest, violas are the first plants to arrive in garden centers in spring. Plant immediately for summer bloom, and again in autumn for bloom from winter to spring (or longer). In cold-winter climates, set out plants in spring for summer bloom.

CLOCKWISE FROM LEFT: *'Pink Shades' pansies; 'Velour Blue Bronze' viola; 'Wine Flash' pansy.*

Where All violas need well-drained soil amended with organic matter, and full sun or partial shade. As summer progresses, plants will need shelter from afternoon sun.

How Water the plants in their nursery containers. Dig planting holes larger than the plants' root balls, spacing them 6 inches apart. To remove the transplants, tip the containers on their sides and use your thumb to push the root balls gently up from the bottom. Loosen the roots, then set the plants in the holes, making sure the tops of the root balls are even with the surrounding soil surface. Firm soil around roots and water well. In containers, add a controlled-release fertilizer to the potting soil and space plants 3 inches apart.

TLC To prolong bloom, pick flowers regularly and remove faded blooms before they set seed. Keep the plants well watered but not soggy. Control slugs and snails. In hot-summer areas, plants will get ragged by midsummer and should be removed. In cool-summer areas, cut back plants lightly in summer to control legginess.

Zinnia

Zinnia

Just when the fairer annuals of spring are swooning in the summer sun, zinnias come into their own. Sturdy plants with thick stems, most zinnias stand stiffly upright, without flopping or drooping. Each flower head has a ray of petals in a bold, unshaded color—usually a warm yellow, orange, pink, or red—surrounding a dark brown or yellow central disk. Forms vary from simple daisies to spiky cactuslike flowers, and on to ruffled types and extravagant dahlia-like pom-poms fairly bursting with petals.

It's hard to beat zinnias for hot colors in the border. Mix up different types for more interest, such as those shown here from the Profusion and Oklahoma series.

If you've found traditional zinnias a little too bright and perky, take heart. Recent breeding programs have brought forth smaller hybrids that are more modest in appearance and some that are even quite subtle. As a bonus, these new hybrids are resistant to the powdery mildew that plagues the older generation of zinnias.

Plop zinnias into the spaces left by departing annuals and perennials. Avoid big blobs of bright color by choosing plants of the same series in closely related shades and then mixing them up when planting. Zinnias make good flowers for a child's garden, as they grow quickly, attract butterflies, and withstand quite a bit of abuse.

PEAK SEASON

Zinnias bloom from midsummer to first frost.

OUR FAVORITES

Zinnia angustifolia Crystal series (also called Star series) has small, long-blooming single flowers in orange, yellow, or white. They grow to 1 foot and require no deadheading.

Z. tenuifolia 'Red Spider' has scarlet flowers with scalloped petals arrayed like Daddy longlegs (to 2 feet).

Z. elegans green 'Envy' (to 2 feet) has pale chartreuse pom-poms.

Z. e. Benary's Giants series has dahlia-type, 5-inch flowers (to 5 feet).

The award-winning Profusion series (*Z. haageana,* sometimes listed as *Z. angustifolia*) grows to 2½ feet.

Z. h. 'Old Mexico' (to 1½ feet) and 'Persian Carpet' (to 28 inches) have wispy habits and double flowers in rich mahogany, gold, orange, and rust.

Peruvian zinnia (*Z. peruviana*) bears tiny (1½-inch) flowers in subtle tones on plants 3 feet tall and wide.

GARDEN COMPANIONS

Z. haageana and *Z. peruviana* complement yarrow, coneflower, salvia, and other casual flowers. Taller zinnias look best with bright flowers such as yellow tickseed or clear blue asters. Temper the heat with silvery or lime licorice plant (*Helichrysum petiolare*).

When These hot-weather plants don't appreciate an early start, so wait until summer has truly begun before setting them out from nursery cell-packs or jumbo packs.

Where Choose an area with full sun. Average soil is acceptable, but if you add compost and all-purpose fertilizer to the soil before planting, you'll get lusher crops. Taller types (to 3 or 4 feet) belong in the cutting garden; lower-growing dwarf types can be tucked in the front of the border or planted in containers.

How Water the plants in their nursery containers. Dig planting holes larger than the plants' root balls (check plant labels for spacing). Tip the containers on their sides and use your thumb to push the root balls gently up from the bottom. Loosen the roots, then set each plant in its hole, making sure the top of the root ball is even with the surrounding soil surface. Firm soil around roots and water well.

TLC Water young plants to get them established—always at ground level to keep the foliage dry. Thereafter, give 1 inch of water per week and feed with an all-purpose fertilizer once a month.

TOP: *'Profusion Cherry' zinnias sport the small, prolific flowers typical of the series.* BOTTOM: *Peruvian zinnias in the Bonita series come in brick red, as shown, and soft gold.*

Vines

TOP

TOP
10
PLUS

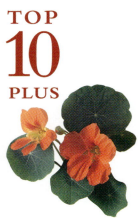

Annual vines make us gardeners feel capable. Plant and water, and in a few weeks these vigorous climbers transform a pergola into a shaded bower, clothe a chain-link fence in leafy green, or screen out the neighbors. Let them romp and bloom all summer, then toss them on the compost pile.

Our Favorites

Mandevilla × amabilis 'Alice du Pont' has lush leaves and deep pink flowers as festive as a summer garden party hat. Pair this with Costa Rican butterfly vine (*Dalechampia dioscoreifolia*) which has dark green leaves and natty, 6-inch, pink, bow-tie–shaped bracts with yellow centers.

Mountain-fringe vine (*Adlumia fungosa*) is a biennial bleeding heart look-alike that prefers shade and grows to 10 feet; the first year its spiral growth supports lacy green foliage, followed the next summer by delicate pale pink hearts.

Sweet pea (*Lathyrus odoratus*) is the queen of annual vines. The blossoms have a clean perfume and come in almost every color, including bicolors. They make wonderful cut flowers.

LEFT: *Deep blue morning glories.*
BELOW: *A stunning potted composition of coleus, purple fountain grass, and chartreuse 'Marguerite' sweet potato vine.*
OPPOSITE PAGE, BOTTOM: *Canary bird flower; sweet pea blossoms.*

those of 'Heavenly Blue' are sky blue. Sweet potato vine *(I. batatas)* has leaves to 4 inches wide; 'Blackie' has deep blackish leaves. Spanish flag *(I. lobata,* sometimes *Mina lobata)* has racemes of little tubular flowers that start out scarlet and fade to yellow for a two-toned effect.

Cup-and-saucer vine *(Cobaea scandens)* has flowers with a honeylike fragrance that bloom yellow-green, aging through violet to purple.

Planting and Care

Most annual vines come from the southern hemisphere, so they like plenty of sun and heat. Plant them after the soil has warmed to 50°F/ 10°C, usually in late May to mid-June. Sow seeds directly into the garden or plant from 4-inch pots; either way, the soil should be fertile and well drained. All annual vines are suitable for containers and hanging baskets. Regular water is essential. Give these vigorous vines a half-strength liquid fertilizer every two weeks throughout the season. Supports for annual vines need not be as sturdy as for perennial vines, but they should be in place before the plants begin their great burst of growth.

Tropaeolum majus 'Jewel of Africa' is a climbing nasturtium with cream-marbled leaves and flowers of yellow, red, and peach-pink. Canary bird flower *(T. peregrinum)* has gray-green leaves and bright yellow flowers with fringed petals like tiny birds' wings.

Chilean glory vine *(Eccremocarpus scaber)* has hot red, trumpet-shaped, fragrant flowers that grow rapidly and attract hummingbirds.

Rhodochiton atrosanguineum 'Purple Bells' is ideal for hanging baskets or to grow up trellises. The richly purple, pendulous flowers are topped with a frill of rosy pink bells and the foliage is toothed and handsome.

Morning glories *(Ipomoea tricolor)* have large, luminous flowers. 'Star of Yelta' has silky, deep purple blooms;

Vines

Vines are the ultimate garnish for the garden, adding color, texture, and perfume to almost any surface. There is no quicker way to dress up an outdoor space than by clothing a cement wall with winter jasmine, growing a clematis through a rose bush, lacing a fence with a supremely sweet-scented *Akebia quinata,* or letting a wisteria engulf an arbor.

Indeed, a vine's great charm lies in its lush liveliness, that expression of energy barely contained. No other type of plant more clearly expresses the life force. One of my most compelling memories is of a huge and bountifully blooming wisteria dripping its purple flowers down through an arbor, warm rain intensifying the heady fragrance. To bring back that feeling of being nearly encompassed by such leafiness and bloom, I've grown at least one wisteria in every garden since.

A VINE FOR EVERY GARDEN

Many of the flashy and colorful vines native to the Southern Hemisphere prefer hot summers, but hardy vines grow vigorously and bloom prolifically in our mild winters, damp springs, and long autumns. And, we can all grow a tantalizing bevy of annual vines that sprout from seed and seem to grow at least a foot a day. In the Northwest's warmer areas, we have even more choices, such as the intricately beautiful passion vine *(Passiflora × alatocaerulea)* and the vibrantly neon-colored bougainvillea.

Vines are so diverse, there is at least one to suit even the most difficult garden situation. In dank, wet soil on the shady north side of my house, I grow a silvervein creeper *(Parthenocissus henryana)* where its silver-etched leaves form a striking backdrop to blue and white hydrangeas. Small-flowering *Clematis viticella* and *C. alpina* are ideal for compact gardens;

they can clamber up trees and shrubs without completely engulfing them.

PLANTING VINES

The best advice my mother ever gave me was always to plant at least two vines in any given hole. Her reasoning was that vines look their best and provide multiseasonal bloom when intertwined. (And as a vine's planting hole should be widely dug and well enriched, you may as well make the most of it.) As a result, all the arbors and fences and a good many of the trees in my garden are dressed with a consortium of vines. Especially effective is evergreen *Clematis armandii* with a deciduous variety, so that when the starry blooms of *C. armandii* fade in springtime, a summer-bloomer will flower against its green leaves.

The Top 10 vines described on the following pages are some of the most carefree types you can grow. Some adhere directly to a surface,

OPPOSITE PAGE: Clematis montana *'Pink Perfection' winds its way up a tree.* ABOVE: *Two* C. viticella *varieties, 'Polish Spirit' and 'Prince Charles', clamber up supports on either side of a curving path.*

others send out twining tendrils, still others have a naturally shrubby habit. Some must be coaxed up a support; others need a firm hand wielding sharp pruning shears to keep them in bounds. But they all do a beautiful job of softening and adorning the garden.

—VALERIE EASTON

Akebia

Akebia

Although akebia is sometimes known as the chocolate vine because of its purplish brown blooms, the flowers actually smell strongly of vanilla. Each plant has both larger, showier female flowers and smaller, male flowers, which makes it look like two plants in one. Despite this floral uniqueness, akebia is more often lauded for its lovely yellow-green foliage. The leaves are divided into three or five oval leaflets (depending on the species) and have such a fine texture that even when the vine achieves its full length of 30 feet, it still maintains a certain delicacy.

This vine grows quickly in mild regions, winding its wiry tendrils around supports. To train it up a tree, give the shoots something to latch onto by winding plastic netting or fishing line around the trunk.

Akebia is one of several vines that are semievergreen in the Northwest. That means it drops its foliage in response to winter cold but will keep it year-round in warmer areas. Gardeners who endure cold winters are rewarded with a

A dense but not overly vigorous cover of akebia shades this bench nestled underneath a wooden arbor.

more pronounced flower show in spring, as the flowers will emerge before the new leaves have filled in. As a further bonus, the flowers are sometimes followed by fruits that look for all the world like little cocktail sausages.

PEAK SEASON

Akebia is attractive from spring through fall.

OUR FAVORITES

Threeleaf akebia (A. trifoliata) has three leaflets per leaf. 'Deep Purple' has smoky purple blooms.

Fiveleaf akebia (A. quinata) has five leaflets per leaf. White-flowered 'Brookside Variegated' has golden splashes on the leaves. 'Alba' is a white-flowered form with solid green leaves. 'Purple Bouquet' has dark purple flowers and darker green foliage.

GARDEN COMPANIONS

Akebia looks terrific with other climbers that have flowers in similar hues, such as deep pink clematis or merlot-colored roses. Underplant it with columbines, hellebores, hardy geraniums, and impatiens.

When Plant akebia in spring or fall from nursery containers.

ABOVE: Akebia trifoliata 'Deep Purple'. BELOW: Clustered blooms of A. quinata 'Albiflorus'.

Where Akebia prefers cool, shaded conditions and rich soil. Use it to cover a fence, to climb into trees, or to train up to balconies or over a shaded arch. Choose the site carefully, as this vine resents root disturbance and doesn't transplant well.

How Water the plant in its nursery container before planting. Dig a hole the same depth as the root ball and twice as wide. Set the root ball in the center of the hole with the crown of the plant at the same level as it was in the nursery container. Amend the dug soil with compost and refill the hole. Firm the soil around the plant and water thoroughly. Spread a 2- to 4-inch layer of mulch around the base of the plant.

TLC Give akebia regular water and an application of 10-10-10 fertilizer in early spring. To keep it looking tidy, trim it lightly after bloom. Prune in winter when it's easiest to see the branch structure; it recovers quickly when cut to the ground. For a tracery effect on a post or column, prune out all but two or three basal stems.

Clematis
Clematis

When it comes to clematis, the sheer number of stunners to choose from can be daunting. Most of these vines have beautiful, abundant, petal-like sepals around contrasting centers. Some have more unusual blooms—with narrow petals, multiple colors, bell-shaped flowers, or double-, triple-, or many-petaled forms. Puffy seed clusters often follow the flowers. Clematis have a reputation as finicky plants that only experienced gardeners can grow, but the fact is, if you choose the right one for your soil and climate, and give it a little extra attention, your clematis will be the envy of even the experts.

Clematis, especially the large-flowered hybrids, are sometimes affected by a curious condition called wilt; the entire plant seems to collapse overnight. If this happens, provide regular water and the plant usually recovers, though sometimes not until the next season.

Clematis armandii blooms in spring. Put it where its fine, sweet fragrance can be appreciated, such as over an entryway or a seating area.

PEAK SEASON

Flowers bloom in spring, summer, or fall, depending on variety.

OUR FAVORITES

The following are deciduous, with the exception of *Clematis armandii.*

Large-flowered hybrids for zones 1–7 and 17 include *C. × jackmanii* (deep purple), 'Niobe' (deep red), and 'Nelly Moser' (pink with reddish stripes).

C. alpina (zones A2, A3; 1a–6, 17) has dangling spring blooms with pointed sepals. It grows to 8 to 12 feet. Favorites include 'Helsingborg' (dark blue) and 'Willy' (pale pink).

Spring-blooming *C. armandii* (zones 4–7, 17) can reach 35 feet.

Montana clematis *(C. montana;* zones 3b–7, 17) reaches 30 feet, with white or pink spring flowers.

Summer-blooming *C. viticella* (zones A3; 2b–7, 17) reaches 15 feet, with purple or red flowers.

GARDEN COMPANIONS

Plant clematis so they twine in and around roses and other flowering shrubs and trees. Overplant the base with fast-growing annuals to help keep the roots cool. Clematis also look wonderful in cottage-style borders with delphiniums, foxgloves, lilies, and peonies.

When Plant clematis in early spring.

Where There's an old saying about clematis: Flowers in the sun, feet in the shade. One way to achieve this is by planting your clematis against an east-facing wall or fence, where it can get morning sun and afternoon shade. Less vigorous varieties can grow up a mailbox or light post; more vigorous forms need a sturdier support.

How Water the plant in its nursery container before planting. Dig a hole twice as wide and deep as the roots. (Clematis should be planted deeply to help them recover from wilt or damage.) Set the root ball in the center of the hole with the crown of the plant at the same level as it was in the nursery container. Amend the dug soil with compost and refill the hole. Firm the soil around the plant and water thoroughly. Spread a 2- to 4-inch layer of mulch around the base of the plant.

TLC Clematis need constant moisture and nutrients to make their great rush of growth. During the growing season, maintain 2 to 4 inches of mulch around the base of the plant, keep the soil evenly moist, and apply a complete liquid fertilizer monthly. Twisting leafstalks may need help climbing; the stems are brittle, so use care when attaching them to supports. Prune spring bloomers a month after flowering; prune summer and fall bloomers in late winter before the leaf and flower buds swell.

TOP TO BOTTOM: Clematis alpina; C.a. *'Betina';* C. hybrid *'The President';* C. montana rubens; C. viticella *'Polish Spirit'.*

Climbing Hydrangea
Hydrangea anomala petiolaris

In a seaside garden on Vancouver Island, this climbing hydrangea ornaments a fence with flowers.

Compared with such flamboyant vines as honeysuckle and clematis, which have flowers that explode with color or fragrance or both, climbing hydrangea has a more modest elegance. But if you are a fan of the related shrubby hydrangeas, consider planting their shade-loving, climbing cousin. This vine's medium green, 2- to 4-inch-long leaves are shaped like plump hearts. Blossoms emerge in spring and summer as clusters of tiny chartreuse balls that open to form lace-cap constellations up to 10 inches across of white, starlike blossoms. The flowers last for weeks and then fade to a brownish gold color. In fall, the leaves turn burnt orange before falling to the ground.

Climbing hydrangea grows something like ivy (for which it makes a well-behaved substitute), with aerial rootlets that cling firmly to vertical surfaces. It takes some time for the plant to get established, but once under way, growth is vigorous and the vine can extend up to 50 feet. As the plant ages, it becomes woody, the branches twist, and the cinnamon-colored bark peels attractively.

When Plant in early spring, or throughout the growing season if you can provide plenty of moisture.

Where Climbing hydrangea should be put in partial shade in rich soil that is moist but well draining. It makes a good choice for the east or north side of a house or fence.

How Water the plant in its nursery container before planting. Dig a hole the same depth as the root ball and twice as wide. Set the root ball in the center of the hole with the crown of the plant at the same level as it was in the nursery container. Amend the dug soil with compost and refill the hole. Firm the soil around the plant and water thoroughly. Spread a 2- to 4-inch layer of mulch around the base of the plant.

TLC Consistent watering is important, especially as the plant is becoming established, but even mature plants will wilt at the first sign of drought. Maintain a 2- to 4-inch layer of mulch at the base of the plant throughout the growing season to help retain moisture in the soil. Fertilize in spring with a balanced 10-10-10 fertilizer sprinkled around the base of the plant and watered in well. These vines bloom on existing wood, so prune after flowering only to shape. It may take up to two years before a vine clings well along a flat surface; you must tie it to supports at first.

PEAK SEASON

Climbing hydrangea flowers from midspring to midsummer. The foliage is an attractive dark green all season and has good fall color. Peeling bark provides winter interest.

OUR FAVORITES

'Mirranda' is a variegated form with bright yellow leaf margins.

GOOD COMPANIONS

Climbing hydrangea looks best against brick or stone walls or wooden fences. Surround it with other shade plants, such as Japanese anemones, astilbe, or cimicifuga. You can also underplant it with glossy-leafed, shade-tolerant ground covers such as wild ginger (Asarum), carpet bugle (Ajuga), sweet box (Sarcococca), or sedges (Carex).

ABOVE: *Climbing hydrangea scales a mature tree.* LEFT: *The variegated leaves of 'Mirranda' climbing hydrangea.*

Grape
Vitis

Try to picture a romantic alfresco dinner under a wooden arbor *without* clusters of grapes hanging from it. Sure, it's a cliché, but there are several good reasons that grapes are the ultimate arbor vine. The stems' tight-gripping, spiraling tendrils can quickly and easily be trained up and over any structure. The leaves are large and a beautiful light green, allowing dappled light beneath. Grapevines can live for many decades; with age, the trunks become venerably gnarled. And the edible fruit hangs down in a most convenient manner for easy picking.

The trick with growing grapevines is to choose the right variety for your climate—one whose fruit will mature before the arrival of autumn. Generally, red wine grapes require the most sun and the longest growing season—conditions found east of the Cascades and in southern Oregon. White wine and table grapes are better selections for coastal areas and where summers are short. Your local Cooperative Extension Office is a great resource for recommended varieties in your area.

Vitis vinifera purpurea is a much-loved variety grown for its ornamental foliage, which emerges green and matures to tones of burgundy and bronze.

PEAK SEASON

Grapevines bear fruit in summer; some have colorful fall foliage

OUR FAVORITES

All grapes are edible, but smaller, seedier kinds are used for wine-making. The following are table grapes unless noted otherwise.

In warmer areas, try 'Concord Seedless' (midseason, seedless, blue-black grapes good for cooking, juice, and jelly), 'Glenora' (large clusters of early to midseason, seedless, dark blue grapes with spicy-sweet flavor), and 'Thompson Seedless' (mid- to late-season, very sweet, seedless, pale green grapes). For winemaking, try 'Chardonnay' (mid- to late-season, small, sweet, seeded, pale red grapes).

In cool-summer areas, good choices include 'Canadice' (early, sweet, seed-less red grapes), 'Flame' (early to mid-season, small, round, seedless, red grapes with crisp flavor), 'Interlaken' (early, seedless, green grapes with crisp flavor sometimes described as slightly foxy), 'Perlette' (midseason, seedless, juicy, white to yellowish, mild-flavored grapes), and the wine grape 'Gewurztraminer' (early to midseason, seeded, reddish brown fruit with a delicious spicy flavor).

'Valiant' (very early, seeded blue grapes) is one of the hardiest—it will grow in Alaska. 'Edelweiss' (early, seeded, greenish white grapes) and

'Swenson Red' (early, seeded red grapes with fruity flavor) are other good choices for northern areas.

Vitis vinifera purpurea ('Purpurea'; zones 4–7, 17) is grown primarily for its striking foliage in summer and its blazing fall colors.

When Nurseries sell year-old grapevines; plant them bare-root when dormant in early spring.

Where All grapes need full sun, good air circulation, and fertile but fast-draining soil. They do well on slopes or can be trained up a sturdy trellis, arbor, or fence. They also make excellent subjects for containers—what could be more appropriate than an old wine barrel cut in half?

How Soak the grapevine roots in a bucket for a few hours before planting. Dig a hole the same depth as the roots and twice as wide. Set the vine in the center of the hole, fanning the roots over a cone of soil. Be sure the graft union (the knobby ring around the base of the trunk) is above ground level, and prune branches back to two buds. Refill the hole, firm the soil around the plant, and water thoroughly.

TLC Grapevines become more drought tolerant with age, but they will need regular watering—drip irrigation or watering at the base of the plant is best. Don't prune the first year; thereafter, prune during winter to guide the vine along its support structure. The first winter, before buds swell, select the sturdiest shoot for the trunk; remove all other shoots at their base. In future winters, thin out entangling growth. For best fruit production, prune shoots to two or three buds. Remove any shoots that sprout on the trunk as they appear.

TOP: *'Flame' is one of most widely grown red table grapes.* BOTTOM: *The hardy, seedless green grape 'Himrod' is well suited to arbors. It fruits early.*

GARDEN COMPANIONS

For a Mediterranean look, pair grapevines with other heat lovers such as herbs, roses, and grasses. *Vitis vinifera purpurea* looks wonderful growing through golden shrubs or intertwined with a pale pink clematis.

Honeysuckle

Lonicera

A honeysuckle clambers up a wooden arch over a gravel path; its exuberance is matched by the daylilies below.

Honeysuckles are country-garden staples, beloved for their carefree exuberance, penetrating perfume, and abundant blooms. Some (such as Japanese honeysuckle) can grow rampantly; others (like goldflame honeysuckle) are more restrained. The same species may be evergreen, semievergreen, or deciduous, depending on the location and the degree of winter cold it must endure. The vine climbs by twining its stems around slender supports such as strings, wires, or branches.

From a distance, honeysuckle flowers resemble brightly dressed ballerinas, each one a cluster of rosy tubular buds with protruding anthers. Some types are flared trumpets; others reveal two-lipped inner petals in pink, yellow, white, or peach, deepening in color with age.

Bees, hummingbirds, and butterflies are irresistibly drawn to the flowers, as are children, fascinated by the multicolored blossoms filled with sweet nectar. The flowers are followed by hard, round fruits colored red, navy, or black; these provide food for many kinds of birds.

ABOVE: *How many colors can you count in this bloom of goldflame honeysuckle (Lonicera × heckrotti)?* BELOW: *A honeysuckle and the red rose 'Blaze' combine color and fragrance atop an arbor.*

PEAK SEASON

Flowers bloom from early spring to late summer; berries follow in later summer through fall.

OUR FAVORITES

Deciduous goldflame or coral honeysuckle *(Lonicera × heckrottii;* zones 2–7, 17) has a 15-foot spread. From spring to fall, fragrant, deep pink blooms expose yolk yellow insides.

Sweet-scented Japanese honeysuckle *(L. japonica;* zones 1–7, 17) has purple-tinged white blooms from late spring into fall; it can reach 30 feet. It may be evergreen, semievergreen, or deciduous. The large white flowers of Hall's honeysuckle *(L. j.* 'Halliana') age to chamois yellow. *L. j.* 'Purpurea' has purple-tinted leaf surfaces and blossoms blushed with maroon.

Fragrant woodbine *(L. periclymenum;* zones 1–7, 17) grows to 20 feet, with creamy, purple-flushed summer blossoms. 'Serotina' has yellow-and-purple blooms; 'Graham Thomas' grows to 30 feet with creamy white flowers that age to coppery yellow.

Trumpet honeysuckle *(L. sempervirens;* zones 2–7, 17) gets its common name from the shape of its large red or orange flowers (unscented), which grow in clusters of six from late spring to summer. 'Sulphurea' has yellow unscented flowers in April. The vine is evergreen or semievergreen and climbs to 20 feet.

When Plant honeysuckle in early spring after the soil has warmed up.

Where Honeysuckles make good screens on fences or trellises, or they can be trained up a post, a large tree trunk, or up to the eaves of a house—anywhere the vine can be tied to supports. Position the more vigorous species, such as Japanese honeysuckle, where they will not smother less robust garden plantings. Honeysuckles are not particular about soil, but they will flower best in fertile soil in full sun.

How Water the plant in its nursery container before planting. Dig a hole the same depth as the root ball and twice as wide. Set the root ball in the center of the hole with the crown of the plant at the same level as it was in the nursery container. Amend the dug soil with compost and refill the hole. Firm the soil and water thoroughly. Spread a 2- to 4-inch layer of mulch around the base of the plant.

TLC Honeysuckles have a twining growth habit, but you will initially need to tie the branches to supports; use a soft material such as flexible plastic. Fertilize in spring with a 10-10-10 fertilizer sprinkled around the base of plants and watered in well. Give moderate to regular water throughout the growing season. If old vines become top-heavy or tangled, thin in late winter or early spring. Cut old, scraggly vines to the ground before spring growth begins; they'll soon regrow.

GARDEN COMPANIONS

Surround honeysuckles with other cottage-garden flowers like foxgloves, lavender, roses, phlox, and Santa Barbara daisy *(Erigeron).*

Hop Vine
Humulus lupulus

A rustic bent-twig bench is beautifully framed by a full surround of hop vine.

Talk about a plant that combines utility and beauty. The common hop is not only beloved by brew-masters for the agreeable bitterness its flowers add to beer and by floral arrangers for how long they last, but it also makes a fast-growing and attractive vine for an arbor, an entranceway bower, or a fence. This vigorous perennial vine can shoot up to 25 feet in a season, twining its growing shoots vertically around string, wire, or a trellis. It dies to the ground in winter only to sprout up again in spring.

The individual leaves are about the size and shape of grape leaves, but they grow in a much thicker mass, making common hop a good plant for creating shade. Summer brings the emergence of the flowers (hops), which are enclosed in pale green bracts that look like soft, 2-inch pine cones and even have a piney fragrance. Eventually these fade to amber brown and remain attractive all winter, or they can be snipped off to use in harvest displays—as trailing dried vines, set in vases, or coiled into wreaths.

PEAK SEASON

Hop flowers from summer through fall; faded hops remain attractive into the winter months.

OUR FAVORITES

Golden hop (*Humulus lupulus* 'Aureus') has bright gold leaves.

Japanese hop (*H. japonicus*) has dark green leaves; 'Variegatus' is marked with white. It is usually grown as an annual and can be planted from seed in spring.

GARDEN COMPANIONS

Think of hop vine as a two-season plant. In summer, surround it with annuals and perennials with colorful flowers, such as penstemons, poppies, and Russian sage (*Perovskia*). In fall, combine it with late-blooming flowers such as asters, and with ornamental grasses.

When Plant dormant roots in early spring, from nursery containers in late spring.

Where Hop does best in good, organically enriched soil, so amend the planting area with compost. Plant in full sun, but in hot-summer regions 'Aureus' may need light shade in the heat of the day to prevent the leaves from bleaching.

How Wear gloves when handling hop vine; the bristly spines on the stems can irritate skin. Water the plant in its nursery container before planting, or soak the dormant roots. Dig a hole the same depth as the root ball and twice as wide. To plant from a container, set the root ball in the center of the hole with the crown of the plant at the same level as it was in the nursery container. Plant dormant roots just beneath the soil surface, with the thick end pointing up. Amend the dug soil with compost and refill the hole. Firm the soil around the plant and water thoroughly. Spread a 2- to 4-inch layer of mulch around the base of the plant.

TLC Provide hops with string, wire, or a trellis for support. The stems twine vertically, so to get horizontal growth along a trellis or fence, twine stem tips by hand. When established, hop vine tolerates drought, but until then give it regular water. At the onset of frosty weather, leaves and stems will turn brown; remove them before new growth starts in spring.

ABOVE AND LEFT: *Golden hop is often paired with deep-colored plants like cerise foxgloves and cobalt blue delphiniums.*

107

Ornamental Kiwi Vine

Actinidia kolomikta

Nurseryman Sam Benowitz at Raintree Nursery in Morton, Washington, describes ornamental kiwi vine as "one of the best backyard ornamentals from Vladivostok to Kalamazoo." This extremely hardy Russian native, sometimes sold as 'Arctic Beauty', is an improbable-looking plant that might have been designed by a preschooler in a "pink phase": the leaves are shaped like elongated hearts and splashed with a mixture of bright green, white—and strawberry pink. The vine climbs by twining and makes a good cover for arbors or fences, growing quickly to a dense mass of foliage up to 15 feet long. In early summer, clusters of small, fragrant, white flowers appear on female plants, followed by smooth, oblong fruits that are eat-off-the-vine tasty.

Some gender issues: For a female plant to produce fruit, you'll need a male plant nearby. In the past, only male plants sported the multicolored foliage, but newer female

varieties are equally splashy. The colors tend to be more pronounced in cool weather and partial shade, so you may want to grow this kiwi along a north- or east-facing wall, especially if you live in a hot-summer climate.

If your newly planted kiwi vine turns all green, don't worry—it takes a few years for the variegation to stabilize.

When Plant kiwi vine as a bare-root vine in fall.

Where Grow kiwi vine up a sturdy support such as an arbor or wall where it will receive partial shade and has fertile, well-drained soil. If you want a female plant to produce fruit, site a male plant within the same garden.

How Soak the vine's roots in water for several hours before planting. Dig a hole the same depth as the roots and twice as wide. Set the vine in the center of the hole, fanning the roots over a cone of soil. Prune the branches back to four or five buds (the undeveloped knoblike shoots that protrude from the branch). Amend the dug soil with compost and refill the hole. Firm the soil around the plant and water thoroughly. Spread a 2- to 4-inch layer of mulch around the base of the plant to keep roots cool and to retain moisture.

TLC Give kiwi vine regular moisture during the growing season. Train the new stems into place as they lengthen. The vine is too heavy to hold itself up, so you will need to tie it to a support. While the plant is young, prune it to 2 feet in late winter or early spring; when it's established, prune only to control its size and shape.

The variegation of kiwi vine differs tremendously from one leaf to another.

PEAK SEASON
Foliage is attractive spring through fall.

OUR FAVORITES
'September Sun' ('Sentyabraskaya') is a variegated female vine that produces fruit in August and September.

'Pasha' is a variegated male kiwi that can pollinate up to eight female vines.

GARDEN COMPANIONS
Kiwi vine is striking on its own, but it can be combined with pink or white climbing roses or clematis for an even more dramatic effect.

Virginia Creeper
Parthenocissus quinquefolia

If you have a chain-link fence or a homely garden shed that you need to make "go away," plant Virginia creeper—it's an excellent camouflage for such eyesores. This plant can grow to 60 feet if left unchecked, clinging with strong suction discs to stucco, wood, brick, or metal. Unlike the familiar ivy *(Hedera)*, though, it won't envelop everything in its path, but has a looser, see-through quality.

This vine is valued for its large deciduous leaves, which are divided into five leaflets like fingers on a hand. The foliage is a glossy green through spring and summer, turning to dazzling orange and red in fall. Although a woodland plant, native to the eastern United States, Virginia creeper can tolerate a lot of sun exposure (it's a common sight grown against stone walls in the south of France). You won't notice the flowers but you can't miss the magnificent fall color, and the birds in your garden will love the clusters of shiny black berries in fall.

Virginia creeper has a lot of the virtues of ivy without sharing its invasive habit. It looks striking against a brick wall.

PEAK SEASON

Virginia creeper is most spectacular in fall, when its foliage turns bright orange-red.

OUR FAVORITES

Parthenocissus quinquefolia 'Engel-mannii' (zones A2, A3; 1–7, 17) will cover any surface in a hurry, but with a smaller, coarser, darker green leaf and a looser growth habit than the species. 'Star Showers' has white-spattered leaves that turn pink and red in fall.

Silvervein creeper (*P. henryana*) is a good alternative in milder areas (zones 4–7, 17). It grows vigorously but to only about 20 feet. Leaves are purplish when new, then mature to dark bronzy green with a network of pronounced silver veining. The color is best in shade; leaves fade to plain green in strong light. The fall color is a rich, deep red.

Boston ivy (*P. tricuspidata;* zones 1–7, 17) has light green, glossy leaves that turn orange to burgundy in fall. It reaches just as far as Virginia creeper but produces a solid foliage cover.

GARDEN COMPANIONS

Virginia creeper makes a good, dark foil for perennial borders, especially those containing grasses, whose golden or buff flower heads contrast beautifully with the vine's fall color.

When Plant in early spring, or year-round if well watered.

Where All *Parthenocissus* species are woodland plants that thrive in organically enriched soil and dappled sun, but they can grow in exposures ranging from full sun to full shade.

How Water the plant in its nursery container before planting. Dig a hole the same depth as the root ball and twice as wide. Set the root ball in the center of the hole with the crown of the plant at the same level as it was in the container. Amend the dug soil with compost and refill the hole. Firm the soil around the plant and water it thoroughly. Spread a 2- to 4-inch layer of mulch around the base of the plant.

TLC Young plants may need initial support or tying, but the tendrils soon make the stems fully self-attaching. Plants need regular moisture to become established; older vines easily get by on moderate watering. Thin and prune as needed for training and untangling before leaf-out in spring. Cut out any stems that detach from their support; discs won't reattach.

ABOVE: *The beautiful rich fall colors of Virginia creeper.* RIGHT: *The pale markings on the leaves give silvervein creeper its common name.*

Winter Jasmine
Jasminum nudiflorum

In warmer climates, pink-and-white flowered jasmines provide almost year-round fragrance and color. In the colder parts of the Northwest, however, winter is prime jasmine time. Winter jasmine is a deciduous shrubby vine with stiff, arching stems; in winter the stems drop their leaves but remain green, tracing striking patterns on a trellis or wall. In late winter, unscented, golden yellow, 1-inch flowers cover the plant and remain for several weeks or even months—a gleaming glimpse of spring glories to come. By the time the glossy leaves unfurl, the first daffodils have emerged from the ground and winter jasmine becomes a handsome background plant for spring flowers.

Winter jasmine has an unusual growth habit for a vine; its branches cascade rather than climb, making it a versatile choice for covering banks or walls—and it will root where the stems touch the soil. If you tie up the stems to a support or weave them through a trellis, winter jasmine can grow upward to about 15 feet.

LEFT: *Summer is not considered winter jasmine's best season, but the deep green leaves are handsome against a painted trellis year-round.*

PEAK SEASON

Bare green stems are decorative throughout winter; yellow flowers bloom in spring.

GOOD ALTERNATIVES

In the warmest parts of the Northwest (zones 5–7, 17), try *Jasminum officinale,* a deciduous vine with fragrant white flowers in summer and fall. The variety 'Fiona's Sunrise' has brilliant yellow stems and foliage.

Another good choice for the same zones is *J. polyanthum,* an evergreen with highly fragrant blossoms that are white inside and rose outside; it blooms in late winter and spring.

GARDEN COMPANIONS

Underplant winter jasmine with yellow-toned grasses such as 'Bowles Golden' sedge (*Carex elata* 'Aurea') and sweet flag (*Acorus*), and with similar-colored bulbs, such as early-flowering daffodils, which will bloom at around the same time as the jasmine.

When Plant winter jasmine from nursery containers in fall.

Where You can put winter jasmine at the top of a stone or brick retaining wall and allow the branches to spill over the side, or you can tie it to a trellis mounted on a wall. Winter jasmine grows equally well in full sun or light shade, though flowering is more plentiful in sunny locations. The plant grows best in good fertile soil, but it does just fine in a wide range of soil types.

How Water the plant in its nursery container before planting. Dig a hole the same depth as the root ball and twice as wide. Set the plant in the center of the hole with the crown of the plant at the same level as it was in the nursery container. Amend the dug soil with compost and refill the hole. Firm the soil around the plant and water thoroughly. Spread a 2- to 4-inch layer of mulch around the base of the plant.

ABOVE: *The pretty, lemon yellow flowers of winter jasmine.* BELOW: *Jasminum officinale 'Fiona's Sunrise' has delicate, golden foliage.*

TLC Winter jasmine needs regular watering at all times. Because of its sprawling habit, maintenance chiefly involves thinning and pruning. You can snip out tangled stems and excess growth anytime; major pruning should be done just after flowering.

Wisteria

Wisteria

There's a good reason wisteria is so often trained above entryways. Walking beneath this vine when it's in bloom is like passing through a perfumed beaded curtain. The effect in the landscape is always stunning and romantic—think of the misty images of Monet's bridge at Giverny, draped with wisteria blossoms dangling above the water lilies.

Two wisterias, Chinese (*Wisteria sinensis*) and Japanese (*W. floribunda*), are similar, but the latter produces longer flower clusters. In late spring these hanging racemes of sweet-pealike blossoms unfurl; they may be lavender, cream, pink, mauve, blue, or a dramatic combination of colors. The ferny foliage emerges at the same time, usually as a soft bronze that gradually changes to green. Some plants will provide a second, lesser flower show in late summer. After the tawny fall leaves have dropped, the plant's gnarled, silvery limbs are revealed.

Wisteria is a vigorous vine that is eager to cover a fence or arbor or to scramble up a porch post, so be sure to provide a sturdy support.

PEAK SEASON

Wisteria blooms in spring and summer. The foliage turns gold in fall.

OUR FAVORITES

Chinese wisteria has a white-flowered form, 'Alba', and a dark lavender form, 'Cooke's Special'. 'Amethyst' bears strongly fragrant, reddish violet flowers. Flower clusters on all three are about 1 foot long.

Flower clusters of Japanese wisteria range from 1½ to 3 feet long, depending on the age and health of the plant. 'Issai Perfect' and 'Ivory Tower' both bear white flowers, as does 'Longissima Alba', which has especially long flower clusters. The double blossoms of 'Plena' are full of medium-violet petals. 'Violacea Plena' ('Black Dragon') is another double-flowered type, with reddish purple blooms. 'Rosea' is pale rose tipped with purple, while 'Texas Purple' is a dark-flowered variety.

GARDEN COMPANIONS

Wisteria looks best underplanted with shade-tolerant shrubs such as camellias or evergreen azaleas; all varieties also look wonderful with shrubs that bloom at the same time, such as deep blue *Ceanothus thyrsiflorus* 'Victoria' and color-matched lilacs.

When Wisteria is available year-round, but it's best to plant dormant vines in late fall or early spring.

Where Wisteria will do fine in less-than-perfect soil but it does prefer good drainage and full sun. Chinese wisteria will bloom in a little more shade than Japanese wisteria, but both species like to have their roots cool. This is a sturdy vine that can live for many decades, so be sure to give it adequate support. You can keep it in a large pot for many years, which helps to control its size.

How Soak the wisteria roots for a few hours before planting. Dig a hole the same

Japanese wisteria has long, dangling flower clusters that look like stringed pearls.

depth as the roots and twice as wide. Set the vine in the center of the hole, fanning the roots over a cone of soil. If there is a graft union (a knobby ring around the base of the trunk), make sure it's above ground level. Amend the dug soil with compost and refill the hole. Firm the soil around the plant and water thoroughly. Apply a 2- to 4-inch layer of organic mulch, keeping it from touching the trunk.

TLC Young wisterias need regular water; once established, though, they will do fine with moderate water. Maintain a 2- to 4-inch layer of mulch around the base of the plant. Let newly planted wisteria grow with a single- or multistemmed structure—whichever you prefer. Remove stems that interfere with the desired framework; pinch back side stems and long streamers. Tie the remaining stems to stakes, wires, or a sturdy trellis, using flexible ties. As the plant matures, prune it to shape in winter, when you can see its structure. During the growing season, remove excess new growth that would produce needless tangle; this late-spring and summer pruning will help stimulate next year's bloom.

*Japanese wisteria grows in zones 2–7, 17. Chinese wisteria grows in zones 3–7, 17.

Ground Covers

The first time I saw kinnikinnick *(Arctostaphylos uva-ursi)* growing as a ground cover along a sunny slope, I had to stop my car to take a closer look at this charming plant. It was spring, and the little pink urn-shaped flowers dangled against the leathery green leaves.

Later I saw Lenten rose *(Helleborus orientalis)* massed beside drifts of yellow-flowering bishop's hat *(Epimedium × versicolor)* in shade beneath deciduous trees. It looked like springtime in winter. These are still my favorite ground covers, and I've planted stretches of them outside all my view windows for a winter lift.

Ground covers at their best form a true tapestry of foliage that gives you long-lasting texture, form, and color. As beginning gardeners, we crave the seasonal garnish of blossoms, but eventually we come to understand that foliage lasts longer than flowers. And beyond providing beauty, ground covers discourage weeds and conserve moisture. In dry shade, they make pools of texture. They fill gaps between shrubs, camouflage the fading foliage of bulbs, and skirt the knobby knees of roses.

HOW THEY GROW

I've learned that there is tremendous variety among ground covers. Some grow slowly in clumps, and can be relied on for the long haul. Others gallop vigorously by underground runners, and although they solve the immediate problem of covering bare ground, ultimately they can become as troublesome as the worst weeds. Yet these same aggressive ground covers are wonderful in dry shade where little will grow, and in places where pavement curbs their appetite. What

may be invasive in one garden with rich soil and plenty of rainfall may be welcome where leaner soil and less moisture beg for thugs. For example, sweet woodruff *(Galium odoratum)* behaves itself in my garden full of heavy clay but is a menace in gardens with loamy soil.

In harsher climates of the Northwest, where extremes of cold, heat, and drought make gardening especially challenging, tough ground covers with gray or succulent leaves and deep or woody roots can be especially helpful. East of the Cascade mountains, woolly thyme, lamb's ears, and the succulent perennial *Sedum spathulifolium* do extremely well in sun, while bishop's hat, evergreen ginger *(Asarum caudatum),* and hardy winter cyclamen *(Cyclamen coum)*

ABOVE: *Stone steps planted with a mix of ground covers wind down a hillside garden.* OPPOSITE PAGE: *A carpet of ground-cover plants woven from lamb's ears, carpet bugle, and creeping Jenny.*

are invaluable in shade. In southern Alaska, plants that are tolerant of cold and drought, such as bunchberry, pussy toes *(Antennaria dioica),* woolly yarrow *(Achillea tomentosa),* snow-in-summer *(Cerastium tomentosum),* and carpet bugle, are just as indispensable in the garden.

Keep in mind that a healthy ground cover that does well in your region is more worthwhile than an exotic specimen that struggles to survive. These workhorse plants free us to enjoy the garden instead of becoming its slave.

—BARBARA BLOSSOM ASHMUN

Bunchberry

Cornus canadensis

If you chance to take a walk in the woods and come across a patch of bunchberry, you could be forgiven for thinking that a shower of dogwood blossoms had fallen out of the trees. But take a closer look under the small, greenish flower bracts and you'll see a little stalk holding a whorl of six oval or roundish green leaves. This low-growing deciduous plant is widely distributed in woods throughout the northern reaches of North America. It creeps by rhizomes across the forest floor and over fallen logs to form large mats about 6 inches tall.

The bright red berries of bunchberry are a cheerful accent in the fall garden.

The name "bunchberry" refers to the clusters of red berries that appear in fall; the berries are soft, with a pulpy yellow flesh, and were a favorite berry of aboriginal peoples. (If you decide to sample them, beware of the hard central seed.) As fall progresses, the leaves turn shades of deep red, purple, then yellow before dying down for the winter.

Bunchberry is suitable for cool, shady areas in the garden, beside streams and ponds, or in naturalistic gardens, where it will ramble amid trees, stumps, and boulders.

When Plant bunchberry from nursery containers in spring. (Never gather wild plants from the woods; they are unlikely to establish.)

Where Bunchberry likes cool, moist shade and moderately acidic soil. Plant it in the wooded areas of the garden; it will gradually carpet the ground.

How Water the plants in their nursery containers. Dig planting holes 6 to 8 inches apart, slightly deeper than the root balls and twice as wide. Gently remove the plants from

ABOVE: *Water glistens on the bright green, ribbed leaves of a bunchberry.* BELOW: *A shower of creamy white petals in spring.*

their containers and rough up the roots on the sides of the root balls with a gloved hand. Set the plants in the holes so that the tops of the root balls are just at soil level. Backfill the holes with soil and firm it around the roots with your hands. Water well and apply a 2-inch layer of compost, well-rotted leaves, or pine needles around the plants, keeping the mulch several inches away from the stems.

TLC Keep bunchberry constantly moist. In late fall, after the plants have died down, apply 2 to 4 inches of organic matter such as compost, well-rotted leaves, or pine needles.

PEAK SEASON

White flowers appear in late spring and early summer; red berries follow in late summer and fall.

GARDEN COMPANIONS

Its preference for slightly acidic soil makes bunchberry ideal for planting under other acid-loving plants, such as azaleas, camellias, rhododendrons, and vine maples *(Acer circinatum)*. Partner it with other woodland treasures such as epimediums, ferns, lily-of-the-valley, and trilliums.

Carpet Bugle
Ajuga reptans

Have you ever found yourself wading through a thigh-high "ground cover"? Rest assured that carpet bugle truly reaches no higher than 4 inches. This evergreen plant spreads by sending out self-rooting runners that form new plants, creating a mat of lustrous foliage that rarely needs mulching and suppresses all but the most robust weeds. Carpet bugle (also called bugleweed) spreads rapidly, and is so popular and easy-to-grow that new varieties appear in the nursery every season. And, as a beautiful bonus, showy flower spikes bring bursts of blue, pink, or white in early spring and summer.

Carpet bugle is a member of the mint family but is not as invasive as its tasty relative. The basic species has crinkly, oblong leaves, each about 3 or 4 inches in length (larger overall in the shade). The plant's shaggy, 6-inch spikes of white, pink, or blue flowers look much like the blossoms on mint or edible sages.

'Bronze Beauty' carpet bugle, violets (Viola labradorica), and 'Georgia Blue' create a symphony of blue and purple tones.

ABOVE AND BELOW: *'Burgundy Lace'* carpet bugle sports abundant flowers of cornflower blue and deep cherry—splashed foliage.

PEAK SEASON

Foliage is attractive year-round; the flowers add color in spring and early summer.

OUR FAVORITES

'Bronze Beauty' has deep bronze leaves and cobalt blue flowers. 'Catlin's Giant' has leaves twice as large as those of the species. 'Valfredda' is a miniature form.

'Alba' and 'Rosea' have white and pink flowers, respectively.

Several variegated forms exist. 'Burgundy Lace' (sometimes called 'Burgundy Glow') has leaves splashed with reddish purple, pink, and white. 'Multicolor' is similar, with cream and pink markings on green leaves. 'Variegata' has leaves edged with light yellow.

Ajuga pyramidalis 'Metallica Crispa' has shiny, metallic bronze foliage with medium-blue flowers; it tolerates more sun than *A. reptans*.

GARDEN COMPANIONS

Carpet bugle is a robust grower and will overwhelm other low-growing neighbors. It makes a good backdrop for spring bulbs like grape hyacinths (*Muscari*) and bluebells (*Scilla*). Plant it in the semishade under leggy shrubs such as hydrangeas, smoke tree, and viburnum, or around black bamboo.

When Plant carpet bugle from cell-packs or 4-inch pots in spring or early fall.

Where Carpet bugle makes a good edging around shrub borders and trees; keep it away from lawns unless you intend to regularly dig out the spreading plantlets. Keep this vigorous ground cover in bounds by installing a 6-inch-deep edging, or by planting it in an area that is bounded by pavement. It will do fine in any well-drained soil, and although it tolerates sun it does better in part shade.

How Water the plants in their nursery containers. Add generous amounts of organic matter such as compost to the planting area. Dig planting holes slightly deeper than the root balls and twice as wide, spacing them about 1 foot apart. Gently remove the plants from their containers and set them in the ground so that the tops of the root balls are just at soil level. Water well. A light layer of mulch will keep the area attractive until the plants fill in.

TLC Carpet bugle isn't demanding, but it does need good drainage and air circulation or it can develop root rot. When flower spikes are spent, simply set the mower on the highest setting and run it over the plants (any sheared foliage will grow back quickly). If clumps die out, dig up and divide the plants, amend the soil, and replant the divisions.

Cotoneaster

Cotoneaster

Rock cotoneaster drapes glossy green accents over these streamside boulders. Birds are drawn to the combination of moving water and late-season berries.

Cotoneasters range from full-size trees to petite rock-garden specimens, including several prostrate forms that make foolproof ground covers. Everything about these low-growing forms is tiny—except for their overall spread, which can be extensive. The lance-shaped leaves are less than an inch in length, arranged in alternating fashion along the stems; the clustered (usually white) flowers are less than 1 inch across; and the bright red berries are no larger than peas. The overall effect is neat and unassertive, which makes cotoneasters perfect foils for showier plants.

Cotoneasters grow vigorously and require little or no maintenance so they can quickly cover bare earth, even where the soil is poor or rocky or on sloping ground. In fact, they look better and produce bigger crops of berries in challenging conditions. You can use cotoneaster for erosion control, for a large-scale ground cover, or to suppress weeds in the wilder reaches of the garden. Both deciduous and evergreen forms are available. Birds are attracted to the fall fruits, which often remain on the plants well into winter.

PEAK SEASON

Cotoneasters flower in spring; attractive berries follow in fall and winter.

OUR FAVORITES

All varieties are deciduous unless stated otherwise.

Cotoneaster apiculatus 'Tom Thumb' is a miniature cranberry cotoneaster that grows 6 inches tall and 10 inches wide. Shiny round leaves turn deep red in autumn. This plant is a good choice for cold-winter climates.

Evergreen bearberry cotoneaster (*C. dammeri*) roots as it grows, soon reaching a height of 8 inches and width of 10 feet. Foliage is glossy bright green. 'Coral Beauty' and 'Lowfast' are both choice selections.

Rock cotoneaster (*C. horizontalis*) has an attractive growth habit with 2-foot-tall branches arranged in an unusual flat herringbone pattern. The spring flowers are pale pink.

Rockspray cotoneaster (*C. lineari-folius*) is an evergreen that measures 2 feet tall and wide. The branches are covered with tiny clusters of dark green, glossy leaves.

GARDEN COMPANIONS

Plant cotoneasters in a mixed-shrub border; combine with smaller conifers or native plants such as ceanothus, or mix them with heaths and heathers in the rock garden.

When Plant cotoneasters from nursery containers in spring or fall.

Where Cotoneasters are not fussy about soil, and they tolerate full sun or part shade. Place them in rock gardens, on slopes, spilling over retaining walls, or in tough spots under trees—anywhere they can spread their branches without regular clipping.

ABOVE AND BELOW: *Evergreen bearberry cotoneaster often sports both flowers and berries at the same time.*

How Water the plants in their nursery containers. Dig planting holes slightly deeper than the root balls and twice as wide, spacing them according to the mature size of the plants. Gently remove the plants from their containers and rough up the roots slightly. Set the plants in the holes so that the tops of the root balls are just at soil level. Backfill the holes with soil and firm it around the roots with your hands. Water well and apply a 2-inch layer of mulch around the plants, keeping the mulch several inches away from the stems.

TLC Give cotoneasters moderate water until established, then put them on a lower-water regimen. Prune only when needed to remove crossing or upright branches—overzealous clipping can disfigure the plants. If you have to limit spread, make cuts at the branch junctures to maintain a natural look. There is no need to fertilize cotoneasters.

Cranberry and rockspray cotoneasters will also grow in zone A3. Rock cotoneaster will grow in zones A3; 2b–7, 17.

Epimedium
Epimedium

When the first 3-inch-wide, heart-shaped leaflets of epimedium emerge from their dense network of underground stems in spring, they are a bronzy pink color. As summer progresses they begin to turn green and overlap to form a nodding 1-foot-high carpet. Finally, in fall, they turn a reddish bronze that adds a sweep of color during mild winters. This delicate tracery of pretty, slightly textured leaves makes a fine ground cover in areas where you'd prefer a lighter texture, such as under a laceleaf Japanese maple, for contrast with a large-leafed hosta, or to fill in a small, shady bed.

Epimedium grandiflorum 'Higoense' makes a pretty edging along a wood-chip path. The delicate looks of this plant belie a toughness of character.

The flower sprays dangle on wiry stems above the leaves. The blossoms are curious little things, sometimes called "bishop's hat" due to their likeness to medieval ecclesiastical miters—soft caps with protruding "ears" or points. The small waxy flowers come in purple, pink, red, creamy yellow, or white, each sporting a combination of inner and outer sepals, as well as petals that have long, curved spurs, giving the blooms the appearance of slightly flattened columbines.

PEAK SEASON

Flowers bloom spring through fall; some varieties of epimedium may retain their colored foliage through winter in milder climates.

OUR FAVORITES

Deciduous *Epimedium grandiflorum* 'Lilafee' has long-spurred, lavender-lilac blossoms; 'Rose Queen' has rosy sepals and white-tipped spurs.

E. alpinum 'Shrimp Girl' has red sepals and yellow spurs; its evergreen foliage grows to 8 inches tall.

E. stellatum 'Wudang Star' emerges bright pink; 1-foot-tall flower stems hold white and orange petals.

E. × versicolor 'Sulphureum' has two-tone yellow flowers and pinkish red fall color. It is semievergreen.

E. × youngianum 'Niveum' is a pure white form; *E. × y.* 'Roseum' has flowers of purple and white. Both are deciduous.

GARDEN COMPANIONS

Plant epimedium in a shaded or woodland garden underneath plants that enjoy the same conditions, such as azaleas, camellias, conifers, rhododendrons, and pieris. Under a katsura tree (*Cercidiphyllum*) or almost any Japanese maple (*Acer palmatum*), epimedium will echo the leaf texture and hues of the tree's foliage.

When Most nurseries offer epimedium in containers in spring, but it can be planted in either spring or fall.

Where Epimedium should be planted in slightly acidic, organically enriched soil with good drainage. In areas that have very dry, hot summers, grow it in full shade.

How Add generous amounts of organic matter such as compost to the planting area. Water the plants in their nursery containers, then dig holes 1 foot apart, slightly deeper than the plants' root balls and twice as wide. Gently remove the plants from their containers and set them in the ground so that the tops of the root balls are just under soil level. Refill the holes with compost-enriched soil and water well. Apply a 2-inch layer of mulch.

TLC Maintain even moisture during the growing season. In late winter, cut back old foliage and apply a balanced fertilizer, then apply a 2-inch layer of mulch. Once every few years in fall, lift and divide clumps of epimedium; replant the divisions in compost-enriched soil.

TOP TO BOTTOM: *E. grandiflorum* 'Rose Queen'; *E. stellatum* 'Wudang Star'; *crimson-purple fall color; E. × versicolor 'Sulphureum', with corydalis foliage.*

Hardy Geranium
Geranium

Although some hardy geranium species are ornamental enough to be border plants, the ones listed here have a spreading or scrambling growth habit that makes them ideal ground covers in situations as diverse as rock gardens, underneath trees, and as filler between other perennials. With their considerable hardiness and preference for mild summers, they grow happily throughout the Northwest. In most areas, plants die down in winter and re-emerge in spring. In mild climates, some will stay green through winter.

Don't confuse these plants with the bedding plant commonly called geranium (*Pelargonium* species). Hardy geraniums, sometimes called cranesbills, have wiry stems and masses of smallish leaves that come in many shapes, usually lobed or deeply cut; some resemble miniature maple leaves, others look like parsley, yet others like little stars. Carried singly or in clusters, the long-lasting blossoms are usually 1 to 2½ inches wide, in purple, magenta, mauve, pink, or white, often with blotches and veins.

Geranium 'Johnson's Blue' spreads up to 2 feet wide and has clear blue flowers that appear in midsummer.

PEAK SEASON

Most bloom in spring and summer, but some varieties flower until fall.

OUR FAVORITES

Geranium 'Ann Folkard' (zones 2b–7, 17) billows to 1½ feet tall and 5 feet across, with chartreuse leaves and magenta blossoms veined with black.

G. × cantabrigiense (zones 1–7, 17) is 6 inches tall, with deeply cut, green foliage, and blue or pink flowers from late spring through summer.

G. macrorrhizum (zones 1–7, 17) grows to 1½ feet tall, with sticky, hairy leaves up to 4 inches across. Fall color is yellow, orange, or scarlet.

G. × oxonianum (zones 2–7, 17) can grow to 2 feet tall and 3 feet wide. 'Wargrave Pink' has glossy, warm pink blossoms. Lipstick pink 'Phoebe Noble' is named for the renowned Victoria, B.C., gardener.

Bloody cranesbill (*G. sanguineum*) (zones A2, A3; 1-7, 1) spreads to 2½ feet wide, 1½ feet tall. The leaves turn to blood red in fall. Commonly available are white 'Album' and reddish magenta 'New Hampshire'.

GARDEN COMPANIONS

Hardy geraniums thrive under trees. They also make a good cover-up for spring bulbs such as crocus, daffodil, and tulips.

When Plant hardy geraniums from nursery containers in late spring or fall.

Where Plant in moist, well-drained soil in open, sunny areas or partly shaded spots under trees. They look great at the edges of patios and pathways.

How Water the plants in their nursery containers. Dig each planting hole twice the width of the container and about the same depth, spacing holes according to the mature size of the plants. Gently tip the root ball from the pot and loosen the roots with your fingers before placing it in the center of the hole; keep the crown of the plant at the same level as it was in the pot. Fill in the hole with soil amended with organic matter such as compost. Firm the soil with your fingers; apply a 2- to 3-inch layer of an organic mulch, and water well.

TLC All types appreciate regular water. Give a complete fertilizer in spring. One of hardy geraniums' most attractive qualities is how quickly they bounce back from an after-bloom shearing, usually ushering in another burst of bloom. If clumps outgrow their allotted spaces, dig up and divide them in early spring, making sure each division has some visible roots.

ABOVE: Geranium macrorrhizum 'Album'. RIGHT: *Bloody cranesbill (Geranium sangineum 'New Hampshire') is the hardiest.*

Kinnikinnick

Arctostaphylos uva-ursi

This evergreen ground cover can be found growing in the wild from Northern California to Alaska and is variously known by gardeners and native-plant enthusiasts as manzanita, bearberry, and kinnikinnick. It is a member of a clan of woody plants that resemble smaller versions of native madrone, with striking crooked branches covered with smooth red to purple bark, and small glossy leaves that take on red or purplish tints in winter.

Kinnikinnick thrives in rocky or sandy fast-draining soil with little water and even less fussing. It can take some time to spread, but once established it ranges up to 15 feet across, rooting as it grows. Charming little bundles of pink or white waxy flowers that look like upside-down urns emerge in late winter and then give way to red fruits, which ripen slowly and often remain on the plant during the winter months. Some varieties produce more fruits than others, so if you are hoping to attract birds, pick the heavy croppers listed at right.

Arctostaphylos uva-ursi 'Massachusetts' is one of the finest ground covers for Northwest gardens. It makes a fine addition to a native or low-maintenance garden.

PEAK SEASON.

Kinnikinnick flowers from late winter to early spring.

OUR FAVORITES

'Massachusetts' is a lower-growing form with tiny leaves, abundant pale pink flowers, and plentiful fruit. 'Vancouver Jade' has a similar growth habit but spreads to only 8 feet; it has jade green leaves that turn red in winter.

'Point Reyes' has darker leaves and is extremely tolerant of heat and drought.

'Radiant' offers especially glossy leaves that are lighter green and more widely spaced than those of 'Point Reyes', with a heavy crop of bright red berries.

'Wood's Compact' is a smaller form with pink flowers.

GARDEN COMPANIONS

This is one of the rare ground covers that can thrive underneath trees (even oaks) with almost no extra watering after it is established. Kinnikinnick looks best with other rugged and native plants, such as dwarf conifers, currants (*Ribes*), Oregon grape (*Mahonia*), rosemary, and salal (*Gaultheria*).

When Plant kinnikinnick from 1-gallon containers in fall or early winter, so that winter rains can help the roots establish before the following summer.

The waxy bells of kinnikinnick flowers add bright contrast to the plant's evergreen foliage.

Where Kinnikinnick will grow on parking strips or dry banks, in rock gardens or on top of rock walls, and in the native or naturalistic garden.

How Water the plants in their nursery containers. Dig planting holes 3 feet apart, slightly deeper than the root balls and twice as wide. Gently remove each plant from its container and rough up the roots on the sides of the root ball with a gloved hand. Set the plants in the holes so that the tops of the root balls are just at or above soil level. Backfill the holes with soil and firm it around the roots with your hands. Water well, and apply a 2-inch layer of compost or well-rotted leaves around the plants, keeping the mulch several inches away from the stems.

TLC Don't baby this plant; it will do just fine without too much fussing—little to moderate water is all it requires. In coastal areas, avoid overhead watering, which can lead to leaf spot disease.

Knotweed
Persicaria

The word "knotweed" can elicit gasps of horror, but there's no reason to panic. Several other, more aggressive plants share this common name, and while those in the *Persicaria* genus can be vigorous, they're not rampant.

Having said that, there is something defiant about these "good" knotweeds: their tough, rhizomatous roots spread in even difficult planting conditions. Rising from these underground roots are jointed crimson stems with 2- to 4½-inch-long, lance-shaped leaves (like peach leaves, hence *Persicaria,* from the Latin *persica,* for peach) that sport striking chevron markings. Slender, even wiry, flower stems emerge in late spring, tipped with bottlebrush-like flowers in shades of pink, red, or white. These perennial plants die to the ground in winter and emerge again in spring.

Knotweeds have legendary qualities: they perform well in the face of indifferent soil, capricious watering, and considerable inattention. They also have jazzy good looks that add interest to the garden. Guard against invasive plants by buying knotweed from a reputable nursery and verifying that you are buying *Persicaria.*

Persicaria bistorta *sends up pale pink candles of bloom in late summer.*

PEAK SEASON

Plants bloom in late summer and early fall.

OUR FAVORITES

Persicaria affinis grows to 1 foot tall and spreads to 2 feet. The 3-inch-long flower spikes bloom on wiry, 5- to 6-inch-tall stems in summer and fall. 'Darjeeling Red' is a lower grower (to 3 inches) with 10-inch-tall, deep pink flowers that age to burnt crimson; the foliage turns red in fall. 'Superba' has pale pink flowers.

P. microcephala 'Red Dragon' is a clumping knotweed that will not run but is nonetheless a vigorous and spreading grower, with metallic-looking, deep burgundy leaves that have a silvery chevron marking, and white flowers in late summer.

P. virginiana 'Painter's Palette' is an eastern native with large leaves (to 10 inches long) marbled in green, pale gray green, and ivory, with a ragged chocolate-maroon chevron on the center of each leaf.

GARDEN COMPANIONS

Create a colorful composition by planting knotweed amid coreopsis, daylilies, euphorbias, New Zealand flax (*Phormium*), or variegated grasses.

When Plant knotweed from nursery containers any time during the growing season that you can give them sufficient water to get established.

CLOCKWISE FROM LEFT: Persicaria microcephala 'Red Dragon' is a clumper, not a runner, yet it spreads quickly to make a great ground cover; P. virginiana 'Lance Corporal'; P. m. 'Red Dragon'.

Where Knotweed thrives in full sun or partial shade in well-drained soil. Use it in informal borders or to cover a sunny, open spot.

How Water the plants in their nursery containers. Dig planting holes slightly deeper than the plants' root balls and twice as wide, spacing the holes about 1 foot apart. Gently remove each plant from its container and set it in the ground so that the top of the root ball is just at soil level. Fill the holes with soil, firming it with your fingers, and water well. Apply a 1- to 2-inch layer of mulch around the plants.

TLC Regular watering is required to keep knotweed looking its best. Give the plants an annual application of a balanced fertilizer in spring before new growth starts; controlled-release pellets offer the longest-lasting benefit.

*Persicaria affinis will also grow in zone 1.

Lamb's Ears

Stachys byzantina

Plants with gray and silver foliage like lamb's ear, make a soothing foil for vibrantly colored flowers, such as these spring tulips and primroses.

Some plants seem to grow well no matter how much abuse is heaped on them. Lamb's ears is a perfect example. This tough little perennial herb can thrive beside a concrete walkway, receiving abuse from bicycle tires and wayward basketballs. It can be pummeled by rain, nipped by frost, or blasted by hot sun—even torn up and replanted. Yet plants recover quickly and continue to produce ground-hugging leafy rosettes that spread to make an inviting mat.

The leaves of lamb's ears are 6 inches long, tongue-shaped, and thickly covered with downy white hairs, giving them a silvery green cast and making them truly touch-worthy. "Bunny ears" might be a more fitting name. Square blossom stalks rise up to 1½ feet, producing spikelike clusters of small crimson-purple flowers in late spring and summer. Some gardeners think these detract from the foliage and snip them off. The flowers are attractive to bees, however, so if you are hoping to attract pollinators to the garden, leave the flowers in place until spent and then snip them off.

When Plant lamb's ears in spring, or throughout the growing season if you give it extra water.

Where Lamb's ears will thrive in a sunny or partially shaded spot. It's useful as an edging plant for beds, lawns, and pathways and an excellent choice as a ground cover in high, open shade, such as under tall oaks.

PEAK SEASON

Foliage is attractive year-round.

OUR FAVORITES

'Silver Carpet' produces no flower spikes.

'Big Ears' ('Countess Helen von Stein') has large leaves to 1 foot in length.

'Primrose Heron' has furry yellow leaves that age to chartreuse then gray-green.

GARDEN COMPANIONS

Gray or silver plants can tone down hotter colors in the border; use lamb's ears for this purpose with magenta, cobalt, and fuchsia-colored blossoms. They blend beautifully with pastel colors, too, such as soft pink, light blue, and pale yellow, so mix them with campanula, columbine, diascia, foxglove, and lavender.

How Water the plants in their nursery containers. Plant lamb's ears 2 feet apart; plants fill in quickly. Dig each hole twice the width of the plant's container and about the same depth. Gently tip the root ball from the pot and place it in the center of the hole. Fill in the hole with soil amended with organic matter. Firm the soil with your fingers, and water well.

ABOVE: *'Primrose Heron' boasts a pretty chartreuse color.* BELOW: *Lamb's ears against maroon Anthriscus sylvestris 'Ravenswing'.*

TLC Once established, lamb's ears needs moderate water and no fertilizer. As clumps die out in the center over time, dig them up, divide into sections, and replant. Keep plants looking tidy by removing spent flower spikes and ragged leaves.

Lily Turf
Liriope and *Ophiopogon*

Many of us have a strong desire for uniform green expanses in the garden, and for most gardeners that means a turfgrass lawn. But traditional lawns come with a price—high maintenance—and they certainly aren't suited to all areas. That's where lily turf comes in. These evergreen perennials will thrive along narrow strips of land, under trees, at the edges of walks and planting beds, between pavers, and even in shallow soil under trees—all those places where grass just can't cut it.

Creeping lily turf *(Liriope spicata)* spreads by fleshy underground stems; it forms a uniform colony under 8 inches tall. Big blue lily turf *(L. muscari)* is more of a clumper, much like many of the sedges *(Carex* species); it can be used to create a more naturalistic meadow planting mixed with other flowers. Black mondo grass *(Ophiopogon planiscapus* 'Nigrescens') is a slow-growing clumper.

All have strappy leaves and produce spikes of blossoms in summer, followed by small black berries. Lily turf is supremely adaptable, tolerating pretty much any lousy soil, lack of light, root competition, and even deer. So who needs a lawn?

PEAK SEASON

Plants look best from spring until cold weather arrives.

OUR FAVORITES

Liriope spicata 'Silver Dragon' ('Gin-ryu') has leaves striped silvery white, and pale mauve flowers. It grows more slowly than the species.

Several varieties of *L. muscari* are widely available. 'Big Blue' has stiffly arching foliage 1 to 1½ feet tall, with dark purple flowers. 'Majestic' (sometimes called *L. exiliflora*) grows to 1½ feet tall; it has clusters of violet blossoms. 'Variegata' has a loose growth habit, forming a soft, 1- to 1½-foot-tall clump of leaves with yellow margins, and lavender flowers.

Tufts of slow-growing black mondo grass (*Ophiopogon planiscapus* 'Nigrescens') grow to 8 inches tall by 1 foot wide. Flowers are white.

GARDEN COMPANIONS

Use sweeps of lily turf underneath trees or between shrubs and perennials. For a meadow effect, interplant different varieties of lily turf with daylilies, bearded iris, and sedges and ornamental grasses.

When Plant lily turf from nursery containers in spring or fall.

Where Lily turf prefers filtered sun to full shade but will tolerate most exposures. Plant in well-drained soil.

How Water the plants in their nursery containers. Plant lily turf 8 to 18 inches apart, depending on the ultimate size of the variety and effect desired. Dig each planting hole twice the width of the plant's container and about the same depth. Gently tip the root ball from the pot and place it in the center of the hole. Fill in the hole with soil amended with plenty of organic matter such as compost. Firm down the soil with your fingers, and water well.

TLC Give lily turf moderate water. Regular fertilizing isn't necessary. Cut back or mow shaggy old foliage before new leaves appear in spring. When clumps become large, divide in early spring, using a sharp spade to cut through clumps, and replant the divisions.

TOP TO BOTTOM: *Black mondo grass; Liriope muscari 'Big Blue'; L. spicata 'Silver Dragon'.*

*Big blue lily turf will also grow in zone 2b. Black mondo grass grows best in zones 5–7, 17.

Thyme

Thymus

Thyme packs a lot of plant into a tiny package. This ground-hugging perennial has leaves that are rarely more than $\frac{1}{8}$ inch long, yet it can withstand tough conditions between paving stones and even on pathways with light foot traffic. It has a pleasant aroma that is strong enough to be enjoyed from several feet away—especially if crushed underfoot. And, of course, thyme is invaluable as a culinary herb that adds flavor to a wide range of savory dishes.

Several types of thyme can be used as ground covers; depending on the variety, they may trail or mound or hug the ground. Lemon, lime, and variegated forms grow 6 to 12 inches tall; shorter, mat-forming kinds—some with woolly foliage—top off at 3 inches. Thymes need almost no care and spread rapidly, filling crevices between bricks and stones or draping themselves with aplomb over stone walls or the edges of troughs and herb planters. The tiny flowers of white, pink, mauve, lavender, or deep purple appear in spring and early summer and continue for months.

Technically, thyme is evergreen, but don't be alarmed if it loses its foliage in winter. It always bounces back.

A mixture of thymes grows around stones and steps, filling in crevices along the way. Established plantings can withstand considerable foot traffic.

PEAK SEASON

Foliage is evergreen; flowers bloom from late spring to late summer.

OUR FAVORITES

Lemon thyme (Thymus × citriodorus) varieties include 'Aureus' (leaves splashed with gold); 'Argenteus' (silver-splashed leaves); 'Doone Valley' (dotted with yellow); 'Lime' (chartreuse leaves). All grow to 1 foot tall and 2 feet wide, except 'Doone Valley', which grows only 5 inches tall.

Woolly thyme (T. pseudolanuginosus) has fuzzy, gray-green leaves that form an undulating mat 2 to 3 inches tall and 3 feet wide. 'Hall's Woolly' (or 'Hall's Variety') is a profuse bloomer.

Mother-of-thyme, also called creeping thyme (T. serpyllum), is low growing (to just 3 inches) and wide spreading (to 3 feet) with roundish, dark green leaves and mauve summer flowers. It is good as a filler between stepping-stones. 'Elfin' is highly fragrant, with lavender flowers, but spreads only 5 or 6 inches. 'Minus' grows less than an inch tall, spreads a foot wide, and bears pale pink flowers. 'Pink Chintz' has darker pink flowers and grows 1 to 2 inches tall and 1½ feet wide.

GARDEN COMPANIONS

Mix several thymes together in ground-cover plantings, matching them for height so one doesn't overrun the other, or combine with other herbs, such as sage and oregano.

When Plant thyme from cell-packs or 4-inch pots in spring.

ABOVE: *Mixed thymes fill in nooks and crannies in a rock garden.* BELOW: *The pretty, tiny flowers of silver lemon thyme (Thymus × citriodorus 'Argenteus').*

Where Like most herbs, thyme likes full sun but it does not like overly rich soil and it needs good drainage. Plant it in rockeries, between paving stones, and at the edges of patios.

How Water thyme in the containers before planting. Dig planting holes 6 inches to 1 foot apart, depending on variety. The holes should be slightly deeper than the root balls and twice as wide. Gently remove each plant from its container and loosen the roots with your fingers. Set the plant in the ground so that the top of the root ball is just at soil level. Fill in the holes with compost-amended soil, and water well.

TLC Thyme has low water needs, but the reflected heat of paving or bricks can dry out plants more rapidly. Give those plantings regular water. They will produce more foliage in response to fertilizer, but it's not necessary for good growth. Cut back plants in early spring to encourage new growth.

*Woolly thyme and mother-of-thyme will also grow in zones A2 and A3.

Spillers and Fillers

TOP 10 PLUS

The plants shown here fall somewhere in between the categories of border perennials and ground covers. All have mounding or trailing habits and grow to less than 2 feet tall, making them ideal for softening the edges of plantings or pathways, as well as for filling in the inevitable gaps that appear in even the best-designed plantings.

Our Favorites

Bellflowers (*Campanula*) are vigorous, spreading plants with bell-shaped blooms. Dalmatian bellflower (*C. portenschlagiana*; zones 2–7, 17), to 8 inches tall, has violet blue or grayish white flowers in late spring and summer. Tussock bellflower *C. carpatica*; all zones) grow to 6 inches tall, with violet bells in summer.

Cinquefoil (*Potentilla atrosanguinea*; zones 2b–7, 17) forms clumps to 2 feet wide and 1½ feet tall, with silvery gray leaves and deep, red 1-inch flowers in summer.

ABOVE: *An edging of coral bells picks up tones from both the gravel path and a pink-blooming spiraea.* LEFT: *The metallic bronzy red leaves of coral bells echo the bloom color of a neighboring wallflower (Erysimum 'Bowles Mauve').*

Coral bells (*Heuchera sanguinea;* all zones) has evergreen clumps of roundish leaves with scalloped edges. Two-foot-tall stems hold dainty red, pink, or white blossoms.

Corydalis flexuosa (zones 2–7, 17) reaches 1 foot tall by 8 inches wide, spreads by underground roots, and has divided foliage and spikelike clusters of blue flowers in summer.

Geraniums (*Pelargonium;* all zones). are trailing or mounding perennials that are grown as annuals in the Northwest. The foliage is generally lobed, deeply cut, or scalloped, and often colored, succulent, velvety, or fragrant. Small flowers on wiry stems bloom all summer.

Dwarf plumbago (*Ceratostigma plumbaginoides;* zones 2b–7, 17) has wiry stems that sport bronzy 3-inch leaves and cobalt blue flowers.

Evergreen candytuft (*Iberis sempervirens;* zones 1–7, 17) grows to 1 foot tall with narrow, shiny, dark green leaves. The pure white flower clusters emerge in spring.

ABOVE: *Lady's-mantle softens the edge of a mixed planting.* BELOW: *Lady's-mantle, masterwort* (Astrantia), *and ferns spill over a mossy rock wall.*

Dead nettle (*Lamium maculatum;* zones A2, A3; 1–7, 17) is a spreading plant to 3 feet wide. Its 1-inch leaves have white markings; early-spring flowers are pink or white.

Lady's-mantle (*Alchemilla mollis;* zones A2, A3; 1–7, 17) is a clump-forming plant to 1 foot tall and 2½ feet wide. The leaves are scalloped rounds; clusters of summer flowers are yellowish green.

Japanese blood grass (*Imperata cylindrica* 'Rubra'; zones 2b–7, 17) is a slow-growing grass to 2 feet tall. Leaves are green at the base, brilliant red at the tips. It rarely flowers.

Planting and Care

Almost all these plants like well-drained soil and full sun or partial shade (dead nettle prefers shade). Plant perennials in fall or spring, annuals in spring only. Add a tablespoon of controlled-released food to the planting holes. Most spillers benefit from an annual shearing to encourage bushy growth; do this in late fall or early spring.

Ornamental Grasses

Fifteen years ago, I came to British Columbia from my home state of Ohio, where just a few small areas of North America's once-great tallgrass prairie can still be found. Drawn here by clean air and pristine mountain streams, I built a nursery where I could grow my favorite plants—ornamental grasses.

One of the things that make the Northwest such an exciting place to garden is the great diversity it offers. It has more than a dozen different geo-climatic zones, including everything from misty rainforests to sagebrush deserts and, of course, the short-season northern regions.

My nursery is located near the border between Washington and British Columbia, between the Okanagan Valley and the Rocky Mountains. It has two different locations, and though they are just 15 miles from each other, I have noticed that as far as the grasses are concerned they are worlds apart.

The first is a heavily treed spot near a lake nearly 2,000 feet above sea level. In winter,

plenty of snowfall protects marginally hardy grasses like maiden grass and fountain grass from the killing combination of freezing and thawing. The other nursery site is farther west, in an arid valley. The summers there are hotter and the winters are colder, with biting winds and little protective snowfall. Blue oat grass (*Helictotrichon sempervirens*) and many of the hardier sedges truly thrive there.

SEASONAL GRASSES

The Top 10 grasses on the following pages (which include some grasslike plants and bamboo) are described as cool or warm season. Cool-season grasses grow in early spring

and flower early. They make good choices in northern areas that have short growing seasons. Warm-season grasses start their big push of growth later in the spring and early summer. These grasses flower in midsummer and hold on to their flowers through fall and even winter. The warm-season grasses look great late in the season and provide the landscape with structure even during the winter months.

ABOVE: *Grasses frame a garden bench.* OPPOSITE PAGE: *A graceful golden sedge with conifers.* BELOW: *Japanese forest grass.*

IN THE GARDEN

With their dense clumps of narrow leaves, grasses contrast conspicuously in shapes and foliage textures with nearly all other garden plants. A single grassy clump is both a focal

point and a means of separating plants of different shapes and sizes. The largest (such as maiden grass and giant feather grass) form imposing columns around which to arrange smaller shrubs, perennials, and annuals. Shorter grasses (such as Japanese forest grass and many sedges) serve as distinct punctuation marks among traditional foreground plants. Medium-size grasses easily form part of the tapestry of foliage in mixed borders. And grasses make great meadow plantings, mixed and matched with easy-care perennials and annuals.

—JIM BROCKMEYER

Blue Oat Grass
Helictotrichon sempervirens

In this Eugene garden, an old camellia tree has been pruned up and surrounded with unfussy, silver-toned plants, including lavender and blue oat grass.

Blue oat grass is a plant of unimpeachable character. It can survive winter temperatures even down to −25°F/−32°C, it remains evergreen in milder parts of the Northwest, and it has silvery blue foliage that makes an exceptional color accent. The neat, stiff, tapering leaves radiate from the center of the plant to form a 2- to 3-foot fountain. Wispy, oatlike flowers sit atop 2-foot-tall arching stems, gradually turning from cream to champagne colored as the season progresses. Flowering may be reduced in hot weather, but the foliage mound is not affected by the heat.

Blue oat grass is attractive in borders or with boulders in a rock garden or terrace. For a low-care meadow, intersperse it with easy-to-grow daylilies, coneflowers, and smaller clumps of blue fescue *(Festuca glauca)*. The steely blue foliage also contrasts well with warm reds—try planting it in a terra-cotta pot or a glazed red urn.

PEAK SEASON

Flowers bloom in mid to late summer; foliage is attractive year-round.

OUR FAVORITE

The variety 'Saphirsprudel' is more rust resistant in humid climates, with deeper blue foliage.

GOOD ALTERNATIVES

Switch grass (Panicum virgatum) is similar to blue oat grass but greener, with upright foliage that grows to 4 feet and flowers rising to 7 feet; it holds up well to wind. 'Rubrum' has striking red fall color.

Blue lyme grass (Leymus arenarius) is a blue-gray grass even hardier than blue oat grass, surviving in southern Alaska, but it can be quite invasive. Plants look best when cut back after bloom to stimulate new growth.

GARDEN COMPANIONS

The blue-gray foliage of blue oat grass pairs well with silver-leafed plants such as lavender, salvia, and rose campion (Lychnis), and also with roses—especially red ones.

When Plant blue oat grass from nursery containers in spring or fall.

Where Blue oat grass tolerates a wide range of soils and some shade, but it does best in well-drained, rich soil in full sun. If the soil is too wet, especially in winter, blue oat grass may get root rot.

How Water the grass in its nursery container. Dig a planting hole the same width and about twice as wide as the container. Gently tip out the plant and loosen its roots. Place the plant in center of the hole, making sure that the top of the root ball is even with the surrounding soil. Fill in around the plant with compost-amended native soil and firm down. Water deeply.

TLC Do not overwater blue oat grass—moderate watering is fine—and don't bother with fertilizer. This evergreen grass doesn't need to be cut back in spring, but do remove dead foliage by combing through the grass with gloved fingers. If you like, you can also clip off the spent flower stalks in late fall. If the plant becomes overgrown after a few years, dig up the plant, divide it into several pieces, cut back the foliage, and replant each piece in a new spot.

ABOVE: *This drought-tolerant planting includes daylilies, Mexican feather grass, and blue oat grass.* RIGHT: *Blue oat grass in front of a fiery orange canna.*

Feather Grass

Nassella tenuissima, Stipa gigantea

The two feather grasses—Mexican *(Nassella tenuissima)* and giant *(Stipa gigantea)*—are now classified as different species, but they still share an important characteristic: shimmery, showstopping flowers. Mexican feather grass grows to about 2 feet tall with a multitude of very thin flowering stems that rise upward and then billow out into puffs of silvery green, turning to a light straw color in fall. Giant feather grass is a much larger plant overall, with a fine-textured mound of foliage to 3 feet tall and narrow flower stems that rise to form an iridescent floral cloud about 6 feet off the ground.

Mexican feather grass is one of the finest plants for spilling out over pathways, as it does here mixed in a border with roses, sedums, and hydrangeas.

   Mexican feather grass is the hardier of the two perennials; in well-irrigated situations it also self-seeds in a charming way—little green tufts peek out of the earth often quite far from the original plant. Evergreen giant feather grass, on the other hand, stays put, and holds onto its flowers until the onset of strong winter rains.

PEAK SEASON

Feather grasses flower from early summer to fall.

GOOD ALTERNATIVES

In Alaska and zones 1–3, plant little bluestem (Schizachyrium scoparium), a hardy prairie native with an upright habit to 4 feet tall.

GARDEN COMPANIONS

Plant Mexican feather grass in groups of three, five, or seven in mixed borders, especially with warm-colored flowers of bearded iris, black-eyed Susans, California poppies, and zinnias. Giant feather grass is spectacular enough to be used as a single specimen but because of the airiness of its flowers, you can also put it in mixed borders and rock gardens.

When Plant feather grasses from nursery containers in fall or spring.

ABOVE: *Mexican feather grass arches over yellow pansies.* BELOW: *The shimmery flower heads of giant feather grass last for months.*

Where Feather grasses prefer sunny spots with average to good soil.

How Water the feather grass in its nursery container. Dig a planting hole the same depth and about twice as wide as the container. Gently tip out the root ball and loosen the roots. Place the grass in center of the hole, making sure that the top of the root ball is even with the surrounding soil. Fill in around the grass with compost-amended native soil and firm down. Water deeply.

TLC Water feather grasses regularly for the first year; once established, they are very drought tolerant. Do not fertilize. In late winter, cut back old foliage of Mexican feather grass; fresh new, green growth will soon emerge. When the foliage clump of giant feather grass becomes overgrown, dig up the plant, divide it into several pieces, and replant.

*Giant feather grass grows in zones 4–9, 17; Mexican feather grass in zones 2b–7, 17.

Feather Reed Grass

Calamagrostis × acutiflora

The sheer speed with which this grass achieves its mature height of 5 to 6 feet—within a year or two of planting—is quite remarkable. Even more gratifying is that it then slows right down, becoming overgrown only after many years. The foliage is a lustrous green, and the flower plumes bloom in a soft rose, then deepen in color during summer before turning gold in fall. The flower stalks sway in the slightest puff of wind but always regain their upright stance regardless of heavy winds or rains.

Although it's one of the earliest-blooming grasses, feather reed grass looks good all summer and maintains its posture and buff-colored flowers into winter. It works well in both mass plantings and mixed borders. Don't be afraid to put a single specimen amid plants

If planted close together, feather reed grasses make an excellent screen due to their height and long season of interest.

that are shorter in stature; the tall stems and flower plumes are transparent enough to create interest rather than obstruction. You also needn't worry about feather reed grass overrunning your other plants, because it doesn't self-sow.

PEAK SEASON

Feather reed grass blooms in early summer, but flowers remain on the plant to add winter interest.

OUR FAVORITES

'Karl Foerster' is the most common variety of feather reed grass.

Variegated feather reed grass (Calamagrostis × acutiflora 'Overdam') has pale white variegation on the leaves; it needs some shade in hottest zones.

GARDEN COMPANIONS

Feather reed grass is best planted in a mass as a screen or for blocks of color. In a sunny border, plant it with wispy, loose-textured Russian sage (Perovskia), lavender, and gaura.

When Plant in spring, or in fall to allow roots to get established over the winter months.

Where Feather reed grass is very forgiving of most soils, including clay. Grow in full sun to light shade.

How Because it establishes so quickly, you can plant feather reed grass from a fairly small nursery container or even mail-order plugs. Water the grass in the container before planting. To plant plugs, remove them from the packing material and water the root balls, or water before removing them. Dig a hole the same depth and about twice as wide as the container. If planting in a mass, space plants 1½ to 2 feet apart. Gently tip the root ball from the container and loosen the roots. Place the plant in the center of the hole, making sure that the top of the root ball is even with the surrounding soil. Fill in the planting hole with compost-amended native soil and firm down. Water deeply.

TLC Give average water and feed in spring with a balanced fertilizer. Cut plants back to about 6 inches tall in late winter. If clumps become overgrown with age, dig up and divide them in spring or fall. Replant the divisions in new planting holes.

ABOVE: *Russian sage* (Perovskia) *and feather reed grass.* RIGHT: *Feather reed grass amid black-eyed Susans and* Sedum *'Autumn Joy'.*

Fountain Bamboo

Fargesia

Bamboo is a plant that offers graceful beauty, impressive height, wonderful texture, exotic color, and year-round interest—yet it requires virtually no maintenance. And those tales of its rampant invasiveness are only half-true: spreading bamboos *will* quickly colonize the neighborhood, but clumpers stay put and are suitable for most gardens.

Two widely available clumpers in the *Fargesia* family are the best choices for the Northwest. Umbrella bamboo (*F. murielae)* and fountain bamboo (*F. nitida)* both grow in partial or filtered shade to about 12 feet tall, making them good choices for urban and suburban gardens. Their common names describe their overall shape: umbrella bamboo has a wider spread of foliage at the top of the plant, while fountain bamboo has arching stems (culms) that droop at the top. Fountain bamboo is also slower growing and has deep purple stems. Umbrella bamboo's culms start out light green and gradually take on a golden cast. Both are extremely hardy, withstanding temperatures to −20°F/−29°C.

Shop around when buying bamboo; prices vary, and you may get the best deal through a bamboo specialist. Also be aware that fountain bamboos have been undergoing a phenomenon of worldwide flowering, after which the plants may not survive. Do not buy a fountain bamboo that is in flower or has recently flowered.

LEFT: *Fountain bamboo (Fargesia nitida) sends out gracefully drooping pairs of leaves all along the purplish culms.*

PEAK SEASON

Foliage is attractive year-round.

OUR FAVORITE

Fargesia nitida 'Anceps' has delicate stems and bluish green foliage. It grows more slowly than the plain species and survives heat better.

GOOD ALTERNATIVES

If you have an expansive garden and want to experiment with other clumping bamboos, try *Bambusa multiplex* 'Alphonse Karr', a clumping bamboo with beautifully striped yellow-and-green culms that grow to 30 feet tall. It is reliably hardy down to 15°F/–9°C.

Clumping giant timber bamboo (*B. oldhamii*) is just as hardy and can grow to 50 feet tall, making an imposing presence in a larger garden.

GARDEN COMPANIONS

Surround the base of bamboos with golden-foliaged shade grasses or tropical-looking plants such as large-leafed hostas. Or leave the soil bare and set a piece of stone sculpture at the base of the culms.

When Plant bamboo from nursery containers in fall or spring.

Where Both umbrella and fountain bamboos appreciate some shade, but too much shade can fade the attractive dark color of the culms. Give bamboos a rich, well-drained soil amended with organic matter. Plants can be used singly as accent plants or massed to form a screen or hedge.

How Water the bamboo in its nursery container. Dig a planting hole the same depth and about twice as wide as the root ball. Gently tip the plant from its container and place the root ball in the center of the hole, making sure that its top is even with the surrounding soil. Fill in around the plant with compost-amended native soil and firm down. Water deeply. There is no need for mulch.

ABOVE AND BELOW: *New culms of bamboos shoot up devoid of leaves; they'll produce those next season.*

TLC Give generous amounts of water for the first two seasons; after that, regular watering is fine. Be patient—most bamboos tend to sit tight the first year after planting and then grow vigorously from then on. After four to five years, cut out old or dead culms at the base and clip the remaining ones to emphasize the architectural quality of the remaining culms.

Fountain Grass

Pennisetum

ountain grass is just the right size for small and medium-size gardens; the largest grow 5 feet tall and wide, but most are smaller. What's more, fountain grass has probably the most "touchable" flowers of all plants, defying passersby not to stroke them. The plumes vary in size and shape from the feathery, foot-long flowers of 'Rubrum' to the little colored puffballs of 'Red Bunny Tails'. The flowers and arching green leaves dance and bounce in the breeze, adding movement to perennial or shrub borders, mass plantings, and containers. Flowers and foliage fade to yellow or brown in fall.

All fountain grasses are warm-season perennials (which means they grow

A beautiful arching form is characteristic of fountain grasses, such as this Pennisetum alopecuroides 'Hameln'.

rapidly during the hot sum–mer months), but tender *Pennisetum setaceum* is grown as an annual throughout the Northwest. It can be found in nurseries in spring, often already in flower, and grows quickly.

When Plant fountain grass from nursery containers in spring, after the last frost.

Where Choose a site in full sun with average to rich, well-drained soil, or plant in pots.

How Water the grass in its nursery container. Dig a planting hole the same depth and about twice as wide as the container. Gently tip out the plant and loosen its roots. Place the plant in the center of the hole, making sure that the top

ABOVE: *A close-up view shows the delicacy of the flowers of P. a. 'Hameln'.* BELOW: *Silky flowers of P. s. 'Rubrum' drape poolside.*

of the root ball is even with the surrounding soil. Fill in around the plant with compost-amended native soil and firm down. Water deeply.

TLC Fountain grass takes average water. In spring, cut perennial types to 3 inches tall and feed with a balanced fertilizer. When the crowns begin to die out, dig up the clumps and divide into several pieces. Replant and water deeply.

PEAK SEASON

Bloom time is midsummer to fall for perennial types, spring through fall for *Pennisetum setaceum*.

OUR FAVORITES

P. alopecuroides 'Hameln' grows to 2 feet tall and wide, with bright green foliage and creamy flowers that bloom in late summer. *P. a.* 'Little Bunny' and variegated 'Little Honey' are smaller (to 1½ feet). *P. a.* 'Moudry' has very fluffy, dark purple flowers.

P. orientale has fine-textured green leaves that form a dense clump that is 1 to 2 feet tall and wide, covered with silky, 4-inch-long pink foxtails in summer and fall.

P. messiacum 'Red Bunny Tails', to 2 feet tall with glossy green foliage and red flowers, makes a good plant for a large container. Its plumes are shorter than most.

Purple fountain grass (*P. setaceum* 'Rubrum') has striking maroon-burgundy leaves and ruddy purple, foot-long flower spikes.

GARDEN COMPANIONS

Pair purple fountain grass with hot orange schemes of black-eyed Susan, salvias, and zinnias. Green-foliaged fountain grasses blend well into mixed borders with shrubs; the smaller varieties are excellent fillers and edgers in a perennial garden.

Japanese Forest Grass
Hakonechloa macra 'Aureola'

In our sometimes muted northwestern light, the lemon-and-chartreuse leaves of Japanese forest grass glow with an otherworldly quality. This is the kind of plant that draws the eye, making it a natural for pathways, side yards, and steps—wherever you want to entice attention in a particular direction.

Growing in height to about 1½ feet, then draping gracefully, it forms a tidy mound about 2 feet wide. Planted in the shade around the base of upright plants like bamboo or dogwoods, it looks for all the world like a luminous hooped skirt. Place several plants together and you create fluid, golden waves. Showcased in a blue glazed pot, it simply shines.

The plant spreads by underground runners but is never invasive. In the fall, the leaves turn pinkish bronze, and the entire plant dies back in winter, emerging in spring with bright new foliage. It is one of the most beautiful of all grasses.

LEFT: *A mature clump of Japanese forest grass, such as this one, can reach several feet across and survive for many years.*

PEAK SEASON

The foliage is attractive spring through fall.

OUR FAVORITES

Hakonechloa macra 'Aureola' is the most commonly grown Japanese forest grass. (The plain species has all-green leaves.)

H. m. 'All Gold' has pure gold leaves with no variegation and grows a little over 1 foot tall and slightly wider. *H. m.* 'Albostriata' ('Albovariegata') is hardier than other varieties, to −30°F/−34°C, grows to 3 feet tall, and is green with white stripes.

GOOD ALTERNATIVES

Greater wood rush (*Luzula sylvatica* 'Aurea') is a golden-leafed, shade-loving evergreen grass with foliage that grows to 1 foot, flower stalks to 3 feet. It tolerates poor soil and is more drought resistant than Japanese forest grass.

GARDEN COMPANIONS

Plant Japanese forest grass in a shady border with variegated forms of masterwort *(Astrantia),* hosta, ivy, and pachysandra. It also stands out beautifully against dark-foliaged plants like carpet bugle *(Ajuga),* coleus, smoke tree, and rodgersia.

When Plant in spring.

Where Japanese forest grass needs a damp, cool spot in partial or dappled shade, with rich soil. Use it to brighten up those dark corners in the garden, to decorate the base of a shrub, or in a container.

How Water the grass in its nursery container. Dig a planting hole the same depth and about twice as wide as the container. Gently tip out the root ball and loosen the roots. Place the grass in the center of the hole, making sure that the top of the root ball is even with the surrounding soil. Fill in around the plant with compost-amended native soil and firm down. Water deeply. Apply a 2-inch layer of mulch around the base of the plant.

ABOVE: *Japanese forest grass paired with meadow rue* (Thalictrum) *and Tellima grandiflora.* BELOW: *In peachy fall tones.*

TLC Keep this grass well watered. Apply a few inches of mulch to Japanese forest grass twice a year, in spring and late summer. In late winter, cut back the previous year's foliage and apply a balanced fertilizer.

Maiden Grass

Miscanthus sinensis

For many Northwest gardeners, this is *the* grass, with a classic arching clump of foliage, often striped or zigzagged with a different color, and huge flowers that resemble tassels, plumes, or fluffy cattails—some up to 6 inches long. Few plants are more beautifully animated by wind. The common names of many varieties—zebra grass and silver feather, for example—hint at their unusual patterns or hues. Some types even provide fall color, including the appropriately named flame grass ('Purpurascens'), which turns a brilliant ruddy orange when days shorten.

Foliage clumps on many types may grow to 6 feet tall and wide with flowers held as high as 9 feet above, so be sure you give these grasses plenty of room to grow. One way to highlight the spectacular flowers is to plant maiden grass where it will be backlit by late-afternoon sun, or beside a pond so its reflection can be seen in the water. In fall and winter the foliage and flower plumes of most types fade, but the plants retain their structure and look especially showy against snow. For regions where winter temperatures get down to −30°F/−34°C, plant 'Silberfeder' or 'Purpurascens'.

A graceful Miscanthus sinensis *'Morning Light' in a mixed border.*

PEAK SEASON

Bloom time is midsummer through fall. Many types provide winter interest.

OUR FAVORITES

Miscanthus sinensis condensatus 'Cabaret' has ribbonlike leaves with a white center stripe and green edges. Pink-suffused stems grow to 9 feet tall bearing coppery pink plumes.

M. s. 'Gracillimus' has a dense, rounded form, growing to 7 feet tall with deep green blades that have silver stripes down the middle. Foliage turns bright orange in fall. Coppery plumes fade to a soft biscuit color in winter.

M. s. 'Morning Light' grows to 5 feet tall with wispy, fine-textured green leaves edged in white and plumes that are reddish bronze.

Flame grass (*M. s.* 'Purpurascens') is hardy to −30°F/−34°C and grows best in cool-summer areas. Narrow green leaves grow to 4 feet tall; silver flower plumes rise to 6 feet. Foliage turns a glowing orange-red in fall.

Silver feather (*M. s.* 'Silberfeder') grows to 6 feet tall with showy silvery pink plumes. It is very hardy (to −30°F/−34°C) and retains its beige flowers through winter.

Zebra grass (*M. s.* 'Zebrinus') grows 4 to 6 feet tall with arching leaves that are cross-banded with yellow stripes; fall plumes are coppery pink.

When Plant maiden grass in spring from a nursery container.

The aptly named zebra grass, with its zigzag stripes.

Where This grass prefers full sun and average, well-drained soil.

How Water the grass in its nursery container. Dig a planting hole the same depth and about twice as wide as the container—make sure the plant will have plenty of room around it, as clumps can grow to 6 feet across. Gently tip the root ball out of the container and loosen the roots. Place the plant in the center of the hole, making sure that the top of the root ball is even with the surrounding soil. Fill in around the plant with compost-amended native soil and firm down. Water deeply.

TLC Water maiden grass deeply to accommodate its extensive root system. In late winter, cut plants to the ground before new growth appears. When crowns start to die out, divide in spring.

GARDEN COMPANIONS

Maiden grass makes a great companion for tall-flowering perennials such as asters, black-eyed Susans, eupatorium, meadow rue (*Thalictrum*), agastache, sedums, yarrow, rudbeckia, *Verbena bonariensis,* and yucca; or, in a more formal perennial garden, as a background for lilies and daylilies.

New Zealand Flax

Phormium

These New Zealand natives are not the most hardy plants, but they have nonetheless become garden staples in the Northwest. That's because there really are no other plants quite like them. With spearlike evergreen leaves that fan stiffly outward from the plant's base, New Zealand flax is among the most effective of foliage plants for the garden, providing year-round color, vertical emphasis, and—most of all—drama. To add to the show, established plants send up branched clusters of tubular flowers several feet into the air.

Most varieties will survive reliably in the ground in coastal Northwest gardens, in southern Oregon, and around Puget Sound and Vancouver Island. Where winter temperatures regularly drop to 20°F/−7°C or below, plant them in containers and bring them into a warm garage or greenhouse until all danger of frost has passed. They take almost any soil, little to regular water, and hot or chilly conditions, and make great seacoast plants due to their ability to withstand wind and salt spray.

Bold blades of New Zealand flax are often colored and striped with vibrant shades of red, purple, pink, or burgundy. This variety is called 'Flamingo'.

PEAK SEASON

Where hardy, these foliage plants are attractive year-round.

OUR FAVORITES

Phormium 'Apricot Queen' is light yellow with green margins, blushed with apricot in cool weather. It grows to 3 feet tall and 5 feet wide.

P. 'Yellow Wave' grows to 5 feet tall and wide, with 2-inch-wide leaves in chartreuse with lime green margins.

P. tenax 'Jack Spratt' grows to 1½ feet tall and wide, with narrow, twisting, reddish brown leaves.

P. t. 'Pink Stripe' grows to 4 feet tall and wide with dark purple spears edged in pink.

P. t. 'Tom Thumb' is one of the smallest varieties, growing just 1 to 2 feet tall and wide. It is useful for massing.

GARDEN COMPANIONS

Plant New Zealand flax in masses or combine it with shrubs that sport complementary flower colors, such as roses, or those with colored foliage, such as burgundy smoke tree (*Cotinus*) or Japanese barberry (*Berberis thunbergii*) or golden-leafed forms of euonymus. In mixed borders, surround it with substantial perennials like bearded iris, peonies, dahlias, or tall coneflowers and with ornamental grasses. Single specimens also make excellent container plants.

When Plant New Zealand flax in spring from a nursery container.

Where Find a spot with full sun to partial shade. New Zealand flax can tolerate almost any amount of irrigation, but it must have well-drained soil.

How Water the plant in its nursery container. Dig a hole the same depth and about twice as wide as the container, with enough room around it to accommodate a mature specimen. Gently tip out the plant and loosen its roots. Place the plant in the center of the hole, making sure that the top of the root ball is slightly higher than the surrounding soil. If the crown of the plant is too low in soggy soil it can develop root rot. Fill in around the plant with compost-amended native soil and firm down. Water deeply.

ABOVE: *'Bronze' New Zealand flax (right).*
BELOW: *'Yellow Wave' has stripes in shades of green and yellow.*

TLC Give New Zealand flax regular water; in spring, fertilize with a balanced fertilizer. When the leaves fade, cut them as close to the crown as possible; likewise, remove spent flower stalks. To increase plantings, take individual crowns from clump edges or divide large clumps. (New Zealand flax can grow to gargantuan proportions—divide plants before they outgrow their spaces.)

Sedge

Carex

It's no exaggeration to say there's a sedge for every site. After all, these grasslike plants are found in nature in almost every habitat, from woodland to wetland, savanna to prairie. That's why they work in such a variety of garden situations.

Sedges may be either clumping or running and the foliage is often evergreen but the flowers are usually inconspicuous. These tough, dependable plants are often over-shadowed by showy large grasses, but they suffer from no pests or diseases, can easily be reproduced by division, and are long lived.

PEAK SEASON

All sedges listed here are evergreen; their foliage looks good year-round.

OUR FAVORITES

Unless otherwise stated, sedges tolerate full sun or partial shade, and average garden soil and water.

Berkeley sedge (*Carex tumulicola*) can thrive in hot inland gardens and cool coastal ones, too. The tussocks grow 1 to 1½ feet tall, making a great lawn substitute or low-growing meadow grass. Plant it in masses, or mix in some low-growing bulbs and annuals.

Blue sedge (*C. flacca* or *C. glauca*) spreads slowly by rhizomes to make a good 6-inch-tall ground cover, especially in coastal gardens, as it tolerates salt. Pair it with golden-foliaged plants or succulents.

For a variegated sedge, try *C. albula* 'Frosty Curls', which has charming

*'Evergold' sedge (*C. morrowii* 'Evergold') pours like a golden shower out of a container at the corner of a garden path.*

coils of fine silvery green foliage to 1 foot tall and wide. Japanese variegated sedge (C. morrowii expallida, also sold as C. m. 'Variegata') has wider, white-margined, drooping leaves to 1½ feet long. C. oshimensis has golden variegations. Mix any of them in the border along with flowering perennials and small shrubs.

C. elata 'Aurea' ('Bowles Golden') forms bright yellow clumps 2½ feet tall by 1½ feet wide that are evergreen in milder parts of the Northwest. It prefers a little more shade and moisture than other species and is excellent for softening the base of bamboos or leggy shrubs.

Two New Zealand sedges are also evergreen: leather leaf sedge (C. buchananii), to 3 feet tall with curly-tipped, erect blades of copper-bronze; and C. flagellifera, which is similar but less erect and more purely bronze. These sedges require moderate water; put them in drought-tolerant mixed plantings or around the bases of roses.

Great drooping sedge (C. pendula) has a graceful, weeping form to 3 feet tall and wide, with dark green leaves and pendulous flower spikes. Combine it pondside with medium-green palm sedge (C. muskingumensis), which grows 3 feet tall and wide.

GARDEN COMPANIONS
See specific species, above.

When Plant sedges from nursery containers or plugs in fall or spring.

CLOCKWISE FROM LEFT: Carex elata 'Aurea'; C. albula 'Frosty Curls'; New Zealand leather leaf sedge (C. buchananii).

Where Sun, soil, and water requirements vary by species. See "Our Favorites" at left.

How For a nursery container–grown sedge, first water the plant in its container. Dig a hole the same depth and about twice as wide as the container. Gently tip out the plant and loosen its roots. Place the plant in the center of the hole, making sure that the top of the root ball is even with the surrounding soil. If planting small plugs, dig planting holes 6 to 12 inches apart in a grid. Remove the plugs from the flat by gently pushing up against the roots from the bottom. Fill in around the plants or plugs with compost-amended native soil and firm down. Water deeply.

TLC Applications of high-nitrogen fertilizer will encourage fast growth, but most sedges don't require regular fertilizer. Give larger sedges a light trim once or twice a year; ground-cover types (Berkeley and blue sedge) can be mown with a lawn mower.

*Blue sedge and Japanese variegated sedge grow in zones 3–7, 17.

Sweet Flag
Acorus

A fragrant ornamental grass? Well, sweet flag may lack the perfumed flowers of a rose or honeysuckle, but it is nonetheless aptly named, although you must crush the leaves or rhizomes to release its slightly spicy, ginger-vanilla scent.

This dependable grasslike plant grows in damp soil or even standing water, spreading gradually by developing new rhizomes that are easy to break off and replant. The glossy green, sword-shaped leaves grow in arching fan-like clumps, showing stripes of attention-grabbing yellow or white. In summer, tufted spikes of inconspicuous tawny flowers appear.

Sweet flag makes a terrific edging plant or it can be interspersed with boulders in a flowing stream or waterfall. It thrives in the shallow water at the margins of pools or ponds and in bog gardens. Plant some in a pot by the door or kitchen window so that you can pluck a few leaves and rub them between your fingers to enjoy the delicious fragrance.

Japanese sweet flag (Acorus gramineus 'Ogon') makes a long-lived and graceful accent for the edge of a stone path. Just be sure to give it adequate moisture.

PEAK SEASON

Sweet flag's evergreen foliage is attractive year-round.

OUR FAVORITES

The Japanese sweet flag *Acorus gramineus* 'Ogon' has upright, yellow-striped foliage to 1 foot tall. *A. g.* 'Variegatus', also to 1 foot, has cream-striped leaves. Solid dark green *A. g.* 'Pusillus' grows only to 3 inches tall and is useful between stepping-stones or as a companion plant for bonsai.

Sweet flag (*A. calamus*) tolerates more cold. The species' solid green leaves grow to 5 feet tall. The form 'Variegatus' has bright yellow or creamy white stripes.

GOOD ALTERNATIVE

For a low-growing variegated grass in drier spots in the garden, try Japanese forest grass *Hakonechloa macra* 'Aureola', which has green-and-yellow-striped leaves that appear chartreuse in deep shade.

GARDEN COMPANIONS

Mix sweet flag with Japanese iris, rushes such as curly corkscrew rush (*Juncus effusus* 'Spiralis'), miniature cattails (*Typha minima*), and other moisture-loving plants.

When Plant sweet flag from rhizomes in fall or spring.

Where Use it in damp borders, at the edges of pools, or in shallow water (to a depth of 6 inches). It will tolerate considerable sun as well as quite deep shade.

How Set rhizomes in rich, damp or boggy soil or shallow water. If planting in water, either submerge the rhizomes in a plastic container or dig them into the soil and then weigh them down with pebbles or gravel.

ABOVE: *The variegated form of sweet flag* (A. calamus *'Variegatus'*). BELOW: *Sweet flag at poolside.*

TLC Keep sweet flag moist. Cut back leaves once or twice a year to encourage new growth. Divide in early spring by removing the plant from the soil and breaking off pieces of rhizome with the roots attached. Replant the divisions. No fertilizer is necessary.

*Acorus calamus *also grows in zones 2 and 3a.*

Deciduous Shrubs

Here in the Northwest, we have an extensive palette of shrubs available to us—everything from reliable standbys to exciting new introductions. With such a veritable candy shop of available choices, how can you decide which shrubs are best for your garden?

The first thing you need to consider is your location. After all, our region includes everything from the nearly frost-free coast of southern Oregon to the frigid alpine areas of Alaska, and the mild weather of the Willamette Valley to much more extreme conditions east of the Cascades. In milder areas, the large-leafed and evergreen species are often the best choices; in extremely hot or cold climates, plants with gray or small leaves usually fare better.

Our Top 10 shrubs include something for every region. Review the climate and zone information given on pages 266–269 to find out the typical highest and lowest temperatures in your area. Next, identify local conditions that might affect plants, such as drying winds or the seasonal shade beneath deciduous trees. Then, place your shrubs where they will do best. For instance, plant your hydrangea on the north side of the house to give it protection from sunburn; locate your lavenders against a sunny, south-facing wall or beside a concrete walk to provide the heat they need to bloom well.

SHRUBS IN THE GARDEN

Taking a walk around your neighborhood is a great way to get ideas. Shrubs that are well established in your neighbor's garden are likely to be long-lived in yours, too. Observing plants at various times of the year also will help you

choose something of interest for every season. Select a few key shrubs and plant several specimens of each throughout your garden as "knitters" to tie together your plantings.

I must admit that I'm a big advocate of pushing convention. I like to think of gardening as an adventure, so I'm willing to take a risk on a shrub that may be a little too tender for its zone. I don't mind tucking it into a warm, protected spot; giving it a blanket of burlap during a hard frost; or even accepting the loss of an occasional specimen as the price to pay for the greatest diversity of

ABOVE: *Rhododendrons and viburnum flank a path leading to a peaceful woodland gazebo.* OPPOSITE PAGE: *The pink winter flowers of heather* (Erica × darleyensis). BELOW: *Common lilac* (Syringa vulgaris *'Fred C. Wilkie') offers beautiful flowers in addition to one of the garden's most beloved spring fragrances.*

form and texture. One note though: It is easier and less expensive to replace a small shrub than a large one, so make sure your largest specimens are suitable.

The Top 10 shrubs highlighted on the following pages are just the beginning. Continue to have fun mixing and matching new finds until you satisfy your gardening sweet tooth.

—SEAN HOGAN

Boxwood

Buxus

When you think of boxwoods, pictures of neatly clipped hedges and formal topiary globes most likely spring to mind. Since new growth sprouts readily from the cut stems of these small evergreens, they are well suited to the pruning needed to maintain those unnatural shapes. And the leathery, deep green leaves are so small and densely packed, they create a surface that looks almost solid—maybe that's why deer rarely bother to nibble on them. Whether you're creating a topiary rabbit or an orderly edging

for a flower bed, boxwood makes great raw material. But don't think that such shaping is a must: left to their own devices, most boxwoods grow into a soft, pleasantly billowing mass.

Boxwoods are long lived and slow growing, and their evergreen, reserved presence brings a sense of order to the garden in all seasons. Plant them in casual groups or as stand-alone specimens. These shrubs have shallow roots that resent distur-bance, so it's best not to plant beneath them. They will grow happily for many years in containers.

Boxwoods trimmed to tidy balls form a border for a heart-shaped pond.

PEAK SEASON

Boxwoods look particularly fresh in spring, when new growth is starting.

OUR FAVORITES

Deep green *Buxus* 'Green Mountain' grows into a dense cone to about 5 feet tall and 3 feet wide.

Common boxwood (*B. sempervirens*) may reach 15 feet tall and wide. True dwarf boxwood (*B. s.* 'Suffruticosa') is extremely dense and eventually reaches 4 to 5 feet tall and wide. *B. s.* 'Vardar Valley' is particularly drought tolerant and cold hardy.

Japanese boxwood (*B. microphylla japonica*) has leaves of lively light green in summer that often turn bronzy in winter. It grows 4 to 6 feet tall and not quite as wide. It's the best choice for dry-summer regions and those with alkaline soil. 'Winter Gem' is the hardiest variety.

Korean boxwood (*B. m. koreana*) is very cold hardy. It reaches about 2 feet tall and 2½ feet wide.

GARDEN COMPANIONS

The uniform green of boxwoods is a perfect foil for bright flowers like daylilies (*Hemerocallis*), irises, rhododendrons, and hardy geraniums. They are great as a clipped hedge around plantings of herbs, roses, or flowering trees like dogwood (*Cornus*).

When Plant boxwood in spring in colder zones, in spring or fall in mild areas.

LEFT: *Boxwoods make fine container subjects.* RIGHT: *The natural, unclipped form of a boxwood.*

Where In most areas, boxwoods do best in partial shade, though they will grow in full sun if watered well. Choose a spot with fertile, well-drained soil that is shielded from winter wind.

How Water the boxwood in its nursery container. Dig a planting hole twice the width of the container and about the same depth. Gently tip the root ball from the pot and place it in the center of the hole. Fill in the hole with the dug soil amended with plenty of organic matter such as compost. Firm the soil with your fingers, and water well. Keep roots cool with a 2-inch layer of mulch.

TLC Keep boxwoods well watered, but avoid soggy conditions. Fertilize in spring with a balanced, controlled-release fertilizer. Prune lightly and regularly to maintain desired form, and periodically clean out debris from the plant's center.

*Common boxwood grows best in zones 3b–6, 17; Japanese boxwood is best in zones 3b–7, 17.

Camellia
Camellia

With their evergreen coat of dark, glossy, leaves and yearly explosion of color, it's no wonder that camellias are among the most beloved flowering shrubs. During the cooler months, when few other flowering plants are at their best, camellias produce blooms in hues varying from deepest red through the full range of pinks to pure white. Flowers may be simple and open, with a single row of petals surrounding a golden center— or have double or ruffled petals packed into dense, ball-shaped masses.

The most widely grown is Japanese camellia *(C. japonica),* which forms a dense pyramid 6 to 12 feet tall and eventually as wide; some varieties can reach 20 feet with great age. Flowers

A mature camellia such as this Camellia japonica 'Debutante' can be left in its natural shrubby form or pruned up into a small garden tree.

appear in winter or spring. Tougher and more resistant to disease is *C. sasanqua,* which blooms in autumn or early winter and will thrive in hotter, drier sites than Japanese camellia. Sasanquas are open growers with a particularly attractive branching pattern; they range in size from 1½ feet tall and 6 feet wide to 12 feet tall and wide, and make excellent ground covers or informal hedges.

When Plant camellias from fall to early spring.

Where Camellias grow best in partial shade (such as the dappled light beneath tall trees or on the north side of the house) and rich, well-drained, neutral to slightly acidic soil. Protect plants from drying winds. Camellias grow well in containers filled with a potting mix suitable for rhododendrons.

How Water the camellia in its container. Dig a planting hole twice the width of the container and 2 inches shallower than the root ball; then dig deeper around the circumference of the bottom of the hole, leaving a firm plateau in the center. Roughen the hole's sides. Set the root ball on the soil plateau so that the top of the root ball is 2 inches higher than the surrounding soil—then refill the hole with compost-amended soil. Firm the soil with your fingers, and water the plant well. Apply 2 inches of mulch, keeping it away from the trunk.

TLC Water your camellias regularly. Maintain a layer of mulch beneath plants. After the first year's bloom, apply a commercial camellia fertilizer (or an acid plant food); thereafter, fertilize according to the package directions. Camellias need little pruning, but if you want to shape plants, do the job just after flowering finishes.

PEAK SEASON

Camellias flower from midfall through winter and into spring.

OUR FAVORITES

Among the best *C. japonica* varieties are dark red (semidouble) 'Bob Hope' and 'C. M. Hovey' ('Colonel Firey', formal double); light pink, peony-form 'Debutante'; coral rose, semidouble 'Guilio Nuccio'; and white 'Nuccio's Gem' (formal double). 'Finlandia Variegated' has white semidouble blooms with petals marked in darkest pink.

Look for *C. sasanqua* 'Apple Blossom' (single, pink-blushed white flowers), rose pink 'Cleopatra' (semidouble), white 'Setsugekka' (semidouble), and 'Yuletide' (single, bright red).

C. × williamsii 'Donation' grows 8 feet tall and wide and is loaded with semidouble orchid pink flowers in late winter or early spring.

GARDEN COMPANIONS

To protect their shallow roots, pair camellias with long-term partners like hellebores or hostas planted at the same time, or very shallow-rooted companions such as impatiens, violets (*Viola*), or primroses (*Primula*). Other broadleaf evergreens like rhododendron, lily-of-the-valley shrub (*Pieris japonica*), and boxwood (*Buxus*) make fine companions for a shrub border.

CLOCKWISE FROM LEFT: *Two types of* C. sasanqua; C. japonica *varieties* 'Anticipation', 'Pink Perfection', 'C. M. Hovey', *and* 'Finlandia Variegated'.

Heath and Heather

Erica and *Calluna*

Most heaths and heathers look so much alike—and need such similar growing conditions—that gardeners can consider them variations on a single lovely theme: low, solid mounds of tiny, needlelike leaves and abundant flowers shaped like miniature urns. The leaves of many change colors with the seasons; foliage may be bright or dark green, silvery gray, gold, or reddish, depending on variety and time of year. That, along with the colorful blooms—in white and every shade of pink and purple—provides a kaleidoscopic effect that few other evergreen shrubs can match.

Heaths and heathers are extremely cold hardy, thriving in sunny, exposed locations where the air is moist and cool. Wind doesn't faze them, but they won't take extended heat or drought. Mass them as a shrubby ground cover on a slope with poor soil, or plant a few to bring dependable color to a rock garden. Join a long line of gardeners who plant "tapestries" of heaths and heathers in various colors, but be warned: once you start collecting these little charmers, you may become hopelessly addicted.

Heaths, Scotch heathers, and mixed conifers carpet this sunny slope. Choose your varieties carefully, and you can have color year-round.

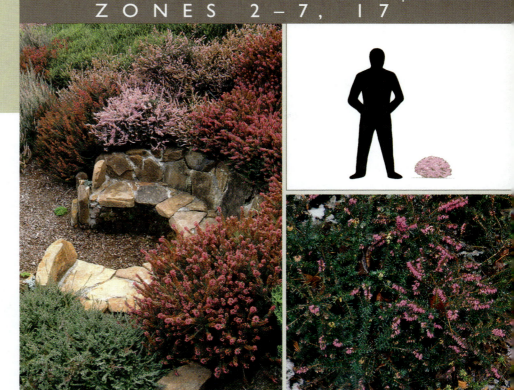

PEAK SEASON

Heaths and heathers bloom in all seasons, depending on type.

OUR FAVORITES

Among the toughest heaths (Erica) is E. carnea, to 1 foot tall and 1½ feet or more wide, with rosy red flowers in winter through spring.

E. × darleyensis grows about 1 foot tall and spreads to around 2 feet. Leaves are medium or dark green; flowers are white or shades of pink.

Scotch heather (Calluna vulgaris) comes in many varieties, with an average size of 1 to 2 feet tall and a bit wider; blooms from summer until late fall. 'Blazeaway', with lavender flowers, has pale gold foliage that turns orange to red in winter. 'Peter Sparkes' has dark green foliage and double, deep pink flowers. 'Robert Chapman' has mauve flowers and gold to orange leaves that shade to red in winter and spring.

GARDEN COMPANIONS

Group heaths and heathers with other plants that thrive in moist, acidic soil, such as conifers, many grasses, and broadleaf evergreens like rhododendron, lily-of-the-valley shrub (Pieris japonica), or salal (Gaultheria shallon). Interplant low-growing types with bulbs such as tulips and ornamental onion (Allium).

When Plant heaths and heathers in spring.

Where These shrubs perform best in full sun in sandy, acidic soil. They need excellent drainage and air circulation; planting on a gentle slope can provide both. In warmer climates, a north-facing slope or afternoon shade is best.

ABOVE, LEFT: Erica × darleyensis 'Mrs. D. F. Maxwell', Calluna vulgaris 'St. Nick', 'County Wicklow', and 'H .E. Beale'.
ABOVE, RIGHT: E. × d. 'Darley Dale' has shell pink blooms through winter.

How Water the plant in its nursery container. Dig a planting hole twice the width of the container and about the same depth. Remove the plant from the container and tease loose the fibrous roots. Set the root ball in the center of the hole and backfill with soil amended with plenty of organic matter, such as compost or wet peat moss. Firm the soil with your fingers, and water well. Keep roots cool with 2-inch-thick mulch.

TLC Heaths and heathers can't tolerate standing water or absolute dryness; regular water is essential. Feed with acid plant food in late winter or early spring. After bloom, clip off faded flower spikes and lightly pinch back growth to keep plants compact. Autumn-blooming types are an exception: don't clip them until early spring. Don't cut back into leafless wood, as new growth may not sprout.

*E. × darleyensis also grows well in zone A3. Scotch heather is best in zones 1a; 2–6, 17.

Hydrangea
Hydrangea

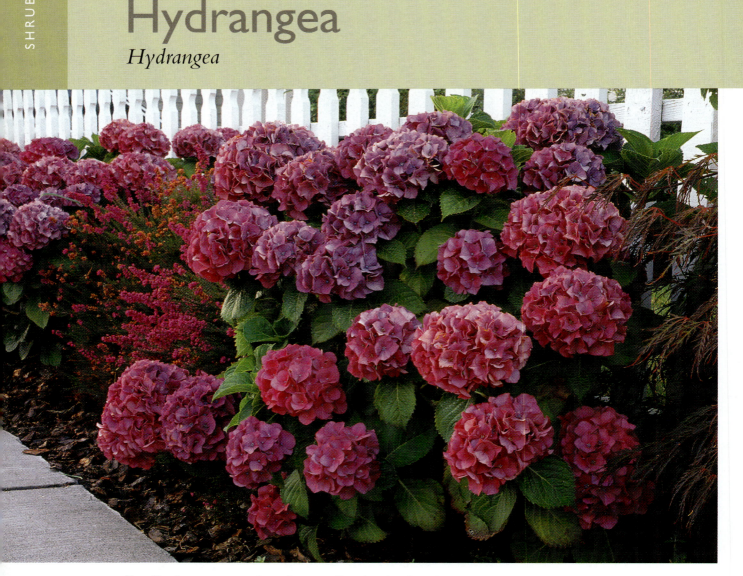

Hydrangeas are big show-offs. They're hand-some, bulky shrubs, usually wider than they are tall, clothed in sturdy, leathery, rich green leaves.

Impressive for size alone, the gargantuan blooms of Hydrangea serrata 'Preziosa' add yet more drama by changing color as they age—from white to pink, blue, or mauve.

The main attraction comes in midsummer, when each stem tip produces an imposing cluster of flowers. Most familiar are the whopping pink or blue spheres you may remember from your grandmother's garden, but the big snowy white cones or lace caps of other types demand just as much attention.

The flower heads are actually composed of two types of blooms: small, starlike fertile flowers and large sterile ones. These intricate floral clusters remain on the plant for a long time and retain their good looks even as their colors fade—which is why they are a favorite cut flower, whether fresh or dried. In autumn, the leaves of many hydrangeas take on bronzy red or purplish hues before they drop.

When Spring is best, but plant any time if you can water them regularly.

Where A spot with morning sun and light afternoon shade is ideal, but hydrangeas can take full sun in cooler areas. In hotter regions, site them on the north side of the house or beneath trees. Rich, well-drained soil results in the best growth and bloom. For bluer flowers on a bigleaf hydrangea, add aluminum sulfate to the soil once a year; to make them pinker, add lime.

How Water the hydrangea in its nursery container. Dig a planting hole twice the width of the container and about the same depth. Gently tip the root ball from the pot and place it in the center of the hole. Amend the dug soil with organic matter such as compost or well-rotted leaves and fill in the hole, firming the soil with your fingers. Water deeply. Keep roots cool with 2-inch-thick mulch kept a few inches away from the base of the plant.

TLC Hydrangeas need regular water, especially during their first 2 years in the ground; if they get too dry, they'll quickly wilt. Established plants benefit from yearly pruning; do this in late winter for those producing blooms on new growth (such as PeeGee and smooth hydrangea), after bloom for those flowering on previous year's growth (such as bigleaf and oakleaf hydrangea). Clipping back the branch tips to the first pair of buds and removing about one-fourth of the oldest stems to the base guarantees the largest flower heads; lighter pruning gives you more clusters of a smaller size.

TOP TO BOTTOM: *Lace-cap blooms of* H. macrophylla; *blossoms in shades of mauve, blue, and soft cream; oakleaf hydrangea* (H. quercifolia).

PEAK SEASON

Hydrangeas bloom in summer and fall; some offer fall leaf color as well.

OUR FAVORITES

Bigleaf hydrangea (*H. macrophylla;* zones 3b–7, 17) grows 4 to 8 feet tall and wide, with white, pink, red, or blue flowers. Mopheads have ball-like clusters of sterile flowers; lace caps have sterile flowers arrayed around a cluster of tiny fertile ones.

Oakleaf hydrangea (*H. quercifolia;* zones 2b–7, 17) forms an elegant 6-by 8-foot mound with oaklike leaves and elongated cones of white flowers. In fall, the leaves turn bronzy red.

The hardy PeeGee hydrangea (*H. paniculata* 'Grandiflora'; zones A2, A3; 1–7, 17) is no peewee: it grows at least 10 feet tall and 8 feet wide. The large, upright white flower clusters slowly fade to pinky bronze. It can take full sun if well watered.

Smooth hydrangea (*H. arborescens* 'Annabelle'; zones A2, A3; 2–7, 17) grows about 4 feet tall and wide, with enormous 1-foot flower clusters. It makes a fine low hedge.

GARDEN COMPANIONS

Plant hydrangeas in a shrub border with rhododendrons, azaleas, dogwoods, and viburnums. In a lightly shaded area, put oakleaf hydrangea with witch hazel (*Hamamelis*) and mountain ash (*Sorbus*).

Lavender

Lavandula

Lavenders are effective massed alongside a sunny path or patio, where you'll get a whiff of the fresh, pungent perfume when you brush against them.

Who doesn't love the sweet, clean scent of lavender? The fragrant essential oil of lavender (most concentrated in the flowers but also found in the leaves) has been used in soaps and various toiletries since the time of ancient Rome. These plants are traditionally included in herb gardens, and some catalogs list them as perennials—but *Lavandula* species are actually evergreen shrubs with narrow gray or green leaves and slender spikes of flowers in white, pink, blue, or shades of—well—lavender. Plants grow quickly into low, broad mounds.

These Mediterranean natives succeed in cool coastal or mountainous parts of the Northwest but may succumb to root rot in areas where heat is accompanied by high humidity or frequent rains. There are many different types to experiment with—both out in the garden and indoors, where you can make crafts such as lavender wands or pillows.

Where winters are too cold for year-round growth outdoors, lavenders make fine container plants; just bring them inside and set them by a sunny window before the first frost.

PEAK SEASON

Most lavenders are their showiest in early spring to early summer.

OUR FAVORITES

English lavender *(Lavandula angustifolia)*, the hardiest and most popular lavender, is found in many varieties; most grow 1½ to 2 feet tall and wide. Flowers come in white, pink, and shades of blue and purple.

Vigorous lavandin *(L. × intermedia)* tolerates warm, humid summers better than English lavender. It grows to 4 feet tall and wide.

Spanish lavender *(L. stoechas)* is a good choice for the warmest, driest areas of the Northwest. It is 1½ feet high and wide. Leaves are mostly gray green; flowers are borne on short, fat 2-inch spikes topped by flaglike bracts resembling rabbit ears.

GARDEN COMPANIONS

Lavender makes a beautiful edging for a bed of roses or irises. Good partners include plants with gray or blue leaves, like blue oat grass *(Helictotrichon sempervirens)*, lamb's ears *(Stachys byzantina)*, and many rockroses *(Cistus)*. Lavender also combines well with other plants that need lots of sun and little water, like penstemon, sedum, and sage *(Salvia)*.

When Plant lavender in spring.

Where Choose the sunniest, driest part of your garden, such as a drought-prone slope or below a south- or west-facing wall. Plants grow best in sandy soil that is neutral to alkaline and not too rich. They also do well in containers.

How Water the lavender in its nursery container. Dig a planting hole twice the width of the container and slightly deeper and mix in a little pumice or sand and a small amount of organic matter. Refill the hole, gently mounding it for improved drainage. Dig a hole in the center of the mound the same size as the container, then slip the plant from its pot and tease loose the roots if they have become tightly matted. Set the root ball in the center of the hole and backfill with the amended soil, making sure the soil level is the same as it was in the container. Firm the soil with your fingers, and water well. Spread crushed gravel, sand, or decomposed granite beneath the plant. Do not mulch with organic materials; they encourage root rot in lavenders. Space plants well apart to make sure they have good air circulation.

TLC Water regularly until your lavender is established, then reduce to moderate irrigation. Avoid overhead sprinkling. To keep plants neat and compact, shear back to just below the flower stalks every year immediately after bloom. Lavenders don't need fertilizing unless they're growing in containers; in that case, apply a balanced, controlled-release fertilizer in spring, using half the amount recommended.

ABOVE: *English lavender.*
BELOW: *Spanish lavender.*

*English lavender also grows well in zones 2 and 3.

Lilac

Syringa

When it comes to lilacs, it's really all about the flowers. The shrubs themselves grow into upright and spreading masses, with oval, pointed leaves of a respectable green; a few types show decent fall color before the leaves drop. But lilac blossoms are legendary for their flamboyant color and the heady perfume that has been called "the essence of spring." Loads of small flared tubes are packed into big upright or arching flower heads at the branch tips; these seem to have been specifically designed for cutting and arranging in vases. Depending on species and variety, the fragrance varies from softly sweet to outrageously rich and spicy, and colors range from white and cream through every shade of pink and purple to blue.

Lilacs are vigorous shrubs, easy to grow in most of the Northwest; unlike many plants that merely tolerate low temperatures, they thrive in cold regions and require a few hard frosts to bloom their best. Compact varieties are perfectly at home in a border of shrubs and flowers. Larger sorts make good screens or informal hedges that burst into glory in spring and then fade quietly into the background during the rest of the year.

The pinky-purple blooms of a common lilac (Syringa vulgaris) frame a birdhouse.

PEAK SEASON

Lilacs bloom early spring to early summer, depending on climate.

OUR FAVORITES

Chinese lilac (Syringa × chinensis) is a graceful, fine-textured shrub to 10 to 15 feet tall and wide, with a profusion of rosy purple flowers in late spring. It needs less winter chill than most other types.

Common lilac (S. vulgaris) eventually grows to about 20 feet tall and wide. Many varieties are available.

Korean lilac (S. pubescens patula 'Miss Kim') is a dense, rounded shrub that stays at 3 feet for many years. Purple buds open to particularly fragrant icy blue flowers.

For mild-winter areas west of the Cascades, try S. × laciniata. It grows about 8 feet tall and 10 feet wide, with fragrant lilac-colored flowers.

S. meyeri 'Palibin', to 4 feet tall, has broad, softly fragrant pink flowers.

GARDEN COMPANIONS

Plant lilacs among summer bloomers like hydrangea and mock orange (Philadelphus). Create a colorful composition with a scattering of tulips or bluebells (Scilla) near lilacs. Or include them in a fragrance garden with roses, honeysuckle, peonies (Paeonia), and daphne. Plant a late-blooming clematis at the base of a lilac to liven up the shrub later in the season.

TOP TO BOTTOM: The blooms of S. vulgaris 'Lucie Baltet', S. v. 'Frank Klager', and S. meyeri 'Palibin'.

When Plant lilacs from fall to early spring in mild climates. In cold zones, mid-spring is best.

Where For best flowering, plant lilacs in full sun in an open area where they'll get good air circulation. The soil should be well drained and fertile. Neutral to slightly alkaline conditions are best; if your soil is strongly acid, dig lime into it before planting.

How Water the lilac in its nursery container. Dig a planting hole twice the width of the container and about the same depth. Gently tip the root ball from the pot and place it in the center of the hole. Fill in the hole with soil amended with organic matter such as compost. Firm the soil with your fingers, and water well. Keep roots cool with 2-inch-thick mulch, but keep it away from the trunk.

TLC Lilacs do best with regular water. Until plants are established, pinch back any overlong stems. Remove spent flowers, cutting back to a pair of leaves. To encourage bushiness on mature plants, cut back a few of the oldest stems right after bloom each year, along with any dead branches and any suckers that arise from the plant's base. Apply a balanced fertilizer after blooms fade.

*Common lilac grows in zones A1–A3; 1–7. S. × laciniata is best for zones 3–7.

Rhododendron and Azalea

Rhododendron

The cool, humid air and acidic soils of the Pacific Northwest combine to create a paradise for rhododendrons and azaleas. In such happy circumstances, these well-known shrubs churn out masses of blooms in a rainbow of colors. Individual flowers are shaped like flaring tubes or trumpets and held at the branch tips in tightly packed clusters called trusses.

Rhododendrons and azaleas both belong to the genus *Rhododendron*. Most familiar are the large, sturdy shrubs we

call rhododendrons, with huge, round flower trusses. The blooms are dramatic in their season—and the leathery, evergreen leaves are handsome year-round.

Azaleas are smaller plants with a finer texture. Evergreen types offer flowers in pinks, reds, orange-red, lavender, purple, or white. Deciduous azaleas bloom in those colors as well as shades of yellow—and many offer an autumnal show. These azaleas tolerate a bit more heat, cold, and sun than their evergreen cousins.

ABOVE: *A 'Hino-crimson' azalea in full bloom under 'Mt. Fuji' flowering cherry.* LEFT: *A woodland gazebo seems to float above puffy clouds of pale lilac rhododendron blossoms.*

When In cold areas, plant azaleas and rhododendrons in spring; in mild-winter climates, plant in fall.

Where Azaleas and rhododendrons prefer filtered sunlight or sun in the morning with light afternoon shade. Where summers are mild or foggy, they can take more sun, and in any exposure they need shelter from strong winds. Provide rich, well-drained acidic soil.

How Water the shrub in its container. Dig a planting hole about three-quarters as deep as the plant's root ball and twice as wide. Amend the soil with organic matter. Remove the plant from its container and place it in the hole. The juncture of stems and root ball should be 2 to 3 inches above soil grade. Replace the amended soil and press it into a gentle mound. Where drainage is poor, grow these shrubs in specially formulated planting mixes in raised beds. Water thoroughly. Mulch with 3 inches of pine needles or shredded leaves.

TLC Give azaleas and rhododendrons regular watering. Feed established plants with commercial acid fertilizer before bloom, again as buds swell, and just after flowers have finished. Pinch young plants to keep them bushy. Replenish the mulch annually, keeping it in place year-round.

CLOCKWISE FROM TOP LEFT: *'Hinode-giri' azalea; foliage of* R. yakushimanum; *Rhododendron hybrid;* R. *'Mrs. Furnivall';* Rhododendron hybrid; R. *'Unique'*.

PEAK SEASON

Azaleas flower from midwinter well into spring, rhododendrons from early to late spring.

OUR FAVORITES

There are countless rhododendrons available. Visit local nurseries to help make your choices.

Most evergreen azaleas are hybrids; among the best for the Northwest are the Harris hybrids, the hardy Kaempferi hybrids (zones 2–7), and the Robin Hill hybrids.

Among the many excellent deciduous azaleas are the Knap Hill–Exbury hybrids (zones 3–7, 17) and the hardy Northern Lights hybrids (zones A2, A3; 1–7). For a sunny spot, try the beautiful Western azalea *(R. occidentale),* with white or pale pink flowers.

GARDEN COMPANIONS

Rhododendrons and azaleas look great in each other's company, but they're also ideal with shrubs like hydrangea, camellia, and lily-of-the-valley shrub *(Pieris japonica).* Good perennial partners include Japanese forest grass *(Hakonechloa macra),* hosta, carpet bugle *(Ajuga reptans),* and shade-loving hardy geraniums like *Geranium phaeum.*

*Except as noted.

Smoke Tree
Cotinus coggygria

Though it's called smoke tree, this plant is really more of a big shrub, growing into a billowing, irregular mass about 15 feet tall and almost as wide. The "smoke" part of the common name refers to the masses of fuzzy panicles that form as the tiny summer flowers fade; these give the distinct impression of creamy or pinkish purple puffs of smoke that practically cover the plant.

What usually draws the eye first, though, is smoke tree's strikingly colorful foliage. The oval or round-ish leaves are bluish green in the species, but the most popular varieties feature some of the richest purples and deepest maroons to be found in the garden. (A bright golden form is also gaining popularity.) Leaves of all types color up beautifully in autumn, taking on tones of yellow to orange-red, coral, or reddish purple before falling.

The namesake puffs of "smoke" are shown here in full bloom. Cherry red sneezeweed (Helenium) is another tough garden customer, tolerating heat and some drought.

Smoke tree is far from finicky; in fact, it grows better in poor, rocky soil than in rich garden loam and is well suited to areas with warm, dry summers. This shrub is just the thing for a difficult "hot spot" in almost any garden.

PEAK SEASON

The "smoke" appears in summer; in fall, leaves are gold, orange, or red.

OUR FAVORITES

'Golden Spirit', to about 8 feet tall and 6 feet wide, has bright golden yellow leaves that turn dramatic shades of coral and orange in fall; puffs are light pink.

'Notcutt's Variety' has maroon-purple foliage; 'Royal Purple' and 'Velvet Cloak' have deep purple leaves. All three have rich pinkish purple puffs.

'Pink Champagne' and 'Daydream' have bluish green leaves and pinkish tan puffs. They grow to about 10 feet tall and wide.

Cotinus 'Grace' is an excellent hybrid to about 15 feet tall and wide, with blue-green foliage shaded purple; large, deep pink puffs; and orange and purple-red fall foliage.

GARDEN COMPANIONS

Group with other shrubs that need just moderate water, such as Pacific wax myrtle (*Myrica californica*), Western redbud (*Cercis occidentalis*), rockrose (*Cistus*), or pink winter currant (*Ribes sanguineum*). Nice perennial partners for smoke tree include sage (*Salvia*), euphorbia, sneezeweed (*Helenium*), penstemon, and Jupiter's beard (*Centranthus ruber*).

When Smoke tree is best planted in its leafless dormant period in fall.

Where Plant in full sun where it will have good drainage. Avoid wet or low locations.

How First, water the shrub in its nursery container. Prepare a planting hole that is slightly shallower than the root ball and twice as wide. Then dig a bit deeper around the edges of the hole's bottom, leaving a firm central core. Set the plant on the firm center, making sure the top of the root ball is slightly higher than the surrounding soil. Fill in with soil around the root ball, firming with your fingers, then water thoroughly. Apply a 2-inch-thick layer of mulch, keeping it away from the stem.

TLC Provide moderate to regular water for the first year or two—long enough to get roots well established. Thereafter, moderate watering is sufficient. You can prune out dead or wayward branches in late winter or in early spring before new growth emerges. If you want just the foliage effect (no flowers) and a smaller plant, you can cut the whole bush to the ground each year in late winter.

ABOVE AND RIGHT: C. 'Grace' glows in autumn, especially when backlit by late-afternoon sun.

Viburnum

Viburnum

Some shrubs score high for fragrant or showy flowers, others for good-looking foliage, and still others for their flashy fruit. Among the large and diverse group of shrubs in the viburnum clan, many get high marks in all three categories.

The leaves of most evergreen types are dark green, glossy, and leathery; those of deciduous species are often heavily textured and pleated, clothing the shrub in rich shades of green before taking on attractive autumnal hues of red or orange. Dainty, often fragrant flowers of white, cream, or pink are carried in tightly packed clusters. Blooms of most species are followed by roundish little fruits in brilliant red, blue, or black—often with a glistening, almost metallic, sheen. They certainly catch the attention of birds, which flock to them. To get the best fruit crop, plant several members of the same variety (but purchased from different sources to ensure genetic diversity).

You can find a viburnum for almost any function in your garden, from tall ground cover to hedge, and from flower-border anchor to lawn specimen. The shrubs are perfect in a woodland garden or along a path, where you can enjoy a close encounter with their intricate leaves, sweet-smelling flowers, and colorful fruits.

One of the loveliest qualities of Viburnum plicatum *is the lacelike tiered effect of their branch patterns.*

PEAK SEASON

Most viburnums bloom from late winter into spring.

OUR FAVORITES

Evergreen *Viburnum × burkwoodii* (zones 2–7, 17) has an open, rounded growth habit and reaches about 10 by 8 feet. Pink buds open to fragrant white flowers.

V. davidii (zones 4–7, 17) grows 3 to 5 feet tall and wide, with handsome evergreen foliage, white flowers, and turquoise blue fruit. It does best in acidic soil and partial shade.

Laurustinus (*V. tinus;* zones 4–7, 17) reaches 6 to 12 feet tall and half as wide, with lustrous evergreen leaves, wine red new stems, early white flowers, and bright blue fruit that lasts through summer.

Cranberry bush (*V. trilobum;* all zones) is deciduous and very cold tolerant. It grows to 15 feet tall and 12 feet wide, with lace-cap flowers in mid-spring and colored foliage in fall.

Japanese snowball (*V. plicatum;* zones 3–7, 17), a deciduous species to 15 feet tall and wide, has horizontal branching and snowball-like flowers. Similar doublefile viburnum (*V. p. tomentosum*) has lace-cap flowers.

Deciduous Korean spice viburnum (*V. carlesii;* zones A3; 2–7, 17) forms a dense bush 8 feet tall and wide, with pinkish white flowers emitting a heavenly spicy fragrance.

When Plant in spring or fall.

Where Site in full sun or partial shade. Most viburnums will adapt to just about any soil, as long as it is well drained.

CLOCKWISE FROM ABOVE: V. davidii; *doublefile viburnum* (V. plicatum tomentosum); *and a pink snowball viburnum* (V. plicatum 'Pink Sensation').

How Water the viburnum in its nursery container. Dig a hole twice the width of the container and roughly the same depth. Remove the root ball from the pot and place it in the center of the hole. Fill in the hole, firming the soil with your fingers, and water deeply. Keep the roots cool with 2-inch-thick mulch kept a few inches away from the base of the plant.

TLC Water regularly. To prevent legginess, lightly cut back branch tips after flowering (though this will prevent fruit from forming that year).

European cranberry bush (*V. opulus;* zones A2, A3; 1–7, 17) has a rounded form and grows 8 to 15 feet tall and wide. It has lacy blooms, bright red fruits, and good fall color. Many varieties feature different berry and leaf colors. It can tolerate moister soils than other viburnums.

GARDEN COMPANIONS

Viburnums are good choices for a shrub border alongside dogwood (*Cornus*), lilac (*Syringa*), mock orange (*Philadelphus*), rhododendron, and daphne. Or pair these tough shrubs with perennials like euphorbia, hellebore, and daylily (*Hemerocallis*).

Witch Hazel

Hamamelis

An extract made from the leaves and bark of witch hazel has long been used as a soothing liniment for scrapes and burns. In the garden, these fascinating shrubs can help alleviate another kind of ache: the gardener's wintertime longing for floral color and fragrance. When most of the garden is shut down for the season, the bare branches of witch hazel are decorated with nodding clusters of strange little flowers that look something like spiders or mop heads. These long-lasting blossoms grab your attention with their bright hues of yellow, orange, or red—and with their sweet, astringent smell. One flowering branch cut for a winter bouquet can fill the whole house with fragrance. The oval leaves that clothe the branches in summer are nothing special, but with the return of cooler weather comes a sequel to the color show: the foliage may take on gorgeous tones from deep yellow through orange to rich red.

Witch hazels grow into an open, spreading vase shape, with angular or zigzagging branches, and their somewhat wild look is perfect for the edge of a woodland garden. They also make good specimen plants, especially against a dark backdrop.

Chinese witch hazel (Hamamelis mollis 'Pallida') has light yellow blossoms and, later in the season, yellow fall foliage.

182

PEAK SEASON

Most witch hazels bloom in winter; fall foliage color is spectacular.

OUR FAVORITES

Among the best hybrids *(Hamamelis × intermedia;* zones 3–7, 17) are 'Arnold Promise' (bright yellow flowers; yellow, orange, and red fall foliage); 'Diane' (dark red to orange-red blooms; reddish purple leaves in autumn); and 'Jelena' (coppery flowers; orange and scarlet fall foliage). All grow 12 to 15 feet tall and wide.

Chinese witch hazel *(H. mollis;* zones 2b–7, 17) reaches 10 feet high and wide with golden yellow flowers; fall color is pure yellow.

Common witch hazel *(H. virginiana;* zones 1–7, 17), about 10 to 15 feet tall and wide, is open and spreading, with small, fragrant yellow flowers.

Loropetalum chinense (zones 6–7, 17) is called Chinese witch hazel in much of the Northwest. These evergreen plants grow slowly to 10 feet tall and wide. Colorful 'Razzleberri' has burgundy foliage and bright pink flowers.

GARDEN COMPANIONS

Witch hazels stand out silhouetted against evergreen hedges; they also make good understory plants beneath tall deciduous trees. Carpet the ground beneath them with hellebores, lily turf *(Liriope),* and early-blooming bulbs such as cyclamen.

When Plant witch hazel in spring or fall.

Where Choose a sheltered spot in full sun or partial shade. Witch hazels prefer moist, rich, well-drained soil.

How Water the witch hazel in its nursery container. Dig a planting hole the same depth as the container and about twice as wide. Remove the root ball from the pot and place it in the center of the hole. Fill in the hole with dug soil mixed with plenty of organic matter such as well-rotted leaves or compost, then firm the soil with your fingers. Water deeply. Spread a layer of mulch about 2 inches thick around the base of the plant but not touching the trunk.

TLC Supply your witch hazel with regular water. Regular pruning is not needed. Remove branches only to guide growth or to remove poorly placed branches and suckers; do the job just after flowering, before the leaves unfurl.

ABOVE: H. × intermedia *'Diane'.* BELOW: *Blooming witch hazels include the spidery blossoms of* H. × intermedia *'Winter Beauty'.*

Native Shrubs

The Northwest is home to a number of magnificent broadleaf shrubs that were thriving here without the benefit of irrigation, fertilizer, or pesticides long before humans arrived. Obviously, not all the plants listed here are native to all parts of the Northwest—but these rugged, adaptable characters will thrive far from their natural home if given the right conditions.

More and more nurseries are offering a selection of native shrubs, and their popularity is increasing as gardeners become familiar with their good looks and easygoing habits. By choosing the right shrub for your site and resisting the urge to lavish it with unnecessary attention, you can create a part of the garden that truly takes care of itself.

For Full Sun

Manzanita (*Arctostaphylos*; zones 4–7, 17) grows into a low, wide mound of striking reddish brown stems clothed in small, leathery leaves and early-spring clusters of urn-shaped white or pink flowers. Species vary in size from ground covers to small trees.

Wild lilac (*Ceanothus*; zones 5–7, 17) is covered in spring with pale to deep blue or white fuzzy blooms.

TOP 10 PLUS

You don't have to travel far to find low-maintenance, drought-tolerant plants with seasonal color and year-round good looks.

ABOVE: *Native salal* (Gaultheria shallon) *and western sword fern.* NEAR RIGHT: *'Pokey's Pink' winter currant.* FAR RIGHT: *Birds love the powdery blue berries of Oregon grape.* OPPOSITE PAGE, TOP: *Pink winter currant.* OPPOSITE PAGE, BOTTOM: *'Elk River Red' winter currant.*

Some are low and wide spreading, but the majority grow quickly into upright mounds 4 to 10 feet tall and a bit wider.

Pacific wax myrtle *(Myrica californica;* zones 4–7, 17) is an excellent large shrub or small tree with glossy, dark green leaves that look good all year. Little purplish fruits decorate the branches in fall and winter. It makes a wonderful informal hedge.

For Partial Shade

Oregon grape *(Mahonia aquifolium;* zones 2–7, 17) grows into a dense, bushy mass of hollylike leaves topped in early spring by bright yellow flowers that are followed by blue-black fruits. Plants reach about 6 feet tall and 5 feet wide.

Salal *(Gaultheria shallon;* zones 4-7, 17) makes a perfect companion for rhododendrons, camellias, and other acid-loving shrubs. It reaches 4 to 10 feet tall and slightly wider, with large, glossy, fresh green leaves and springtime clusters of white or pink flowers; in exposed locations, salal may be lower-growing.

Pink winter currant *(Ribes sanguineum;* zones A3, 4–7, 17) is deciduous but loses its maplelike leaves only at winter's end, just before producing long, drooping clusters of white, pink, or red flowers. New foliage quickly follows. This shrub rapidly grows to 6 to 12 feet tall and wide.

Planting and Care

Choose the appropriate site for your native shrubs, and plant them in fall so winter rains can settle them in. The sunlovers appreciate maximum light and heat, and they demand good drainage, so plant them on a south-facing slope or in an area with sandy or rocky soil. Natives adapted to partial shade do well in dappled or morning sun and somewhat richer soil, so you can add organic amendments at planting time and treat them to a layer of compost around their bases each spring. For either group, dig the planting holes the same size as the nursery pots, slip the root balls into place, then water well. They'll need regular irrigation during their first dry season, but after that you can taper off to only occasional deep watering for the full-sun natives (except for wild lilac, which won't tolerate summer water after its first year in the ground) and moderate irrigation for the shade lovers.

Roses

Northwesterners love roses. The proof of that is in the vast array found in nurseries, garden centers, and catalogs. Truly, there's a rose for every garden: huge climbers that can cover a barn; spreaders for ground-cover plantings; and bushes of all shapes and heights to add color and texture to your planting beds.

Roses are often separated into complex categories based on age, size, or provenance, but we've kept our Top 10 guide simple. The six categories of roses in these pages are primarily distinguished by their growth habit—which is what matters most to home gardeners (along, of course, with the flowers).

When I moved to the Northwest from Arizona, I realized that the growing conditions for roses were very different here. In the desert, there's plenty of sun, which almost all roses crave—but some parts of the Northwest get only 3 or 4 hours a day. The trick is finding the right varieties for your area. The instructions on the next page are applicable to all our roses; special pruning and training instructions are given for individual categories. —ED CHAVEZ

When The best time to plant roses is in spring, after all danger of frost has passed.

Where Plant roses in well-drained soil where they'll receive at least 6 hours of sun each day. Choose an area with good air circulation but not strong, direct wind.

How Before planting, water container-grown roses in their nursery pots; bare-root roses should be soaked in water overnight before planting. Space plants 1½ to 3 feet apart, depending on their mature width; locate climbing roses about 1½ feet away from their support. Dig each planting hole twice as wide as the root ball and 1½ to 2 feet deep, and amend the dug soil with organic matter such as compost. Set container-grown roses at the same level they were growing in their nursery containers; for bare-root roses, use the amended soil to form a central mound in the planting hole, then spread the roots over the mound. Set climbing roses in the hole at a 45-degree angle so the canes lean toward the support. Backfill the hole with the amended soil. In areas where winter temperatures are unlikely to fall below 10°F /−12°C, plant with the bud union at or slightly above soil level. In colder areas, position the bud union 1 to 2 inches below soil level. Water deeply.

ABOVE: *'Sally Holmes' landscape rose.*
OPPOSITE PAGE: *'Ballerina' landscape rose (top) and the English rose, 'Mary Rose' (Bottom).*

TLC Keep the soil evenly moist throughout the growing season (spring through fall). Water deeply, and try not to wet the foliage. Maintain a 3- to 4-inch layer of organic mulch such as shredded leaves or bark around the plants but not touching the canes. In late winter or early spring, feed established plants with a complete fertilizer (many brands of "rose food" are sold); repeat applications every six to eight weeks until weather cools in fall. Control pests and diseases as needed, using the least toxic method first.

Winter Protection If you live where winter temperatures routinely drop below 10°F /−12°C, you will need to protect your rose bushes from freeze damage, and you're better off forgoing climbing roses altogether. Once nighttime temperatures are consistently below freezing, mound a foot of soil from another part of the garden over the base of each rose bush; when the mound has frozen, cover it with insulating material like straw or evergreen boughs. Gradually remove the protection in spring, after the danger of frost is past.

Climbing Roses

The climbing form of 'Cécile Brunner' has been popular with generations of gardeners. It's nicknamed the "sweetheart rose" for its sweet pink blooms.

PEAK SEASON

Some climbing roses bloom only once in spring, but many repeat their waves of bloom from spring or summer until fall.

TEN FAVORITES

'Aloha' has large, sweetly scented pink flowers from summer to fall on a plant that reaches about 10 feet; it's a good choice for training up a pillar or post. This hardy rose tolerates some shade.

'Cl. Cécile Brunner' is a lush grower to 20 feet, with small, sweet-scented, light pink flowers over a long period.

'Cl. Iceberg' produces waves of white blossoms from spring to fall on a vigorous plant that grows to 15 feet. It is considered by many to be the finest climbing rose available.

'Dublin Bay' sports velvety, bright red flowers from spring into autumn against dark green, glossy leaves. It grows to about 10 feet and is excellent trained on a column or an upright trellis.

'Fourth of July' reaches about 10 feet, with fragrant blooms that are striped or splashed in various combinations of red and white.

What could be a more gracious welcome to a garden than an arching trellis laden with fragrant roses? Consider the climbers. They may look like flowering vines, but these plants don't twine around supports like honeysuckle or attach themselves to walls like climbing hydrangea. Rather, they have long, flexible canes that can be tied to or woven through a support. Whether fanned out on a wall trellis, threaded through a fence, draped over an arbor, or even clambering up into a small tree, a climbing rose can add vertical pizzazz to just about any garden.

'New Dawn' is an old favorite that delivers plenty of fragrant, pearl pink flowers—both individually and in small clusters—over a long season. It grows to about 15 feet, is cold hardy, and tolerates some shade.

'Royal Sunset' grows to about 10 feet and has nicely shaped flowers with a fruity scent; blooms are orange in bud, fading to buff apricot or creamy peach tones. It's not the best choice for colder climates.

'Stairway to Heaven' grows to about 10 feet, with mildly fragrant, velvety red flowers from summer to fall.

'William Baffin' has carmine pink blooms in large clusters over a long season. This disease-resistant, cold-hardy rose grows to about 12 feet.

'Zéphirine Drouhin' has practically thornless canes that grow 8 to 12 feet and are easily trained over an arch. Richly fragrant, deep pink flowers appear in late summer.

GARDEN COMPANIONS

The classic companion for a climbing rose is clematis. For a long bloom period, plant a climbing rose with three different clematis: an early type that will blossom before the rose, a midseason bloomer that will complement the rose's color, and a late type to extend the season into fall.

*Hardy types may survive in zones 1–3 with winter protection.

Training Climbing roses naturally send their new shoots straight up and produce most of their flowers at the tips. To bring the flowers closer to eye level, train the long canes horizontally; the smaller ones will then bear lots of blooms. Use plastic tape or nylon twine to tie the tips of the canes to a support so that they point downward. To grow a rose against a wall, install wires and screws or attach a trellis to the wall, inserting 4-inch spacer blocks between the wall and trellis. When it comes time to repaint or repair the wall, remove the wires or trellis with the rose attached and lay it gently on the ground.

Pruning For the first few years, remove only weak or dead wood. Thereafter, prune climbing roses that bloom only in spring just after their bloom, removing old canes that show no signs of strong new growth. Prune repeat-flowering climbers at the end of their dormant season, when growth buds begin to swell. Remove the oldest, unproductive canes and any weak, twiggy growth—then cut back all the side branches on the remaining canes to within two or three buds of the main canes.

TOP TO BOTTOM: 'Fourth of July', 'Cl. Iceberg', 'Royal Sunset', 'William Baffin'.

Ground Cover Roses

Most gardeners probably think of roses as upright, mounding shrubs or climbers. But some roses are low growers, spreading their arching or creeping canes widely but rising to a height of no more than a few feet. These are the ground cover roses, and much work has been done by breeders in recent years to produce vigorous, disease-resistant, hardy varieties with dense foliage and a profusion of fragrant blooms. Many also have colorful hips (fruits) in autumn.

Plant ground cover roses in any sunny spot that needs a dash of color; they're available in the same wide range of hues as other types of roses. Their spreading habit makes them ideal for scrambling down a slope, spilling over a wall, or fanning out next to a path or at the front of a flower border. The larger, bushier types can cover sizable areas and can even double as low hedges. Smaller varieties are excellent in containers, where their graceful canes can overflow with bloom.

Pruning Ground cover roses need little trimming, though deadheading encourages more flowers. After the danger of frost has passed, prune shrubby types by removing any dead or damaged canes, and open up the center of the plant. For lower, more spreading types, just cut back any wayward or overlong stems. To spread your roses over a larger area, peg down the shoots rather than cutting them back.

OPPOSITE PAGE: *A raised bed of scarlet ground cover roses.* ABOVE: *'Sea Foam'.* BELOW: *'Flower Carpet'.*

PEAK SEASON

These roses bloom most heavily in summer but continue into fall.

TEN FAVORITES

'Baby Blanket' grows 3 feet tall and 6 feet wide, with long-blooming soft pink flowers and shiny foliage.

'Fire Meidiland' has lush green foliage and large clusters of fire engine red blooms on a plant that grows about 2 feet tall and 6 feet wide.

'Flower Carpet' roses are available in apple blossom pink, coral, red, white, and yellow. They're easy to grow and highly resistant to disease. Sizes vary, so check the label when purchasing.

'Fuchsia Meidiland' sports masses of purplish pink blooms over a very long season. It grows 2 feet tall and 4 feet wide with light green, plentiful foliage.

'Magic Blanket' grows to 3 feet tall and twice as wide. Its peachy buds open into white blooms. Foliage is medium to dark green.

Vigorous 'Red Ribbons' has glossy leaves and crimson red flowers centered with glowing golden stamens. It grows to 3 feet tall and 4 feet wide.

'Scarlet Meidiland' grows to 4 feet tall and 6 feet wide and has generous clusters of bright red flowers. It makes an excellent slope or bank cover.

'Sea Foam' produces creamy white flowers on a plant that grows to 3 feet tall and twice as wide. It has small, glossy leaves. It's a good choice for coastal gardens and for mild-winter areas with dry summers.

'Sun Runner' (sometimes sold as 'Stardust') has cheery yellow blooms and a dark green mat of foliage that grows quickly to about 1½ to 2 feet tall and twice as wide.

'White Meidiland' has dark green, glossy foliage that sets off its pure white flowers to perfection. Plants grow to 2 feet tall and 6 feet wide.

GARDEN COMPANIONS

Ground cover roses consort well with other sun-loving plants, like lamb's ears (*Stachys byzantina*), kinnikinnick (*Arctostaphylos uva-ursi*), artemisia, and lavender (*Lavandula*). They're lovely softening the base of a New Zealand flax (*Phormium*)—or even hiding the bare ankles of their cousins, the hybrid tea roses.

*Hardy types may survive in zones 1–3 with winter protection.

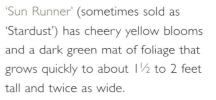

Hybrid Teas and Grandifloras

The glamorous roses you see in florist shops and garden catalogs are almost certainly hybrid tea roses. These are the movie stars of the rose world, grown for their refined flowers (usually one per stem) that spiral open from long, pointed buds into gorgeous, high-centered blossoms. The bushes themselves grow 2 to 6 feet tall. Grandiflora roses are similar but can be larger (8 to 10 feet tall), and they bear blooms both singly and in small clusters.

Both types grow rather stiffly upright, so you may want to plant them in groups of at least three for a bushier look. To hide their typically leafless bases, plant them behind billowing perennials or a low hedge—but give them a foot or two of "breathing space." Generally, these roses are susceptible to diseases and pests; the ones listed have resisted both in Northwest gardens. And even if the leaves have a few spots or a touch of mildew, the beauty of the flowers will more than make up for it.

LEFT TO RIGHT: *'Double Delight', 'Elina', 'Mister Lincoln', 'Pristine', 'Olympiad', and 'Sunset Celebration'.*

PEAK SEASON

Most hybrid tea and grandiflora roses bloom from spring until frost.

TEN FAVORITES

'Dainty Bess' has fragrant, picture-perfect, single pink blooms, usually borne in small clusters. This 4-foot-tall hybrid tea does well in both hot and cool summers.

'Double Delight' is a hybrid tea that grows 4 to 5 feet tall. Its sweet-scented blooms are pale pink, edged and flushed with red.

'Earth Song' is a 4-foot-tall grandiflora that was bred to withstand cold (to at least −30°F/−34°C). Its large, sweetly fragrant flowers open dark pink and age to a lighter pink.

'Elina' has large, creamy yellow blooms with perfect form and a light perfume. This vigorous hybrid tea grows well in all areas and reaches 4 to 5 feet tall.

'Love and Peace' is a hybrid tea derived from the classic 'Peace'.

The elegant pointed buds of 'Queen Elizabeth' open into radiant and regal pink blooms with a mild fragrance. It tolerates cool summers.

It grows to 5 feet tall and has mildly fragrant, soft yellow blooms blushed with pink. The blossoms are large, with a high-centered, spiral form.

'Mister Lincoln' holds its powerfully fragrant, velvety red flowers on very long stems. This heat-tolerant hybrid tea grows to about 5 feet tall and blooms over a long season.

'Olympiad' grows to an impressive 6 feet tall, with velvety, bright red flowers on sturdy stems; the lightly scented blooms last a long time in a vase. This hybrid tea grows well practically anywhere in the Northwest.

'Pristine', another hybrid tea, produces lightly fragrant blooms in a tasteful ivory flushed with pale pink. This is a bushy plant that grows 4 to 6 feet tall.

'Queen Elizabeth' is a classic grandiflora, vigorous (to 7 to 12 feet tall) and bushy enough to use as a tall hedge or background planting.

Pruning

Remove faded blooms to encourage repeat flowering and to keep plants looking tidy. Remove any suckers growing from the roots whenever they appear by grasping them with a gloved hand and pulling them straight down. In late winter or early spring, use sharp pruning shears to remove any dead or diseased canes, along with old canes that produced no strong growth during the previous year. Also remove any branches that cross through the center of the plant; then shorten the remaining canes by about one-third.

'Sunset Celebration' is a hybrid tea that blooms over a long period, with fragrant, peachy salmon flowers opening from long, tapered buds. It reaches 4 to 8 feet tall and is a good performer even in areas that have cool summers.

GARDEN COMPANIONS

Plant these roses behind a low hedge of boxwood (Buxus) or lavender. Or surround them with perennials like artemisia, catmint (Nepeta), thyme, twinspur (Diascia), smaller ornamental grasses, hardy geraniums, lamb's ears (Stachys byzantina), baby's breath (Gypsophila paniculata), daylily (Hemerocallis), or Siberian iris.

*Hardy types may survive in zones 1–3 with winter protection.

Landscape Roses

This diverse group includes many types of bushy roses—as opposed to upright hybrid teas or vinelike climbers—such as polyantha, floribunda, English, and hybrid musk roses. All are valued for the masses of color they bring to the landscape rather than for individually stunning flowers (although some have blooms every bit as lovely as those of a hybrid tea rose). They are easy to grow, with disease-resistant foliage that keeps the plants looking handsome even when they're out of bloom. Some of the cold-hardiest roses on the market fall into this group, too.

As their name implies, landscape roses perform a variety of functions in the garden. Larger types serve beautifully when lined up to form a casual hedge. They're tough enough to work as a low border along a driveway, and their usually thorny canes make a formidable barrier. With a little pruning for symmetry, many of these plants make striking stand-alone specimens. Smaller types can be incorporated beautifully into flower borders (at the back or as anchors at either end, for instance). These versatile players even thrive in large pots on a patio or deck.

Landscape roses have many flower forms and colors. CLOCKWISE FROM BELOW: *'Bonica', 'Sally Holmes', 'Graham Thomas', 'Ballerina', and 'Iceberg'.*

PEAK SEASON

Bloom time varies among varieties and locations, but most landscape roses bloom from spring to fall.

TEN FAVORITES

'Aunt Honey' is disease resistant and very hardy (down to −20°F/−29°C). It reaches 4 to 5 feet tall and not quite as wide. It is loaded with clusters of fragrant, medium-pink blooms over a long period.

'Ballerina' has a nicely rounded shape and grows to 3 to 5 feet tall and almost as wide. It is covered with clusters of small, single, light pink flowers (resembling those of dogwood or apple) that develop into pretty orange-red hips in fall.

Pruning There's nothing complicated about pruning shrub roses. In late winter or early spring—just before new growth starts—trim them lightly to a pleasing shape. Remove any dead or diseased growth, and old or weak canes.

'Sexy Rexy' reaches 5 feet tall and wide, producing huge pink trusses of mildly scented blooms.

Easy-to-grow 'Bonica' forms a mound 3 to 5 feet tall and at least as wide, with dark, glossy leaves and sprays of clear pink blooms over a long season. This shrub makes a nice hedge.

'Easy Going' is medium green with glossy leaves and an attractive, 4-foot-tall form that looks good even when the plant is not in bloom. The abundant, deep yellow blooms have an apricot tinge, and their scent is sweet and fruity.

'Graham Thomas' boasts sweet-smelling, butter yellow blooms that are packed with petals. It reaches 5 to 8 feet or taller and is rather slender, just 2 to 3 feet wide.

'Heritage' forms a compact, leafy shrub about 4 to 5 feet tall and wide. It bears very full pink blooms that are darker in the center and exude a wonderful citrus fragrance.

'Iceberg' is a vigorous shrub that grows to about 6 feet tall and 4 feet wide, with clusters of sweet-scented white blooms over a long season. It has particularly attractive light green foliage.

'Lavender Lassie' produces bouquets of fragrant, ruffled blooms in a pleasing lilac-pink shade. This is an open-growing plant that reaches 6 to 8 feet tall and wide.

'Mary Rose', to about 4 to 6 feet tall and wide, has dark green leaves and lightly fragrant, gorgeously full flowers of a deep rose pink. Blooms are produced over a long period.

'Sally Holmes' produces large clusters of scented, creamy white flowers that resemble oversize apple blossoms. This is a vigorous, upright grower to about 6 to 8 feet tall and roughly half as wide. It is a nice choice for a specimen plant.

GARDEN COMPANIONS

Surround landscape roses with irises, daylilies (Hemerocallis), delphiniums, hardy geraniums, lavender, and ornamental grasses. You can grow a small vining clematis up into the larger landscape roses.

*Hardy types may survive in zones 1 and 2 with winter protection.

Old Roses

In the words of a popular song, "everything old is new again." That is undoubtedly the case with old roses, sometimes called antique or heirloom roses. After hybrid teas came on the scene in 1867, the gardening public was spellbound for well over a century by the huge, shapely blooms of those new hybrids and their modern descendants. Eventually, however, the charms of old roses reasserted themselves in the gardening imagination (they're also much less finicky and disease-prone than some of their modern offspring) and they continue to be more popular with each passing year.

Several types of roses fall under the "old rose" heading, but among those best suited to Northwest gardens are hybrid perpetual, Bourbon, centifolia, damask, and Portland roses (the latter named for an 18th-century English duchess and not for Oregon's "City of Roses"). Fragrance may be the strongest selling point of old roses: their rich perfume may be spicy, sweet, musky, or citrusy. Size and cold hardiness vary considerably, so be sure to check both carefully when purchasing your living antique.

CLOCKWISE FROM BELOW LEFT: 'Rose de Rescht', 'Mme. Isaac Pereire', 'Mme. Hardy'.

PEAK SEASON

Many old roses bloom in late spring or early summer, then again in fall. A few bloom once a year, in spring.

TEN FAVORITES

'Baronne Prévost' has large buds that open to very full, bright rose pink blooms with a heady perfume. It is a compact plant, growing about 5 to 6 feet tall and half as wide, and blooms heavily in summer with occasional repeat in autumn.

'Boule de Neige' sports richly scented flowers packed with creamy white petals that may be lightly touched with pink, especially in the bud stage. This upright grower (to about 5 feet tall and 4 feet wide) blooms from spring to fall.

'Comte de Chambord' is an upright, bushy plant about 3 feet tall and almost as wide, with extremely full, fragrant, rich pink flowers from midsummer to fall.

'Crested Moss', also sold as 'Cristata', has intricately fringed buds that open into highly scented silvery pink blossoms in spring. It grows about 6 feet tall and 4 feet wide; the rather lax canes can use some support.

'Mme. Hardy' grows 5 to 6 feet tall and not quite as wide, with especially attractive leaves. Gorgeous, full, fragrant blossoms are pristine white with a small, green button eye center. It blooms in late spring.

Pruning For old roses that bloom over several seasons, prune in late winter. For those that bloom only once in spring, you can prune immediately after flowering. Remove any dead, weak, crossing, or damaged canes and thin out a few of the oldest canes in older plants that have become dense and overcrowded. Then cut back the remaining canes lightly (by no more than one-third).

Many old roses, such as this hybrid perpetual 'Baronne Prévost', were developed in France more than 150 years ago.

'Mme. Isaac Pereire' carries intense purplish pink blooms with an intoxicating aroma in early summer and autumn. This vigorous plant reaches at least 7 feet tall and nearly as wide. It is excellent climbing a sturdy pillar.

'Mutabilis' is a big, spreading shrub, to 10 feet tall and 6 feet wide, that grows well in the warmest areas of the Northwest in protected spots, such as near a wall. Fascinating blooms start off as buff yellow buds that open pink and age to light wine red. It blooms summer into fall.

'Rose de Rescht' is a bushy, upright plant to 3 feet tall and wide, with clusters of small, pink pompon flowers with a powerful perfume. Blooms appear midsummer to fall.

'Salet' has full, clear pink flowers that are packed with petals and exude a wonderful perfume when they appear in early and late summer. This plant may reach 4 feet tall and almost as wide, with bright green leaves that are soft to the touch.

'Souvenir de la Malmaison' sports big, incredibly full, light pink flowers with a spicy scent. It grows rather slowly to 3 or 4 feet tall and wide. Rain may spoil the summer-to-fall blooms, but they're so magnificent, they're worth the risk.

GARDEN COMPANIONS

Lilies (Lilium) are classic cohorts for old roses in a romantic flower border. The blue and purple tones of lobelia contrast beautifully with the mostly white and pink shades of these roses. Dahlias and ornamental alliums also make nice spring and summer companions.

Species Roses

Species roses bloomed in the Northern Hemisphere long before gardens ever existed. These are the wild plants from which every garden rose descended. Use them to cover a slope, to make the transition from a casual part of the garden to more formal areas, or as a flowering hedge. Almost all species roses bloom in spring.

Rosa rugosa has crinkly leaves, fragrant blooms, and tomato red hips.

RUGOSA ROSES AND HYBRIDS

One of the most useful species roses for northwestern gardens is *Rosa rugosa*, a cold-hardy, disease-resistant shrub that will stand up to wind, dry soil, and even salt spray. The basic species has been crossed with various other roses to produce a host of hybrids, and some of the best are listed here. They'll grow well in all zones of the Northwest.

'Blanc Double de Coubert' is a dense grower 6 feet tall and 5 feet wide; it may spread wider by suckers. White blooms are full and loose.

'F. J. Grootendorst' has cherry red, carnation-like flowers and no hips. This thorny plant grows 5 feet tall and spreads wider.

'Fru Dagmar Hastrup' ('Frau Dagmar Hartopp') blossoms are silvery pink. It grows to 4 feet tall and wide.

'Hansa' makes an excellent 6-foot-tall hedge, with purplish red flowers.

Vigorous 'Henry Hudson' has pink-tipped buds that open to white flowers. It grows 2 to 3 feet tall and wide.

'Jens Munk' reaches about 5 feet tall and wide, with lilac-pink flowers.

'Moje Hammarberg' has large, reddish violet flowers and particularly large, abundant hips. It grows to about 5 feet tall and wide.

'Robusta' ('Kordes Robusta') reaches 6 feet tall and wide and is loaded with scarlet flowers. This one makes a good flowering hedge.

'Roseraie de l'Haÿ' has fresh-looking apple green leaves and purplish red flowers; it's another good choice for a 6-foot-tall hedge.

'Wild Spice' grows about 4 feet tall and 3 feet wide, with pure white, single flowers.

Pruning Species roses need very little pruning, but on established plants, you may want to cut the oldest canes to the ground each year to shape plants and encourage more bloom.

LEFT: *Lady Banks' rose.* BELOW, LEFT TO RIGHT: *Nootka rose, Harison's yellow rose, nootka hips, sweet briar.*

TEN FAVORITES

Austrian brier (*Rosa foetida;* zones A2, A3; 1–7, 17) grows 6 feet tall and wide and covers itself in bright yellow blooms with an interesting scent. *R. f.* 'Bicolor' ('Austrian Copper') is a bit smaller, with yellow-backed coppery orange flowers. Both are good choices for gardens east of the Cascades.

Chestnut rose (*R. roxburghii;* zones 2–7, 17) is decked out in light green, fernlike foliage, cinnamon-colored bark, and soft rose pink flowers that are deliciously fragrant. It grows 6 to 10 feet tall and up to 15 feet wide, but if the stems are pegged down it makes a good bank cover.

Father Hugo's rose (*R. xanthina hugonis;* zones 2–7, 17) forms a dense shrub reaching about 8 feet tall and 5 feet wide. Its dark green leaves contrast nicely with the lightly scented, bright yellow flowers that appear all along the branches.

Harison's yellow rose (*R. × harisonii;* zones 1–7, 17) is a tough, disease-free plant that reaches at least 6 feet tall and 4 feet wide, with fragrant, bright yellow flowers; dark, bristly hips appear in fall.

Lady Banks' rose (*R. banksiae;* zones 4–7, 17) holds onto its light green leaves unless temperatures drop to 0°F/–18°C. Practically immune to diseases and pests, it grows vigorously to 20 feet or more and can cover an arbor or fence with countless blooms. 'Alba' has white, scented flowers.

Nootka rose (*R. nutkana;* zones A1–A3; 1–7, 17), native from Alaska to Northern California, is cold-hardy and grows at least 6 feet tall and 4 feet wide (though it can spread to form thickets). The scented flowers are deep pink; showy hips are red.

R. glauca (*R. rubrifolia;* zones A1–A3; 1–7, 17) is grown for its gorgeous foliage in tones of gray green and coppery purple; small red hips are attractive in fall. This 6- to 9-foot tall, cold-hardy shrub makes a good informal hedge.

Scotch rose or burnet rose (*R. pimpinellifolia,* also known as *R. spinosissima;* zones A1–A3; 1–7, 17) grows 3 to 4 feet tall and wide and may spread by suckers with age. The upright stems are set with ferny leaves and needlelike prickles, and the small flowers are white to pink.

Sweet briar, sometimes called eglantine (*R. eglanteria* or *R. eglanteria;* zones 1–7, 17), is a vigorous shrub that can reach 12 feet tall and 8 feet wide; it can be grown as a climber. The soft pink flowers are centered with glowing golden stamens, and the dark green leaves smell of apples.

Winged thorn rose (*R. sericea pteracantha;* zones A3; 1–7, 17) has unusual huge, red-brown thorns. This arching shrub grows about 10 feet tall and nearly as wide and sports single white flowers.

Trees

I have been passionate about trees for as long as I can remember, and people often ask why. To me, trees are comforting, beautiful, and inspiring. In gardens, they can make or break the mood with the sheer force of their commanding size. A treeless garden has the unfinished look of a room devoid of furniture.

Trees frame views, give us shelter from sun or wind, offer food and habitat for wildlife, and eventually provide the reassuring appearance of maturity. In addition, deciduous trees offer a striking seasonal clock of living color, presenting four different appearances through the year. As if by magic, spring's tender buds unfold from bare winter branches. The leafy luxuriance of full summer follows, and then the tree is painted with warm color before autumnal leaf fall.

CHOOSING TREES

Because the climates of the Northwest range from lush, dripping rainforest to arid sagebrush scrubland, a wide variety of trees from many different areas of the world grow beautifully here. Warm, protected gardens can be graced with relatively tender trees; gardeners in the coldest zones will need to choose from hardier types. If your garden is in a site that is markedly wet, dry, shady, windswept, or otherwise extreme, be sure to take that into consideration when making selections. And be aware of the eventual size to which your tree will grow, and site it accordingly. Too often I see trees shoehorned next to buildings or planted beneath utility wires or other trees, where they become obstacles rather than enhancements.

Deciding which annual flowers to plant is no big deal because they live only a year—if you make a bad choice or site them poorly, the next year brings entirely new possibilities at minimal cost. Even more substantial perennials and most shrubs can be moved readily, if need be. But trees usually cost more than these smaller plants, and once they've grown large cannot easily be transplanted. That's why it pays to give deliberate thought before planting them.

In the following pages you'll find our Top 10 choices, from small flowering trees to stately shade trees. All have proved their merit in the Northwest, so most are readily available from well-stocked garden centers or nurseries.

ABOVE: *A magnificent spring shower is provided by this 'Mt. Fuji' flowering cherry.* OPPOSITE PAGE: *An arrangement of Himalayan birch* (Betula jacquemontii) *is carefully spaced at the edge of a curving lawn.*

A few rarer kinds are included for those who want to get ahead of the Joneses rather than just keep up with them. Take a look through our choices and then mull them over. Trees are potent symbols and they move us deeply; even the act of *planting* a tree can eventually become a cherished memory. Choose for form, for flowers, for fall foliage color, or for winter interest. But most of all, remember than when you choose trees, you choose not only for yourself but also for posterity.

—ARTHUR LEE JACOBSON

Birch
Betula

It's no wonder birches are so often featured in photographs and paintings—their open, elegant form and gorgeous bark make them natural subjects for artists. The clean-looking green leaves turn yellow before dropping off in autumn, and in winter the delicate limbs, white or patterned shaggy bark, and hanging seed tassels continue the show. What could be more dramatic than a leafless, white-barked birch against a background of dark conifers or bright blue sky?

Birches grow throughout the Northern Hemisphere in a variety of soil conditions, but their shallow roots need a regular supply of moisture; drought-stressed trees fall victim to various diseases and pests. Because they grow quite fast when young, you often see birches planted right next to new homes for quick effect—but they look and grow much better when given plenty of space. Also, they're frequent hosts to aphids, which can drip sticky honeydew on cars and patios, so place them where you can admire them from a distance.

A weathered bench echoes the ghostly color of these young Himalayan birches (Betula jacquemontii).

PEAK SEASON

The bark is attractive all year, nicely complemented in summer by the fresh green leaves.

OUR FAVORITES

Paper birch *(Betula papyrifera)* grows 50 to 90 feet tall and half as wide, with bark that varies from pure white to reddish brown. It resists diseases and is extremely cold hardy, growing in zones A1–A3 and 1–6.

In warmer regions, try river or Himalayan birch. River birch *(B. nigra;* zones 1–7, 17) has bark that is smooth and pinkish when young, then shaggy reddish brown, developing deep ridges with age. These disease-resistant trees grow 50 to 90 feet tall and 40 to 60 feet wide, often with trunks that fork near the ground. 'Heritage' is a popular selection with creamy white bark. White-barked Himalayan birch *(B. jacquemontii* or *B. utilis jacquemontii;* zones 3–7, 17) is a tall, narrow tree, growing 40 to 60 feet tall and half as wide, with striking pure white bark.

GARDEN COMPANIONS

The dappled shade beneath a birch is a good spot for low growers such as coral bells *(Heuchera),* hardy geraniums, hostas, and spring bulbs and annuals. For a stunning contrast with white bark, plant a sweep of black mondo grass *(Ophiopogon planiscapus* 'Nigrescens').

When Plant in spring or early fall from a nursery container.

Where Your birch will do best in full sun in an open situation, where it won't have to compete for light or nutrients. Provide moist, rich, acidic soil.

How Water the tree while it's still in the nursery container. Dig a hole the same depth as the container and about twice as wide. Remove the tree carefully, keeping the root ball intact. Set the root ball in the center of the hole, making sure its top is level with the surrounding soil. Refill the hole and firm the soil around the plant. Water thoroughly. Spread a 2-inch layer of mulch around the base of the plant but not directly against the trunk.

TLC Be sure your tree is not allowed to dry out between rains, and water deeply to encourage deep root growth. Birches need little trimming (most branches and twigs that die fall off by themselves) but do prune out any dead wood as needed. You may also wish to remove some of the lowest branches so that you can see more of the trunk's decorative bark. Do any pruning in late summer or early fall in mild-winter areas and at the end of January in cold-winter areas. If you prune in late winter or early spring, sap will drip profusely from the cuts.

ABOVE AND RIGHT: *Paper birches are beloved for their glimmering, snow-white or silvery bark that peels off in thin layers to reveal darker bark beneath.*

Dogwood
Cornus

The native Pacific dogwood *(Cornus nuttallii)* is one of the most beautiful trees in the natural landscape. The bad news is that it doesn't fare well in gardens, where it often succumbs to a fungal disease. The good news is that there are several other equally beautiful dogwoods that are disease resistant.

In late spring and early summer, dogwood flowers (actually bracts that surround the tiny flowers) are produced in such quantities that trees can look shrouded in white or pink. Many dogwoods also have striking fall color and fruits. Because they are usually smaller trees, they make good subjects for entry gardens or around a patio or water feature. On larger properties, dogwoods are ideally placed where the garden makes the transition to surrounding woodland. Because of their spreading branch structure, they are good sculptural elements for the winter garden.

A pink-flowering Eastern dogwood explodes with color in spring above a bed of blue bulbs.

PEAK SEASON

Most dogwoods flower in late spring through early summer; leaves and fruit provide fall interest.

OUR FAVORITES

Cornus 'Eddie's White Wonder', bred in Vancouver, B. C., bears big clusters of cream-colored flowers in late spring. It eventually reaches 25 feet tall and wide. Fall color is superb.

Varieties of Eastern dogwood (*C. florida*) flower in shades of pink, deep rose, and near white. They top out at about 30 feet tall and wide.

Kousa dogwood (*C. kousa*) blooms in June with creamy flowers; it reaches 20 feet tall and wide, eventually with horizontal branching.

Pagoda dogwood (*C. alternifolia*) grows to 20 feet tall and wide, with an open, tiered form. Small white flowers are followed by blue-black fruit and red foliage.

Cornelian cherry (*C. mas*) carries masses of small, cheerful yellow flowers and bright red, cherry-size fall fruits. Shrubby and dense, it reaches 20 feet tall and 15 feet wide.

GARDEN COMPANIONS

Dogwoods look great in a shrub border with rhododendrons and azaleas. Underplant them with spring bulbs and flowers such as erythronium, hellebores, carpet bugle (*Ajuga*), and hardy geraniums.

When Plant in spring from a nursery container.

LEFT: *A Cornelian cherry in late winter, with yellow flowers on bare branches.* RIGHT: *The blooms of Cornus 'Eddie's White Wonder'.*

Where Give your dogwood well-drained, slightly acidic soil. Locate in full sun or light shade; east of the Cascades, where summers can be blistering, it will need protection from afternoon sun.

How Water the tree in its nursery container. Dig a hole that is the same depth as the container and twice as wide. Remove the tree from its container, keeping the root ball intact. Set the tree in the center of the hole, making sure the top of the root ball is level with the surrounding soil. Refill the hole and firm the soil around the plant. Water thoroughly. Add a 2-inch layer of mulch around the tree, but keep the mulch away from the trunk.

TLC Give dogwoods regular water. These trees need little pruning, but you should remove crossing or crowded branches to allow good air circulation through the center.

Pagoda dogwood and cornelian cherry grow best in zones 2–6. Eastern dogwood does well in zones 2b–7, 17.

Flowering Cherry
Prunus

A venerable flowering cherry (Prunus serrulata 'Mt. Fuji') spreads its parasol of pale pink blossoms over a sidewalk.

Just when you think winter will never end, flowering cherries burst into bloom and remind you that spring is on the way. Masses of white or pink flowers seem eager to emerge, appearing before or along with the fresh green or bronzy new leaves—and a couple of weeks later, the delicate petals are released to dance in the breeze like confetti. To bring the feel of spring indoors, cut a branch or two just as the buds begin to open and place them in a deep vase of water.

Spring is not the only season when flowering cherries shine. Many types have colorful fall foliage—and shiny, banded bark that adds winter interest to the garden. These are relatively small trees that are just the right size for urban gardens.

Flowering cherries do suffer from various pest and disease problems that can make them short lived—but they're so beloved that northwestern gardeners go right on planting them. The varieties listed here are among the most resistant to disease, but it's a good idea to check with your local nursery regarding the best flowering cherries for your area.

When Plant in spring from a nursery container.

Where Choose a spot in full sun. These trees require fast-draining, well-aerated soil. If that doesn't sound like yours, consider planting in raised beds.

How Water the tree while it's still in its nursery container. Dig the planting hole slightly shallower and twice as wide as the tree's root system. Gently tip the root ball from the container and loosen the roots. Set the plant in the center of the hole, with the top of the root ball slightly higher than the surrounding soil. Refill the hole and firm the soil around the plant with your fingers, creating a gentle mound for the tree. Water thoroughly. Spread a 2-inch layer of mulch around the tree but not directly against the trunk.

TLC Keep the soil moist until the tree is well established, then continue to provide moderate water; don't flood it or let it dry out completely. Prune in September or October to remove any awkward or crossing branches.

ABOVE: *Gleaming cherry tree bark.* BELOW: *Prunus serrulata 'Kwanzan' sits at the top of a streetside bank covered with spring bulbs, grasses, and perennials.*

PEAK SEASON

Bloom time is early to midspring. Many also have vibrant fall foliage.

OUR FAVORITES

'Akebono' is a disease-resistant Yoshino cherry (*Prunus × yedoensis*; zones 3–7, 17) that grows to 25 feet tall and 40 feet wide, with pink flowers and yellow and orange fall color.

Amur chokecherry (*P. maackii*; zones A1–A3, 1–7) grows to about 30 feet tall and wide, with small white flowers and attractive honey brown bark. Fall color is yellow.

'Schubert' is a variety of common chokecherry (*P. virginiana*; zones A1–A3, 1–3). It sports purplish red leaves and white flowers, and reaches 30 feet tall and wide.

Most Japanese flowering cherries (*P. serrulata*; zones 3–7, 17) reach to 30 feet tall and 25 feet wide.

Sargent cherry (*P. sargentii*; zones 2–7, 17) grows upright to 40 to 60 feet tall and wide. It features early, fragrant white or blush pink flowers and orange-red fall color. The variety 'Columnaris' is only 10 feet wide.

GARDEN COMPANIONS

Plant spring bulbs like daffodils (*Narcissus*), grape hyacinths (*Muscari*), and tulips (*Tulipa*) beneath flowering cherries. These trees stand out nicely in front of an evergreen hedge.

Flowering Crabapple
Malus

Flowering crabapples have loads of character. They're densely branched little trees—most top out at 25 feet or so after many years—that grow into a casually rounded shape. In spring, red or pink buds open into a short but vivid display of white, pink, or red blossoms. The leaves are deep green and often tinted purple or burgundy; these appear along with the flowers. Orange, red, or yellow fruits 1 to 2 inches across decorate the branches in late summer or fall and (in some varieties) hang on right through until winter. A few flowering crabapples bear fruit that can be made into jelly, but they're too tart for eating fresh off the tree. Birds, however, relish them.

Because crabapples look so good all year, a single tree easily holds its own as a street tree or in a front yard. If you plant one in a lawn, dig up the sod up to 1 foot away from the trunk to prevent its delicate bark from being nicked by the mower. Keep the sod-free area mulched.

The luscious, deep pink blooms of flowering crabapple 'Prairifire' are accompanied by leaves that emerge reddish maroon and then eventually turn a dark green.

PEAK SEASON

Crabapples bloom in spring; the fruits add fall and winter interest.

OUR FAVORITES

'Adirondack' has white flowers with hints of red; the fruits are orange-red. Its form is strongly upright, to 18 feet tall and 10 feet wide.

'Evereste' has white flowers and pretty red fruits that make tasty jelly or cider. It grows into a rounded shape about 20 feet tall and wide.

'Prairifire' grows into a dense dome 20 feet tall and wide, with deep purplish red flowers and dark red fruit.

'Professor Sprenger' eventually reaches 20 feet tall and wide, with dark pink buds that open to white flowers followed by orange-red fruits.

'Red Jewel' bears white flowers and bright red, very long-lasting fruits. It has an upright form and grows to 15 feet tall and 12 feet wide.

'Sugar Tyme' has pale pink buds, fragrant white flowers, and long-lasting bright red fruit. It grows upright to 18 feet tall and 15 feet wide.

GARDEN COMPANIONS

Low-growing spring flowers like primrose (Primula), daffodil, and snowdrop (Galanthus) are perfect for carpeting the ground beneath crabapples. Mature trees cast dappled shade that is ideal for impatiens, hellebore, or hosta.

When Set out container plants any time the soil can be worked. Balled-and-burlapped trees are best planted in spring.

TOP: *The fruits of 'Sugar Tyme' crabapple.*
BOTTOM: *Fall color of 'Professor Sprenger'.*

Where Crabapples do best in full sun but will tolerate partial shade, and grow in most soils as long as drainage is good.

How Water the tree in its nursery container. Dig a hole the same depth as the container and about twice as wide. Gently tip the tree from the container, keeping the root ball intact. Set the root ball in the center of the hole, making sure the top is level with the surrounding soil. Plant a balled-and-burlapped tree so that the root flare is right at the soil surface, cutting and removing as much of the burlap and wire as possible without injuring roots. Refill the hole and firm the soil. Water thoroughly. Spread a 2-inch layer of mulch around the tree, avoiding the area directly next to the trunk.

TLC Keep the soil evenly moist with moderate to regular watering. Irrigate deeply to encourage deep root growth. Give plants a balanced fertilizer in spring. Prune lightly to shape the tree's framework and to open up the interior at any time, but too much wintertime pruning causes ugly water sprouts (these can be cut out at their base in late May or June).

Katsura Tree
Cercidiphyllum japonicum

Until it finishes up the year in an amber blaze, the katsura tree has a fairly under-stated presence in the garden—it's charming in a delicate way thanks to its heart-shaped leaves, which are arrayed in pairs along drooping branches. The leaves emerge in spring with a bronze tint, then change to a fresh apple green in summer. As the weather cools, the whole tree seems to turn coppery shades and then bursts into brilliant fall tones of apricot, gold, and orange. Before the leaves drop to the ground, there is a final surprise in store: they emit a heady state-fair fragrance that is variously described as brown sugar, caramel, cotton candy, cinnamon, and toffee apples.

When young, the katsura tree has an attractive pyramidal form; as it matures, it grad-ually extends its upper branches to an ultimate height and spread of 40 or even 60 feet. The tree may be single trunked or forked into multiple trunks. Plant it as a focal point for a large lawn, or choose a dwarf or weeping form for a smaller garden.

LEFT: *'Pendulum', the weeping form of katsura tree, makes a fine focal point behind a small patio.*

PEAK SEASON

Autumn is when the katsura tree really shines.

OUR FAVORITES

'Heronswood Globe' has a rounded crown and ultimately reaches 15 feet tall and wide.

'Red Fox' ('Rotfuchs') has ruddy purple leaves that mature to greenish bronze tones in summer and a more columnar shape than the species, reaching to 40 feet tall and 30 feet wide. Fall color is not as bright as the others listed here.

'Pendulum' is a weeping form that grows slowly to 20 feet tall and 25 feet wide; it has bright golden fall color. 'Amazing Grace' and 'Tidal Wave' are similar to 'Pendulum'; 'Morioka Weeping' grows a bit taller and is decidedly taller than wide.

GARDEN COMPANIONS

Plant colorful spring-blooming bulbs beneath a katsura tree. To complement the tree's fall colors, plant *Sedum 'Autumn Joy'*, witch hazel (*Hamamelis*), or smoke tree (*Cotinus*) nearby.

When Plant katsura tree in spring as a container-grown or balled-and-burlapped plant.

Where Although the tree takes full sun or part shade, it needs a sheltered position away from intense sun or drying winds—which means that it doesn't do as well east of the Cascades. The soil should be rich and moist; trees in acidic soil will have the best color.

How Water the tree in its nursery container. Dig a hole the same depth as the container and twice as wide. Remove the tree from its container, keeping the root ball intact. Set the tree in the center of the hole so that the top of the root ball is level with surrounding soil. If the tree is balled-and-burlapped, set it in the hole so that its root flare is level with the soil surface, then cut and remove as much of the burlap and binding as possible without injuring the roots. Refill the hole, and firm the soil around the plant. Water thoroughly. Surround the plant with a 2-inch layer of mulch.

TLC Give the plant regular water, especially during the first two years. Pruning is necessary only to remove damaged branches. Katsura trees suffer from no major pests or diseases.

ABOVE: *The striking fall color of katsura tree.* RIGHT: *The variety 'Heronswood Globe' has a more rounded shape than the species.*

Magnolia
Magnolia

Deciduous magnolias are not reticent trees. Starting in very early spring, they throw open sumptuous blooms in hues of white, cream, pink, crimson, and yellow. And, as if it weren't enough to have big, fragrant flowers, many varieties flaunt them on the trees' naked branches before leaf-out. After bloom, the trees' glossy green leaves and handsome gray bark look good in the company of flowering shrubs and perennials. In winter, magnolias have strongly patterned, typically gray limbs that make interesting silhouettes. Larger types are most effective set against a background that accentuates their flowers; others show up well in larger flower or shrub borders and are choice in Japanese-style gardens.

Magnolias are woodland trees and do well in the rich soils and moist air of the Northwest. The greatest dangers to these plants are dry, strong winds, and frosts that can literally nip the flowers in the bud. In zones 2 and 3, play it safe by choosing types that bloom in late spring and summer.

The blooms of saucer magnolia are shaped like drinking goblets or bowls and open in mid- to late spring. This variety is 'Speciosa'.

PEAK SEASON

Magnolias bloom from early spring through summer.

OUR FAVORITES

Magnolia 'Elizabeth', to 40 feet by 20 feet, has sweetly scented, soft yellow blooms in late spring.

Vigorous *M.* 'Galaxy' has scented pink flowers in midspring. It grows to 40 feet tall and 25 feet wide.

M. 'Wada's Memory' grows to 25 feet tall and not quite as wide, with slightly fragrant, pure white blooms to 4 inches across in midspring.

Saucer magnolia (*M.* × *soulangeana*) is a bushy tree that grows to 20 feet wide and tall. The striped flowers vary from pure white to burgundy.

Star magnolia (*M. stellata*) grows to 10 feet tall and wide with glistening white blooms in early to midspring; *M. s.* 'Rubra' has rosy blossoms.

Yulan magnolia (*M. denudata*) has scented, ivory white, tulip-shaped flowers to 7 inches across in spring. It reaches 35 feet tall and wide.

GARDEN COMPANIONS

Plant with spring-blooming camellias and rhododendrons. Underplant with bluebells (*Scilla*), crocuses, and grape hyacinths (*Muscari*). To avoid damaging the sensitive surface roots of magnolias, plant shrubs at the same time as the tree.

TOP TO BOTTOM: *Hybrid 'Butterflies' magnolia;* Magnolia × soulangeana *'Speciosa'; the shaggy, star-shaped petals of star magnolia (*M. stellata*).

When Although magnolias are sold as container-grown plants all year, you should plant in spring, when temperatures are still cool and soil retains moisture best. If the tree is not actively growing when planted, its delicate roots may fail to take hold.

Where Plant in full sun or partial shade in a spot where the tree has room to grow. The soil should be rich and high in organic matter, as well as being slightly acidic; alkaline soils can cause chlorosis in magnolias.

How Water the tree in its nursery container. Dig a planting hole the same depth as the container and twice as wide. Remove the tree from its container, keeping the root ball intact. Set the tree in the center of the hole, making sure the top of the root ball is level with the surrounding soil. Refill the hole, and firm down the soil. Water the tree thoroughly. Add a 2-inch layer of mulch around the plant but not touching the trunk.

TLC Magnolias like the soil to be moist but not soggy. Mulch around young plants to conserve moisture and keep the soil cool, and replenish the mulch each spring. Avoid digging or cultivating too close to the trunks or you may damage the sensitive roots. Magnolias need pruning only to remove dead, damaged, or unsightly limbs.

*Magnolia 'Elizabeth', M. 'Galaxy', and Yulan magnolia grow in zones 3b–7, 17.

Maple

Acer

Delicate-looking little Japanese maples may seem out of place in parking strips and gas stations, but that's a testament to the toughness of these trees. They—and most other maples—also grow remarkably well in the cool, moist climate common to much of Cascadia. As maples are woodland trees, they flourish in rich, moist soil and can tolerate considerable shade.

Maples of all types are grown for their graceful form and lovely foliage. In spring, the fresh new leaves,

often blushed red, unfold on dainty twigs. The flowers that follow are

Acer palmatum 'Bloodgood' (above) holds its red color all season. 'Orangeola' (left) blazes red in spring and bright orange in fall.

not much to look at, but they develop into fascinating winged seed capsules technically called samaras but known to children as "whirligigs," which helicopter down to the ground. A few maples have colorful leaves all through the season, but in autumn most can be counted on to bring warm shades of red, orange, or yellow to the garden.

When Plant maples in spring.

Where Filtered shade is perfect, but maples can take full sun if provided with adequate moisture. Fertile, well-drained soil is best. Choose a location that is sheltered from heavy or constant wind. Maples are excellent near patios and entryways, and well suited to growing in large pots or tubs.

How Water the tree in its nursery container. Dig a hole slightly shallower than the depth of the container and twice as wide. Remove the tree from its container, keeping the root ball intact. Set the tree in the center of the hole, with the top of the root ball slightly higher than the surrounding soil. Refill the hole and firm the soil around the plant with your fingers, creating a gentle mound for the tree. Water thoroughly. Add a 2-inch layer of mulch around the plant.

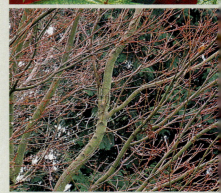

TLC Keep the soil evenly moist. Replenish mulch each spring. Pruning is needed only to accentuate the natural shape or to remove dead wood; prune in summer or early fall in mild-winter areas, or from summer to the end of January in areas where temperatures frequently fall below freezing.

PEAK SEASON

Maples are famous for their brilliant fall color.

OUR FAVORITES

Amur maple *(Acer tataricum ginnala;* zones A1–A3; 1–7, 17) is the best choice for gardeners in the coldest parts of the Northwest; it adapts well to different soil types. It reaches 15 to 25 feet tall and at least as wide, with bushy growth and vibrant red fall color.

Fernleaf fullmoon maple *(A. japonicum* 'Aconitifolium'; zones 2–6, 17) is a shrubby tree featuring elegantly divided leaves that turn fiery red in fall; it grows slowly to about 20 feet tall and 25 feet wide.

Refined-looking Japanese maple *(A. palmatum;* zones A3; 2–7, 17) grows slowly to 20 feet tall and wide. Among the countless varieties are 'Katsura', with foliage that is soft orange and yellow in spring and fall, green in summer; and coral bark maple ('Sango Kaku'), with soft green leaves and brilliant coral bark. Paperbark maple *(A. griseum;* zones A3; 2–7, 17) reaches 25 feet tall and half as wide. Fall color is crimson.

Vine maple *(A. circinatum;* zones A3; 2b–6, 17) native from British Columbia to Northern California, is a shrubby, open grower to 15 feet tall and a little wider in sun and up to twice that in shade. The fall color is orange, scarlet, or yellow.

GARDEN COMPANIONS

Small maples grow well beneath oaks and look at home with ferns, azaleas, and rhododendrons. Shade-tolerant hardy geraniums and Japanese forest grass *(Hakonechloa macra* 'Aureola') are wonderful beneath maples.

TOP TO BOTTOM: *Leaves of the Japanese maple 'Shigitatsu-sawa'; the coral bark maple 'Sango Kaku' in winter; the handsome peeling bark of paperbark maple.*

Mountain Ash
Sorbus

Many flowering trees struggle to survive the harsh winters of the mountainous parts of the Pacific Northwest, but mountain ashes absolutely thrive there. In fact, they need those cold winters to grow well.

Korean mountain ash is decorated with berries from fall through winter.

Despite their ironclad constitution, these small to medium-size trees look light and open in the garden. Most types have finely cut, fernlike leaves that flutter in the breeze and cast dappled shade. Broad clusters of creamy white flowers develop into hanging bunches of small berries that turn orange, red, pink, gold, or white in late summer or early fall, when the foliage is also taking on autumnal tones. These berries are the most appealing feature of the mountain ash; many hang onto the leafless branches well into winter, and are particularly stunning when capped with snow. If that's not decoration enough, look for robins and waxwings among the boughs; these and other birds savor the fruits at a time of year when little other food is available.

Mountain ashes make great lawn specimens, and most are the right size for smaller gardens, but don't plant where fruit drop will make a mess on walkways or patios.

PEAK SEASON

Spring is prime time for flowers, fall for colorful fruit and leaves.

OUR FAVORITES

European mountain ash *(Sorbus aucuparia;* all zones) is erect and oval, growing to 40 feet tall and 25 feet wide. Fernlike leaves turn yellow, red, and reddish purple in fall while orange berries mature to red.

Korean mountain ash *(S. alnifolia;* zones 1–7, 17) grows to 50 feet tall and 30 feet wide, with dark green, shiny, undivided leaves that turn gold in fall. Berries are reddish pink.

Whitebeam *(S. aria;* zones 3–7, 17), to about 40 feet tall and 30 feet wide, is prized for its spring foliage of silvery green: the bold, undivided leaves have undersides covered with handsome white felt. In fall, the leaves form a golden backdrop for plump, deep red berries.

When Plant in spring, as soon as the soil can be worked.

ABOVE: *The white flowers of Korean mountain ash.* BELOW: *Sorbus hupehensis has fernlike blue-green leaves and white fruit blushed with pink.*

Where Choose a spot with full sun or light shade. Acidic, well-drained soil is best.

How Dig a hole the depth of the container and twice as wide. Remove the tree from its container, keeping the root ball intact. Set it in the center of the hole, making sure the top of the root ball is level with the surrounding soil. Refill the hole with soil, and firm the soil around the plant. Water thoroughly. Add a 2-inch layer of mulch around the tree but not up against the trunk.

TLC Mountain ash grows best with regular water, especially during the first few years. Replenish organic mulch each spring. Pruning is not usually necessary.

S. hupehensis (zones 2–7, 17) forms a broad column to at least 25 feet tall and wide. It has white or pink fruits and orange-red foliage in late fall.

GARDEN COMPANIONS

Plant mountain ash with evergreens like pine or holly to highlight its delicate form and seasonal colors. The shade beneath the tree is perfect for hosta, primroses *(Primula),* and hardy ferns like five-finger fern *(Adiantum aleuticum)* and Western sword fern *(Polystichum munitum).*

Sourwood
Oxydendrum arboreum

Sourwood (sometimes called sorrel tree) grows slowly into a slender, round-topped pyramid, eventually reaching about 25 feet tall and 15 feet wide. This beautiful tree has something to offer in every season. In spring, its new leaves are tinted with bronze before maturing to a lustrous dark green. Sweet-scented flowers like little creamy white bells are held in drooping sprays up to 10 inches long. These develop into light brown seed capsules that are almost as decorative as the blossoms, and they hang on the tree well into winter. In autumn, sourwood's foliage turns spectacular shades of orange, scarlet, and blackish purple. The brilliant display is long lasting, too: the leaves stay in place for many weeks after they've started coloring up.

Sourwood offers an unusual combination of vivid fall tones, ranging from pale green to deep purple.

During winter's leafless months, you get a better view of the tree's elegant form and drooping branches and reddish or gray bark, which has a rough, cobbled pattern reminiscent of an alligator's hide.

This distinctive tree is perfect as a single specimen in an open area or planted near a patio. It will also grow well in a container filled with a potting mix formulated for rhododendrons and azaleas.

PEAK SEASON

Late summer flowers are small but fragrant, and fall color is breathtaking.

OUR FAVORITE

'Chameleon' grows slightly more upright than the species and has particularly intense fall color.

GARDEN COMPANIONS

Plant sourwood as part of a fall-color show with oakleaf hydrangea (*Hydrangea quercifolia*) or witch hazel (*Hamamelis*). Or plant with spring bloomers like rhododendrons and azaleas to add color after these plants have finished blooming.

When Plant in spring from a nursery container.

Where Sourwood trees tolerate light shade but will flower and develop fall color best in full sun. They require acidic, well-drained soil and shelter from strong winds. These trees do not perform well in areas where air pollution is a problem.

How Water the tree in its nursery container. Dig a hole the same depth as the container and twice as wide. Remove the tree from its container, keeping the root ball intact. Set tree in the center of the hole, making sure the top of the root ball is level with the surrounding soil.

TOP AND BOTTOM: *Sprays of sourwood's small, bell-shaped blooms. The fragrant clusters of white flowers appear in late summer or early autumn.*

Mix the dug soil (3 parts) with compost (2 parts) and peat moss (1 part), then refill the hole, firming the soil around the plant. Water thoroughly. Add a 2-inch layer of acidic mulch such as pine needles around the base of the tree but not directly against the trunk.

TLC Sourwood trees need regular, deep irrigation. Pruning isn't usually necessary, but you can thin out crossing or awkward branches in late winter.

Stewartia
Stewartia

If you live in a place where rhododendrons grow well, consider adding a stewartia to your garden. These lovely small trees flourish in the same woodland conditions—rich, moist, acidic soil and partial shade—but they flower in summer, after the spring "rhodie show" is over. Blooms resemble single white camellias with golden centers.

Stewartia is just as striking in fall, when the rich green leaves turn shades of orange, deep red, or purple. But winter—when its irregular branching pattern and multiple trunks are revealed—is when your stewartia is likely to get the most attention. The bark is among the most ornamental of all trees, peeling off in patches to reveal tones of rich brown, cinnamon, orange, tan, olive, or gray, depending on the species.

Trees are small and vase shaped, and they don't drop a lot of litter—making them ideal for framing an entryway or planting near a patio.

PEAK SEASON

Stewartia has year-round appeal, including beautiful bark in winter.

OUR FAVORITES

Japanese stewartia (*S. pseudocamellia*) grows to 40 feet tall and 25 feet wide. The fall foliage color is orange-red to purple, and very showy bark is a patchwork of green, gray, cream, brown, and red.

Tall stewartia (*S. monadelpha*), sometimes called orangebark stewartia, reaches 25 feet tall and 20 feet wide; it is smaller in all its parts (and more heat tolerant) than Japanese stewartia. Fall foliage is orange to burgundy, and rich brown bark matures to cinnamon tones.

GARDEN COMPANIONS

Stewartia is excellent among rhododendrons, azaleas, and ferns. Plant low-growing ground covers like bunchberry (*Cornus canadensis*), carpet bugle (*Ajuga*), epimediums, or lily turf (*Liriope* and *Ophiopogon*) beneath specimen trees. A dark background enhances the winter bark display.

LEFT: *Japanese stewartia ushers in a blaze of fall color. This small tree is a good choice in small gardens, as it grows to full size only after many years.*

When Plant in spring or fall from a nursery container.

Where Stewartia will grow best in partial shade, though the tree will take full sun if it is kept well watered in summer. It prefers soil that is rich in organic matter and well drained.

LEFT AND RIGHT: *The graceful tall stewartia has fresh green foliage in spring. Its orange-brown bark looks even more striking when the foliage turns pinkish red in fall.*

How Water the tree in its nursery container. Dig a hole that is the same depth as the container and twice as wide. Remove the tree from its container, keeping the root ball intact. Set the tree in the center of the hole, making sure the top of the root ball is level with the surrounding soil. Amend the dug soil with compost and refill the hole. Firm the soil around the plant. Water thoroughly. Add a 2-inch layer of mulch around the tree, but keep mulch a few inches away from the trunk.

TLC Stewartia prefers moist soil but is forgiving, surviving dry spells after a few years. Replenish mulch each year and sprinkle compost beneath the tree in spring. Pruning is rarely needed, as the tree has a naturally open habit.

Evergreen Trees

The recommended way to plan a garden is to establish a strong, clear framework. Unfortunately, as a beginning gardener, I didn't follow these wise instructions. I was seduced by the lure of fashionable perennials. With these colorful blooming plants, I could quickly "paint" garden pictures, but that satisfaction was to be short lived.

I saw that at the end of the season much of my garden disappeared. Gradually, my approach to gardening evolved, from painting to building a permanent structure and creating moods with evergreen trees. Over time, my admiration for these living bones of the garden has deepened. No matter how long you have gardened, it is never too late for structure.

good candidates for the Northwest, being hardy and pest free. Some of them can be clipped and used as boundary hedges, making simple, calming backdrops to more dramatic specimens that are better left to assume their natural form. These trees all grow to ten feet but can often be taller, so be selective when choosing varieties.

I am head gardener at Abkhazi Garden in Victoria, British Columbia. This heritage garden has gone through a few periods of neglect and renewal, and the evergreens are the most stalwart survivors. They are bent and touched by time, which gives the garden a sense of history and a feeling of permanence. The thick

EVERGREENS IN THE GARDEN

Evergreen trees, broadleaf and coniferous, have practical roles as well as an aesthetic ones in the garden. They provide shelter and privacy and also add interesting textures and colors. The ten chosen for this chapter have proved to be

trunk of a venerable Spanish fir *(Abies pinsapo)* reclines against a rock at a 45-degree angle before growing straight up another 20 feet. Was it trained or was that an accident? 'Reflexa' Norway spruce *(Picea abies)* have been placed so they flow like waterfalls down the face of rocky outcroppings. In another part of the garden, the new growth on the conifers is not as dramatic as emerging bulbs, but it is still a delight of the spring garden. The handsome leaves of *Magnolia grandiflora* give

pleasure throughout the year, with the wonderful flowers being almost a bonus. I am also experimenting with new evergreens that are coming from countries as diverse as Australia, China, and Chile and are well worth trying in mild areas.

It may be hard to envision planting a tree for its appearance in 10 or 15 years, but patience is rewarded. Enjoy your perennials but remember to plant trees. It is an act of optimism that embraces the future. —VALERIE MURRAY

ABOVE: *A stone angel wonders at a mix of conifers.* LEFT: *Clipped evergreens can denote formality in the garden.* OPPOSITE PAGE: *Colorado blue spruce.*

Boxleaf Azara

Azara microphylla

This charming little tree from Chile and Argentina is probably the least well known of our Top 10 evergreens, but it has so much going for it that Northwest gardeners are planting it more and more. Its size makes boxleaf azara a good fit even for small gardens: though it can reach 30 feet tall and 12 feet wide in its native setting, it's more likely to reach only half that size in gardens.

A variegated boxleaf azara sparkles against the darker backdrop of tall conifers.

With its open growth and shiny, roundish leaves (each less than an inch long), boxleaf azara lends a certain lightness to the garden—a bit like an upright fountain spray. In late spring or early summer, the petite yellow flowers all along the branches may not shout for attention, but they'll announce their presence with a delicate fragrance that reminds some people of chocolate, others of vanilla. Tiny reddish berries follow the blooms.

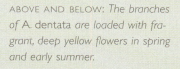

PEAK SEASON

The flowers perfume the air in late winter or early spring.

OUR FAVORITES

Azara dentata is similar to boxleaf azara, but it's a little smaller (topping out at about 10 feet) and has deeply toothed leaves that create an interesting visual texture. It benefits from frost protection in zone 5.

A. microphylla 'Variegata' has leaves edged in creamy yellow.

GARDEN COMPANIONS

For an exotic garden scene, plant boxleaf azara with hostas, large ferns, coleus (Solenostemon scutellarioides), impatiens, and Japanese forest grass (Hakonechloa macra 'Aureola').

Plant a boxleaf azara as a focal point at the center of a courtyard garden or near a light-colored wall, where the delicate tracery of its branches will be highlighted. Or surround your tree with boxwood (Buxus) or evergreen azaleas. These trees can take heavy pruning, so you can shape them to fit just about any garden niche.

When Plant in early spring.

Where Site boxleaf azara in partial shade, with protection from hot afternoon sun and cold winds. Provide fast-draining soil.

ABOVE AND BELOW: *The branches of A. dentata are loaded with fragrant, deep yellow flowers in spring and early summer.*

How Water the tree in its nursery container. Dig a hole the same depth as the container and twice as wide. Remove the tree from its container, keeping the root ball intact. Set the tree in the center of the hole, making sure the top of the root ball is level with the surrounding soil. Amend the dug soil with compost and refill the hole. Firm the soil around the plant. Water thoroughly. Add a 2-inch layer of mulch around the tree, but keep the mulch a few inches away from the trunk.

TLC Water boxleaf azara regularly during dry spells, and fertilize with a balanced plant food monthly (or apply a controlled-release fertilizer in spring). After bloom, prune to remove crowded branches; keep plants shapely by lightly trimming back branch tips at the same time. If older plants become leggy, you can cut them almost to the ground in spring and start over with fresh new growth.

*Azara dentata *does not grow well in zone 7.*

False Cypress

Chamaecyparis

If the soil conditions in your garden aren't ideal for the cypresses you wish to grow, put them in containers. There you can carefully control their soil and fertilizer needs.

Chances are you've used products made from Lawson false cypress *(Chamaecyparis lawsoniana)*. The fine, fragrant timber from this Western native conifer (also called Port Orford cedar) has been used to make everything from cabinets and lawn furniture to yardsticks and toys. The tree itself is the parent of dozens of popular garden varieties in a wide range of shapes, sizes, and colors. Sadly, this species is being wiped out by a root-rotting fungus for which no cure has been found. On the bright side, other disease-resistant species of false cypress are excellent garden performers.

The most popular species grow at a moderate rate into pyramids or columns that are usually branched all the way to the ground, which makes them excellent for use as screens. Their bold form also makes them good specimen plants in lawns or for anchoring corners.

Tiny, scalelike leaves are held in flattened sprays that look something like the delicate fronds of a fern—but these handsome trees are sturdy. Oils in the leaves can cause a skin reaction in some people, so keep the tree hugging to a minimum.

PEAK SEASON

False cypresses look good all year, but their contribution of green is particularly welcome in winter.

OUR FAVORITES

Among the best varieties of Hinoki false cypress (Chamaecyparis obtusa) are 'Crippsii', with rich golden foliage and an eventual size of 50 feet tall and half as wide; and dark green 'Gracilis', which is slender and upright to 20 feet tall and 8 feet wide.

The Northwest native Nootka cypress (C. nootkatensis) has drooping branchlets and forms a slender pyramid that may eventually reach 80 feet tall and 25 feet wide. C. n. 'Pendula', to 30 feet tall, has an open habit and branchlets that droop even more dramatically.

Plume false cypress (C. pisifera 'Plumosa') grows 20 to 25 feet tall and wide, with feathery foliage that gives it a soft, full look.

GARDEN COMPANIONS

Smaller varieties are effective in a shrub border with other evergreens like boxwood (Buxus) and camellia. Low-growing ground covers like bunchberry (Cornus canadensis) and kinnikinnick (Arctostaphylos uva-ursi) are naturals for carpeting the area beneath larger false cypresses.

When Plant in spring or fall.

Where False cypresses grow in full sun or light shade in rich soil with good drainage. They fare best in areas with high humidity and protection from drying winds.

How Water the tree in its nursery container. Dig a hole the same depth as the container and about twice as wide. Remove the tree from its container, and try to keep the root ball intact. Set the tree in the center of the hole, making sure the top of the root ball is level with the surrounding soil. Refill the hole and firm the soil around the plant. Water thoroughly. Add a layer of mulch at least 2 inches thick around the base of the tree, but keep the mulch a few inches away from the trunk.

TLC Keep plants well watered but avoid soggy conditions. Pull off old brown leaves from the base; other than that, these trees need no pruning.

*Nootka cypress grows in zones A2, A3; 2–6, 17.

BELOW: *Dwarf varieties of Hinoki false cypress, such as 'Nana Gracilis', make good potted plants.*

Fir

Abies

Oregon and Washington are top producers of commercially grown Christmas trees, and as almost half of those holiday staples are firs, it's clear that these conifers grow well in the Northwest. Most do best in moist, cool-to-cold areas, but a few tolerate warmer climates. Firs are highly sensitive to polluted air.

As erect, symmetrical pyramids with horizontal branches, firs bring a certain formality to the landscape—and the narrow shape and slow growth of many varieties make them ideal for small suburban gardens. Firs are sometimes confused with spruces, but firs have needles that are flatter and blunter; they are often silvery on the undersides, and many have a citrusy scent. Fir cones are held upright, like elongated eggs standing on end, and come in beautiful shades of deep violet to purplish blue or soft brown.

A sturdy little Spanish fir (Abies pinsapo) anchors a corner of this naturalistic garden.

PEAK SEASON

Colorful cones are very decorative in midsummer.

OUR FAVORITES

Blue Spanish fir (*Abies pinsapo* 'Glauca'; zones 5–7, 17) features striking blue-gray needles. It is very slow growing, reaching 25 feet tall and 10 feet wide in 40 years, and tolerates heat and resists diseases.

Korean fir (*A. koreana*; zones 3b–7, 17) grows slowly into a pyramid about 30 feet tall and 15 to 20 feet wide, with dark green needles and particularly lovely violet-blue cones.

White fir (*A. concolor*; zones A2, A3; 1–7, 17), which grows to at least 80 feet tall and 15 feet wide, is suitable for large gardens. It needs less water than the others listed here. Needles are bluish green in the species, but varieties 'Glauca', 'Violacea', and 'Candicans' are more intensely blue.

GARDEN COMPANIONS

Simulate a mountain meadow by surrounding a fir with grasses like blue oat grass or feather grass and a variety of bulbs. Good companion shrubs include Oregon grape (*Mahonia aquifolium*) and purple smoke tree. Blue-needled firs stand out beautifully when planted in front of evergreen hedges.

When Plant fir trees from nursery containers in spring.

Where Firs need a site with full sun or light shade, and they do best when sheltered from heavy or constant wind. Plant in rich, moist, well-drained soil that is slightly acidic. Be sure to take into account the ultimate size of your tree; firs look miserable when crowded and don't take well to pruning.

How Water the tree in its nursery container. Dig a hole the same depth as the container and twice as wide. Remove the fir tree from the container, keeping the root ball intact. Set the tree in the center of the hole, making sure the top of the root ball is level with the surrounding soil. Refill the hole, and firm the soil around the plant. Water thoroughly. Add a 2-inch layer of mulch around the tree, but keep the mulch a few inches away from the trunk.

TLC Give fir trees regular water for the first 2 years; once established, they'll do fine with just moderate irrigation. Firs rarely need pruning, but remove dead or damaged branches as needed.

ABOVE, LEFT: *Firs hold their handsome and distinctive cones upright.* ABOVE, RIGHT: *Some firs are too big for any but the largest of gardens. Allow ample room at planting; trying to prune a fir will ruin its natural shape.*

Hemlock
Tsuga

The hemlock is easy to recognize in the land-scape by its unusual nodding tip that looks something like a wizard's cap. These big, elegant, cone-shaped trees are regarded by many as the most graceful of all conifers, with horizontal or drooping branches clothed in sprays of delicate, dark green needles. A multitude of small brown cones hangs down from branches, with scales outlined in such fine detail that they look like handmade tree ornaments. The cinnamon-colored bark becomes deeply furrowed with age. Hemlocks take so well to clipping that they are frequently used as hedges—but left to grow into their natural shape, they make wonderful accent plants for lawns. Plant one in a protected corner of a large garden as the centerpiece of a woodland scene. Birds will flock to it.

A mature Canada hemlock presides over a mix of conifers. Hemlocks do best in such woodland conditions, with summer humidity and protection from sun.

Legend has it that these trees were called hemlock because the crushed foliage smells like that of the poisonous herb that ended Socrates' life—but don't worry if you're inexplicably tempted to nibble on your tree: the two plants are unrelated.

PEAK SEASON

Hemlocks look good year-round.

OUR FAVORITES

Dark green Canada hemlock (Tsuga canadensis) grows 40 to 70 feet tall and half as wide, usually with two or more trunks; its outer branches droop gracefully. It will grow in all zones but A1, A2, and 1. 'Golden Splendor' is a fast grower with golden yellow leaves. 'Pendula' (sometimes called Sargent weeping hemlock), with pendulous branches eventually reaches 10 to 15 feet tall and twice as wide.

Mountain hemlock (T. mertensiana) is a superb tree that reaches 20 to 30 feet tall and half as wide; its blue-green needles have a silvery cast. 'Glauca' has silver-gray foliage and reaches only 10 feet by 6 feet.

Northwest native Western hemlock (T. heterophylla) grows 70 to 130 feet tall and 20 to 30 feet wide, with a narrow crown and dark green to yellowish needles. It tolerates more shade than the others listed here, and grows in all zones but A1 and 1.

GARDEN COMPANIONS

Rhododendrons, azaleas, camellias, and ferns all like the same woodsy conditions that hemlocks do. Create a Northwest native garden with a hemlock surrounded by evergreen huckleberry (Vaccinium ovatum) and Oregon grape (Mahonia aquifolium).

When Plant hemlocks in spring or fall.

ABOVE: A butterfly alights on a branch of Western hemlock. BELOW: The unique pendent branches of Sargent weeping hemlock (T. canadensis 'Pendula').

Where Choose a spot in full sun or partial shade with rich, acidic soil, high humidity, and protection from wind. Hemlocks need a cool, damp climate and do not thrive where summers are hot or where the air is polluted.

How Water the tree in its nursery container. Dig a hole the same depth as the container and twice as wide. Remove the tree from its container, keeping the root ball intact. Set the tree in the center of the hole, making sure the top of the root ball is level with the surrounding soil. Amend the dug soil with compost and refill the hole. Firm the soil around the plant. Water thoroughly. Add a 2-inch layer of mulch around the tree, but keep the mulch a few inches away from the trunk.

TLC Keep the soil around hemlocks moist at all times— these trees do not tolerate drought. During hot, dry spells, hemlock foliage benefits from occasional spraying with water from the hose. At the first sign of hemlock woolly adelgid (a white cottony mass at the base of the leaves), spray with insecticidal soap. Hemlocks may be pruned during summer.

Except as noted.

Holly

Ilex

Variegated hollies make sparkling garden accents. This English holly has leaves edged with golden yellow; other forms have white, cream, or light green markings.

Although hollies may be more familiar as shrubs, a few larger members of the genus make fine garden trees. Their dense, symmetrical form is a strong presence in the garden, and their glossy leaves are handsome in all seasons. Nearly all hollies are either male or female, and as a rule both must be in the garden if female plants are to set fruit. Once they do, you can "deck the halls" at holiday time with clipped branches bearing the brightly colored berries that appear in autumn and hang on well into winter.

Hollies branch low to the ground, which makes them a natural choice for screening. They are often planted at the edge of a garden or alone, so their majestic form can be appreciated—and the sharp spines of their leaves avoided. Be sure to mulch the area around the base of these trees, as their roots need to stay cool and moist.

PEAK SEASON

Cheerful red berries decorate the hollies' branches in winter.

OUR FAVORITES

American holly *(Ilex opaca;* zones 2–7, 17) reaches about 40 feet tall and half as wide, with spiny, dark green leaves and berries that are red in most varieties, yellow or orange in others. Check with your local nursery for types best suited to your area.

English holly *(I. aquifolium;* zones 4–7, 17) grows slowly to form a dense pyramid 40 feet tall and 25 feet wide, with glossy, dark green leaves and bright red berries. It is not recommended for coastal gardens, as it can spread invasively there.

Wilson holly *(I. × altaclerensis* 'Wilsonii'; zones 3b–7, 17) takes heat and wind better than other types. Easily trained to a single trunk, it grows 15 to 20 feet tall and 10 to 12 feet wide, with bright green leaves and large scarlet berries.

GARDEN COMPANIONS

Plant near other berry-producing trees and shrubs, such as barberry *(Berberis),* cotoneaster, and mountain ash *(Sorbus),* for a profusion of autumn and winter fruits that will have birds flocking to your garden.

When Plant hollies in spring or fall.

Where Choose a site in full sun or partial shade. Hollies grow best in rich, well-drained soil. In cold-winter areas, choose a spot that offers some protection from winter wind.

How Water the tree in its nursery container. Dig a hole the same depth as the container and twice as wide. Remove the tree from its container, keeping the root ball intact. Set the tree in the center of the hole, making sure the top of the root ball is level with the surrounding soil. Amend the dug soil with compost and refill the hole. Firm the soil around the plant. Water thoroughly. Add a 2-inch layer of mulch around the tree, but be sure to keep the mulch a few inches away from the trunk.

TLC Replenish mulch beneath your holly tree each spring. Prune only to correct shape or remove dead or broken branches; winter is a good time to do this, when the cut foliage can be used for your holiday decorations.

TOP TO BOTTOM: *Blue-green leaves and yellow berries of American holly; a variegated English holly; bright red English holly berries.*

Japanese Cryptomeria
Cryptomeria japonica

This refined-looking conifer is highly valued in Japan, where it has long been considered a sacred tree; centuries-old groves are still thriving where they were planted near temples. The fragrant, soft wood is used there in the construction of everything from dolls to buildings.

Japanese cryptomeria shoots up fast when young—as much as 3 feet per year under ideal conditions—and forms a stout, straight trunk with horizontal branches and attractive red-brown bark that peels off in strips. It matures into a narrow cone 50 to 60 feet tall and 20 to 30 feet wide (very old trees may reach 100 feet tall), with luxuriantly soft, needlelike leaves that are bright green to bluish green, turning brownish purple in cold weather. Small, round, red-brown cones are held at the tips of branches.

This 15-year-old evergreen screen on Whidbey Island features false cypress (Cryptomeria japonica 'Elegans'), fir, and hemlock backed by a plume cedar (back, left).

PEAK SEASON

The new foliage is particularly lush in spring; winter color is also striking.

OUR FAVORITES

For interesting variations on foliage texture, plant 'Cristata' (with branch tips fused into cockscombs) or 'Spiralis' (with twisted leaves that curl into ringlets). Both reach about 10 to 20 feet by 6 to 12 feet.

Plume cedar (*C. j.* 'Elegans'), which forms a dense pyramid 20 to 30 feet tall and 10 feet wide, is even more feathery than the species, with grayish foliage that turns rich coppery red or purplish in winter. 'Elegans Compacta' is similar, but grows only 12 feet tall. 'Elegans Aurea' is full size, with light green summer foliage turning lime green in winter.

'Sekkan-sugi' grows about half the size of the species and sports foliage dramatically tipped in creamy yellow.

'Yoshino' is like the species but reaches only 30 to 40 feet tall and 20 feet wide, with blue-green foliage.

GARDEN COMPANIONS

Japanese cryptomerias make a verdant background for colorful trees and shrubs like witch hazel, dogwood, and flowering cherry. To lend the garden a Japanese-style, combine these conifers with Japanese maples, maiden grass, bamboos, and Japanese forest grass.

When Plant in spring or fall.

Where A single Japanese cryptomeria can be a focal point, or you can mimic a venerable Japanese grove by planting several on your property. These trees grow best in full sun but will tolerate partial shade. Provide rich, acidic, well-drained soil.

CLOCKWISE FROM LEFT: *Red-brown older cones; light green young cones; beautiful rust-colored mature bark.*

How Water the tree in its nursery container. Dig a hole the same depth as the container and twice as wide. Remove the tree from its container, keeping the root ball intact. Set the tree in the center of the hole, making sure the top of the root ball is level with the surrounding soil. Amend the dug soil with compost and refill the hole. Firm the soil around the plant. Water thoroughly. Add a 2-inch layer of mulch around the tree, but keep the mulch a few inches away from the trunk.

TLC Water regularly; these trees will not tolerate hot, dry conditions. During dry spells, spray foliage with water from the hose. Pruning is rarely necessary, but if you inherit an older tree that is ragged from neglect, you can cut it down to 2 to 3 feet tall; new growth will quickly sprout.

Pine

Pinus

Pines come in just about every shape and size, from compact little cushions to towering, open giants. They are the best known and most widely grown conifers, and no matter where you live in the Northwest, there's almost certainly one that's suited to your climate. Check with your local nursery for recommended species, and be sure to choose one of an appropriate size for your garden. If you fall in love with a tree that's too large for your space, don't give up hope: there may be a dwarf or small, weeping variety of that species that will be a better fit.

All pines carry their needles in clusters around the branches, and their attractive, patterned cones hang straight down. In spring, the branch tips are decorated with upright, light-colored bundles of new growth, aptly named candles.

With their rugged, handsome looks, these trees make good choices for specimen plantings. Most are tolerant of high wind and are often planted as windbreaks. They're also good for attracting birds to the garden: their branches offer shelter, and their nutritious seeds are popular with the winged set.

Japanese black pine (Pinus thunbergii) often develops a leaning trunk with age. This carefully maintained specimen appears to bow toward a stone lantern.

PEAK SEASON

New growth is attractive in spring, but pines look beautiful in winter when dusted with snow or frost.

OUR FAVORITES

Beach pine (*Pinus contorta;* zones A3; 4–7, 17), with dark needles, grows to 20 to 30 feet tall and wide, often contorted by coastal winds.

Japanese white pine (*P. parviflora;* zones 2–7, 17) is 20 to 50 feet tall and wide. This pine forms a dense, blue-green pyramid in youth, but is more spreading with age.

Swiss stone pine (*P. cembra;* zones A1–A3; 1–7) grows slowly to 70 feet tall and 25 feet wide, with dark needles and a dense, narrow form.

Shrubby mugo pine (*P. mugo mugo;* zones A1–A3; 1–7, 17) is a symmetrical little pine useful for small yards, containers, and rock gardens. Needles are dark green; choose specimens with dense form.

White pine (*P. strobus;* zones 1–6) is a fast grower to 50 to 80 feet tall and 20 to 40 feet wide, with soft, blue-green needles that give it a fluffy look. It's best protected from winds.

Japanese black pine (*P. thunbergii;* zones 3–7, 17) grows quickly to 100 by 40 feet with bright green new growth. Tolerates much pruning.

TOP: *The Japanese white pine 'Kokuho'.*
BOTTOM: *Mugo pine thrives in containers and raised beds.*

When Young trees can be planted in spring or fall.

Where Pines require full sun. They'll grow in most soils, as long as they're well drained.

How Water the tree in its nursery container. Dig a hole the same depth as the container and twice as wide. Remove the tree from its container, keeping the root ball intact. Set the tree in the center of the hole, making sure the top of the root ball is level with the surrounding soil. Amend the dug soil with compost and refill the hole. Firm the soil around the plant. Water thoroughly. Add a 2-inch layer of mulch around the tree, but keep the mulch a few inches away from the trunk.

TLC Though they'll take drought once established, pines will grow better and faster with regular water. Fertilizing is not recommended. Pruning is fun and easy: just cut back the candles when they emerge in spring. The more you cut off, the more you'll increase the bushiness and limit the size of the tree.

GARDEN COMPANIONS

Rhododendrons, azaleas, heaths (*Erica*), heathers (*Calluna vulgaris*), and lily-of-the-valley shrub (*Pieris japonica*) all grow well in the company of pines, whose dropped needles help to acidify the soil.

Southern Magnolia
Magnolia grandiflora

This magnificent broad-leafed tree hails from the southeastern United States, but it grows well in many parts of the country, including much of the Northwest. Granted, the Southern magnolia loves heat: so no matter where you live, it's best to plant your tree in the warmest part of your garden, such as in front of a south-facing wall or in another spot where it will get full sun all day long.

Southern magnolia grows into a spreading tree to 60 feet tall and almost as wide, but if you don't have a plantation-size garden, there are plenty of smaller varieties to choose from. All types offer big, creamy white, cup-shaped flowers with a heavenly fragrance in summer and fall. The leaves are impressive in their own right: they can reach 8 inches long, with a glossy dark green top and paler green or russet underside. Leaves fall a few at a time practically year-round, so you may want to rake them up—or just let them create a natural mulch and enjoy their dry crackle underfoot.

As the large, creamy white petals of the magnolia flowers fall away, they're followed by vivid crimson seedpods.

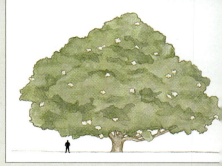

When Plant in early spring, just as new growth is beginning.

Where Plant in well-drained soil in full sun or partial shade. Don't place near sidewalks or pavement, as surface roots can lift those surfaces.

How Water the tree in its nursery container. Dig a hole the same depth as the container and twice as wide. Take the tree from its container, keeping the root ball intact. Set the tree in the center of the hole, making sure the top of the root ball is level with the surrounding soil. Amend the dug soil with plenty of compost and refill the hole. Firm the soil around the plant. Water thoroughly. Add a 2-inch layer of mulch around the tree, but keep the mulch a few inches away from the trunk.

TLC Water Southern magnolia regularly, and apply a controlled-release fertilizer in spring. Prune in late winter to remove crossing or awkward shoots.

A young Southern magnolia displays its glossy leaves, which catch the light—and your attention—in the garden.

PEAK SEASON

Expect gorgeous blooms in summer and fall, though trees may need to settle in for a few years before they begin to bloom.

OUR FAVORITES

'Alta' is quite upright, almost columnar, and very slow growing to 20 to 40 feet tall and 10 to 20 feet wide—perfect for a small garden or to anchor the end of a flower border.

'Edith Bogue' is the hardiest of all, surviving down to −24°F/−31°C, and its stout branches resist breakage from heavy, wet snow. It grows to 35 feet tall by 20 feet wide.

'Little Gem' is upright and compact, to 20 feet tall and half as wide.

'Victoria' is hardy to −10°F/−23°C and resists snow breakage. It grows to 20 feet tall and 15 feet wide.

GARDEN COMPANIONS

Smaller varieties of Southern magnolia are well suited to a shrub border surrounded by boxwood, camellia, rhododendron, and azalea. The area directly beneath the tree's canopy is best left unplanted.

Spruce

Picea

By far the most familiar of these conifers is the chubby little Colorado blue spruce *(Picea pungens glauca),* which looks so Christmasy standing in a front yard, with its stiff, horizontal branches forming a broad pyramid. With names like 'Baby Blue Eyes' and 'Fat Albert', the dwarf varieties practically invite you to squeeze them as you would a big blue teddy bear. Resist that temptation, though, as the soft-looking needles of spruce, arranged bottlebrush-style around the branches, are actually quite prickly.

Colorado blue spruce is a good choice for areas with cold winters; in milder areas such as Puget Sound, it is prone to attack by insects, leaving it brown and unattractive in the center after a decade or so. Unless you live high in the mountains, you're better off choosing one of the more adaptable spruces listed on the opposite page. Spruces are very attractive to birds, which enjoy their seeds and take shelter among their spreading branches.

Colorado blue spruce grows well in mountainous areas throughout the Northwest, including zones A2 and A3. This variety is 'Baby Blue Eyes'.

LEFT: *A weeping form of Norway spruce.* RIGHT: *A pleasing contrast between spruce branches and a euphorbia.*

PEAK SEASON

Spruces bring structure and color to the garden in winter.

OUR FAVORITES

Brewer's weeping spruce *(Picea breweriana),* native to the Siskiyou Mountains, forms an upright pyramid 30 to 50 feet tall and 10 to 12 feet wide, with elegantly drooping branches and deep green needles. It prefers cool, moist conditions.

Norway spruce *(P. abies)* grows fast to 80 feet tall and 20 feet wide. It tolerates wind and cold.

Oriental spruce *(P. orientalis)* forms a shapely pyramid, growing slowly to 60 feet tall and 20 feet wide. Needles are rich, dark green and hang prettily from horizontal branches. Spring foliage of 'Aurea' is creamy gold; 'Skylands' stays gold year-round.

Serbian spruce *(P. omorika)* forms a dense, narrow, formal-looking spire 50 to 60 feet tall and 10 to 20 feet wide, with deep green needles that are silver-blue beneath. This is an adaptable species that resists insects and diseases.

GARDEN COMPANIONS

Spruces are often planted as focal points, but they look at home with other bold growers like holly *(Ilex),* smoke tree *(Cotinus),* and viburnum as neighbors. Suitable ground covers include cotoneaster and sedum.

When Plant in spring or fall.

Where Spruces need full sun or light shade and grow best in moist, well-drained soil. Be sure to give them room to spread to their full width: don't plant large types next to buildings, fences, or walks.

How Water the tree in its nursery container. Dig a hole the same depth as the container and twice as wide. Remove the tree from its container, keeping the root ball intact. Set the tree in the center of the hole, making sure the top of the root ball is level with the surrounding soil. Amend the dug soil with compost and refill the hole. Firm the soil around the plant. Water thoroughly. Add a 2-inch layer of mulch around the tree, but not directly against the trunk.

TLC Once established, these trees get by on little to moderate water. Each winter, check your spruce for the presence of small, dull green aphids; if you see them, spray with insecticidal soap. Pruning usually isn't needed, but a light trimming to correct the tree's shape can be done in midsummer.

*Brewer's weeping spruce grows in zones 2b, 3–7, 17. Norway spruce grows in zones A2, A3; 1–6, 17.

Yew
Taxus

Yews are survivors. Unlike many conifers, they grow equally well (if slowly) in sun or shade, take much or little water, adapt readily to coastal conditions, and don't seem the least bit bothered by air pollution. Their dense foliage, made up of tightly packed needles that are dark green above and lighter beneath, gives them a solid, formal look. They're often sheared as hedges and are among the very best plants for that purpose, but left to grow into their natural shape, they ultimately make handsome trees. Attractive red berries appear on female trees in late summer and fall. (Except for the fleshy cups that surround the berries' hard seeds, all parts of a yew plant are poisonous.)

The densely packed needles of Taxus × media 'Hicksii' make it a good candidate for use as a tall screen or hedge. New growth is a much lighter green.

Yews work well as screening plants, individual specimens, or formal sentinels flanking a driveway. But please don't plant them right against the house: they'll eventually need continual topping to fit beneath the eaves, which will destroy the natural columnar shape of the trees.

PEAK SEASON

The deep green foliage of yews is especially striking in winter.

OUR FAVORITES

English yew *(Taxus baccata)* grows to 25 feet tall and 15 feet wide, with dark needles. The species is less common than garden varieties. 'Aurea' has new foliage that is golden yellow from spring to fall, then turns green.

Irish yew *(T. baccata* 'Stricta', sometimes listed as *T. b.* 'Fastigiata') forms a dark green, narrow column 15 to 30 feet tall and 3 to 10 feet wide. Branches may spread near the top, especially in snowy regions, but they are easy to tie together with wire.

Japanese yew *(T. cuspidata)* reaches 10 to 25 feet tall and only half as wide and is an excellent, cold-hardy choice east of the Cascades.

T. × media 'Hicksii' forms a column of dark green about 10 to 12 feet tall and 3 to 4 feet wide. It's a bit more open growing than Irish yew.

GARDEN COMPANIONS

In the shade, yews look at home with hosta, ferns, hellebore, and epimedium. In the sun, use the dark foliage as a contrasting background for bright flowers of daylily *(Hemerocallis)*, penstemon, coreopsis, iris, and lily *(Lilium)*.

When Plant in spring or fall.

Where Yews will grow in most well-drained soils but do not tolerate extremes of acidity or alkalinity. They thrive in sun or shade but don't like extreme heat; avoid planting near a wall that faces south or west.

How Water the tree in its nursery container. Dig a hole the same depth as the container and twice as wide. Remove the tree from its container, keeping the root ball intact. Set the tree in the center of the hole, making sure the top of the root ball is level with the surrounding soil. Amend the dug soil with compost and refill the hole. Firm the soil around the plant. Water thoroughly. Add a 2-inch layer of mulch around the tree, but keep the mulch a few inches away from the trunk.

TLC Water regularly for the first year or two, until roots are well established; after that, moderate watering should be sufficient. During prolonged spells of hot, dry weather, hose off plants every 2 weeks. Pruning isn't usually needed, but the job is best done in summer or early fall.

RIGHT, TOP: *The waxy red berries of yew.* RIGHT: *A waist-high hedge of clipped yew nicely borders a quince tree entwined with a blue clematis.*

*Japanese yew grows in zones A2, A3; 2–6, 17. T. × media 'Hicksii' grows in zones 2–6, 17.

Here's a down-in-the-dirt secret. Fruits, vegetables, and herbs are as beautiful as any other garden plants, and they fit into just as many niches in the home landscape. So you can think of them as ornamentals with a bonus: they supply you with fresh, healthy produce.

You don't need to plant edibles in tidy rows. Instead, think about the plants' shape, bloom, fruit color, fragrance, and cultural needs just as you would any other plant, then place them where they'll show to best advantage. For instance, you might choose to plant blueberries because they are versatile and beautiful in every season. Some are evergreen, others deciduous. Some grow only 1 foot tall and are right at home in a rock garden, while others reach 7 feet tall and make great edible hedges. Apple trees, depending on their rootstocks, can grow from 4 feet tall to 40 feet tall, so an apple can be a glorious specimen tree in your yard, with a swing and tree house for the kids, or a for-

mal espalier against the wall of your house. Or a minidwarf apple in a pot might be perfect on your apartment balcony overlooking a cityscape.

MAKING CHOICES

For more than 30 years, we have been selling edible plants from our nursery in southwest Washington. We work with state Cooperative Extensions that test thousands of varieties to determine which ones succeed in the Northwest. So why don't we recommend the same varieties that you find in the local supermarket? It's because home gardeners and commercial growers have very different needs. Commercial growers need varieties that they can pick before they are

ripe and that will ship well and keep a long time in controlled temperature storage. Home gardeners, on the other hand, want varieties that are disease resistant, have great flavor, and thrive in their area.

CLIMATE IS CRUCIAL

Each edible plant has very specific growing requirements, so you must match your crops to your growing conditions. For instance, the abundant rainfall west of the Cascades calls for varieties that resist the fungal diseases that are encouraged by excessive moisture. Likewise, the lack of summer heat means that edible plants need to ripen early in the season and still develop their flavor. Gardeners east of the mountains have more summer heat and less rain, which favor edible plants that need extended periods of hot weather to achieve their best flavor. Farther north, the situation is complicated by the short season. The Top 10 edible plants in the following pages will get you started with tried-and-true choices for each region. When you are ready to expand your edible gardening horizons, your local Cooperative Extension Office is a great place to learn more. —SAM BENOWITZ

ABOVE: *Edible gardens can contain innovative landscaping and structures.* LEFT: *'Lumina' pumpkin.*
OPPOSITE PAGE: *A pretty blend of culinary thymes.*

Apples and Pears

Apples thrive throughout the Northwest, from the coldest to the mildest regions. That's why so many yards still boast gnarled specimens that continue to bear fruit a century after planting. Pears are slightly less hardy, but equally long lived. The trick for both is finding a size that suits your garden.

Like any grafted fruit tree, these have two parts: the "variety" (the top, fruiting section of the tree), which is grafted onto the "rootstock" (the root system). This combination determines the tree's height at maturity. You might find the same variety of apple tree as a 6-foot-tall minidwarf, a 10- to 12-foot-tall dwarf, or a tree of 30 feet or more. Pears on dwarfing rootstocks range from 12 to 20 feet tall; full-size trees to 40 feet.

For pollination, most apples and pears require a different variety nearby that blooms at the same time.

PEAK SEASON

Apples and pears ripen through summer and fall.

OUR FAVORITES

The following apples and pears are good for eating fresh.

Apples

West of the Cascades, choose scab-resistant 'Akane', with medium-size, crisp, juicy red fruit that ripens in September; 'Fiesta', with October-ripening, medium to large, red-striped fruit with delicious flavor; or 'Pristine', with medium-size, crisp, mildly tart yellow fruit that ripens in August. 'William's Pride', which produces medium-size, crisp, juicy, flavorful red fruit that ripens in August, bears well in southwest Alaska, although somewhat later in the season.

LEFT: *Espalier is both practical and decorative. These multi-variety, semi-dwarf apple trees have been trained on horizontal wires against a cement-block wall.*

East of the Cascades, try 'Fuji', which has flavorful red fruit that ripens in October. It resists fireblight.

'Honeycrisp' is suitable for all areas. Its large, juicy red fruit ripens in September.

Pears

In coastal areas, plant scab-resistant 'Orcas', which produces large, flavorful yellow fruits blushed with carmine in September; or 'Rescue', which produces heavy crops of large, sweet yellow fruit with smooth flesh, also in September.

An old favorite for east of the Cascades is 'Bartlett', with large, yellow, sweet fruit that ripens in September.

'Bosc' has firm, crunchy flesh and brownish skin. It grows throughout the Northwest and ripens in September. Also suitable for both sides of the mountains is 'Comice', a French favorite with greenish yellow skin and a classic buttery flavor. It ripens in early October.

When Plant in winter when trees are dormant.

Where Apples like deeply tilled, well-drained soil, but they can survive with less-than-ideal conditions. Pear trees can tolerate slightly wetter soil than apples. A full day of sun is best for both. If you plant in a lawn, remove the sod down to bare earth at least 6 feet in diameter around the plant.

How Water the trees while they're still in their nursery containers, or soak bare-root plants in a bucket. Dig each planting hole slightly deeper and wider than the tree's root system and mix in a cup of bonemeal. Gently remove the root ball from the container or bucket, snip off any broken roots, and gently loosen the roots. Make a small mound in the center of the hole and set the plant on the mound with the roots facing outward and downward. The tree should be at the same level as in its nursery container. Refill the hole and firm the soil around the plant. Water thoroughly. Spread 2 inches of mulch around the tree, but don't put it directly against the trunk.

TLC Water young trees generously. Thin heavy crops when fruit is small to prevent the limbs from breaking. Fertilize only in the spring. Take care not to break the "spurs"—the short, knobby branches that produce fruit. During winter dormancy, remove any crossing branches to create an open canopy that allows in plenty of sun. Train pear trees against their natural tendency to grow upright; they produce the most fruit on the branches that grow out from the trunk at an angle between 10 and 45 degrees.

Harvest Pick apples as they ripen, but pick all except the earliest-season pears when hard, and then ripen them at room temperature for a week or more. To know when to pick a pear, cup your hand under the fruit and lift up; if the stem breaks off the tree, the pear is ready to pick.

'Bosc' is long-necked, attractively russeted yellow to brown fruit.

247

Beans

Nurseries and seed companies stock a dizzying variety of beans, but that doesn't mean these are specialty plants. In fact, beans continue to be so popular with gardeners because they are easy to care for and so fast growing.

Beans fall into one of three groups based on when they taste best: snap, shell, or dry. Snap beans (also called string or green beans) have stringless edible pods. Shell and dry beans are grown for the seeds inside, whether cooked fresh or stored for later use.

All types are available as either bush or pole (vine) beans—terms that refer to the way they grow. Bush beans are self-supporting plants that mature quickly, and produce a single, heavy crop. Pole beans are slower to mature but they continue to produce more beans in response to harvesting. Pole beans need support— either a trellis or tepee at least 6 feet tall made of sturdy wood, metal, or bamboo.

After trying the beans listed here, sample some of the more unusual varieties that are readily available.

In this fenced vegetable garden, bush and pole beans mingle with snapdragons and Swiss chard.

PEAK SEASON

Beans ripen from midsummer to the first frost.

OUR FAVORITES

The following are all snap beans.

Pole Beans

'Cascade Giant' has large pods that grow to 10 inches long.

'Kentucky Wonder' is an heirloom favorite that produces heavy crops of tender, 7- to 9-inch-long pods.

Scarlet runner bean has 8-inch pods and beautiful crimson-orange flowers. Children enjoy its colorful blooms and large leaves. Young pods can be eaten as snap beans; beans from older pods can be shelled and cooked.

Bush Beans

'Contender' is a heavy cropper for cold climates. The dark green, 6-inch-long pods are splashed with purple.

'Goldkist' is a yellow wax bean with sweet flavor. It produces heavy crops of 5-inch-long pods.

'Purple Queen' sports shiny, 6-inch-long, purple-green pods that turn green when cooked.

'Tendercrop' produces round, dark green pods up to 6 inches long.

Available as Pole and Bush

'Blue Lake' has tender, 6-inch-long pods with white seeds.

When After the last frost date, sow successive crops every 2 weeks. Beans will not germinate unless the soil is consistently above 55°F/13°C, so in cold areas plant in raised beds, where soil warms faster.

ABOVE: *Scarlet runner beans smother an arbor with leaves and blooms.* BELOW: *'Blue Lake' pole beans.*

Where Beans need a sunny location and well-drained, rich soil. Place pole beans along the north side of the garden, where they won't shade other sun-loving vegetables.

How Sow seeds 1 inch deep, 2 to 3 inches apart. When bush seedlings reach 4 inches in height, thin to 5 to 6 inches apart; give pole beans a little more room—6 to 8 inches. Water well and keep soil moist until seeds germinate.

TLC As they grow, mulch beans with 2 inches of chopped leaves, grass clippings, or other fine-textured organic material. Give beans regular water. Feed with a low-nitrogen fertilizer when plants start growing, and again when pods start to form.

Harvest Harvest snap beans when the pods are about $\frac{1}{8}$ inch thick, before the seeds begin to swell. Harvest shell beans when the pods are plump and fully colored.

Berries

There are dozens of berries native to the Northwest, but home gardeners grow raspberries, blackberries, blueberries, and strawberries. All are delicious fresh or in jams and jellies.

Raspberries may be red, yellow, purple, or black; blackberries are purplish black. Most self-pollinate. Raspberries and blackberries bear fruit only on second-year canes (except everbearing raspberries, which fruit on each year's canes). These plants need a sturdy trellis, preferably one made of two strong posts strung with strong wire.

Blueberries need no support and make fine landscape plants. They range in height from 1 to 6 feet, and some are ever-green. Plant two varieties for pollination.

Strawberries are self-pollinating and are either June-bearing (producing one crop a year) or everbearing (bearing from early summer through fall). They grow well in containers or raised beds.

Most berries are subject to diseases and pests, so it's important to start out with healthy plants from a rep-utable supplier and to give them good soil and care. You'll find the TLC is worth it the first time you pop a just-ripe berry into your mouth.

PEAK SEASON

Most berry fruits ripen in summer and early fall.

OUR FAVORITES

Raspberries

'Meeker' is an old-time favorite that produces red fruit in July. It is hardy to a little below 0°F/–18°C. 'Summit' is a good everbearing type, producing plenty of red, juicy fruit from August until frost. If cut down and mulched in winter, it can withstand tempera-tures to –20°F/–29°C or lower. Both grow in all zones.

LEFT: *Rotate raspberries and blackberries to a different place in the garden every 10 years; rotate strawberries every three or four years. Blueberries can stay put.*

Blackberries

'Arapaho' (zones 1–7, 17) is a thornless variety. It produces large, flavorful fruit. 'Triple Crown' (zones 1–7, 17) is a vigorous, thornless variety hardy to –20°F/–29°C, with very large, sweet fruit. 'Marion' (zones 4–7, 17), sometimes sold as marionberry, has medium-size fruit with excellent flavor. It is hardy to –10°F/–23°C.

Blueberries

'Patriot' grows to 5 feet tall and is extremely hardy (to –30°F/–34°C). It ripens early and produces large, tasty fruit. 'Toro' is equally hardy and fruitful, with extra-large berries; it ripens in midseason. Evergreen 'Sunshine Blue', hardy to 0°F/–18°C, to 4 feet tall, bears delicious fruits in August and September. It makes an outstanding landscape plant west of the Cascades. All grow in zones 2–7, 17.

Strawberries

'Shuksan' is a disease-resistant June bearer with great fresh flavor. It is hardy to –15°F/–26°C. 'Tristar' is an everbearing type that produces very flavorful, medium-size fruit from June through November. It is hardy to –30°F/–34°C. Both grow in all zones.

When Plant most berries bare-root in spring; in mild-winter areas, you can plant container-grown berries in fall.

Where All berries enjoy full sun. Strawberries prefer a fast-draining, humus-rich soil (acid rather than alkaline). Cane berries need deep, well-drained soil. Blueberries require an acidic soil. Don't plant berries of any kind in an area where water settles; if the area does not drain well, mound up the soil to 1 foot before planting.

How Amend the planting bed with organic matter; if planting blueberries, add an acidic amendment such as peat moss. If planting bare-root berries, soak the roots for half an hour in a bucket of water. Water container-grown plants before transplanting them to the garden. Space raspberries 20 inches apart, blackberries 4 to 8 feet apart (depending on variety), blueberries 6 to 8 feet apart, and strawberries 1 foot apart. Dig planting holes and spread each plant's roots over a cone of soil, then cover with more soil and press firmly. With strawberries, make sure the crown is slightly above soil level. Water deeply, and mulch with straw.

TLC All berry plants need regular water. Most also benefit from a 3- to 4-inch layer of an organic mulch in spring and fall. Strawberries are heavy feeders. Give them diluted fish emulsion every 2 weeks until flowering begins. Feed June-bearing strawberries again lightly when growth begins, then again more heavily after fruiting; everbearing types prefer weekly light feedings. Feed potted strawberries monthly with a liquid fertilizer. If birds and other wildlife find the fruit before you do, cover plants with netting. Control chewing pests such as slugs, snails, and earwigs. For most cane berries, prune second-year canes in the fall after fruiting, leaving the current year's canes to bear fruit the next summer. Cut everbearing raspberries to just above ground level in late fall; the new canes will bear the next year's fruit. Prune blueberries only to remove damaged, overlapping, or dead branches.

'Quinault' is an everbearing strawberry grown in Alaska as an annual plant.

Harvest Ripe berries are easily removed by hand. Don't allow overripe fruit to remain on the plant; this encourages fungal diseases.

Herbs, Annual

No matter where you live in the Northwest—north or south, mountain or coast, apartment or suburban house—you can tuck a few annual herbs into your garden. Most can be grown from seed sown in place and many do fine in pots and window boxes. They grow quickly, suffer from virtually no pests or diseases, and reward you with a bounty of flavors.

Some annual herbs prefer cool weather; like lettuce, they'll go to seed ("bolt") in the heat of midsummer. Others, such as basil, flourish with high temperatures.

PEAK SEASON
Herbs ripen from spring through fall.

OUR FAVORITES
Basil (*Ocimum basilicum*) is so flavorful you can pluck the leaves right off the plant and eat them fresh. Plants may reach 2 feet tall, with bright green or striking purple leaves. Basil needs regular water and plenty of sun. Many varieties are used in cooking, including 'Genovese', 'Mammoth', 'Purple Ruffles', 'Red Rubin', 'Siam Queen', and 'Sweet Basil'.

Dill is one of the largest herbs for the garden, reaching up to 4 feet, with airy crowns of tiny yellow flowers above feathery leaves.

Cilantro *(Coriandrum sativum)*, also known as coriander, fares best in spring and fall. The fernlike, foot-tall, fresh green foliage is used in many Mexican and Asian dishes.

Dill *(Anethum graveolens)* has willowy 4-foot stems. The feathery leaves can season soups, fish, poultry, and salad dressings. The dried seeds can also be used in pickling and vinegar.

Parsley *(Petroselinum crispum)* has deep green, either flat or curly leaves and grows in clumps to 2 feet tall. Curly types turn a rusty color in fall, and make good edging plants. 'Giant Italian', a flat type, is best for cooking; 'Extra Curled', 'Forest Green', and 'Moss Curled' are curly parsleys that make pretty garnishes and can be used in salads and casseroles.

Summer savory *(Satureja hortensis)* has a loose, open habit and grows to about 1½ feet tall. Its leaves can be used fresh to flavor meats, fish, eggs, soups, and vegetables.

Sweet marjoram *(Origanum majorana)* has oval, gray-green leaves on foot-tall plants that have a nice, rounded form. It may be perennial in the warmest zones. The flavor is like a sweeter version of the perennial herb oregano. Use sweet marjoram to flavor pastas and rice dishes, poultry, fish, meat, soups, stews, and vegetables.

When Sow seeds in place or plant from nursery six-packs after all danger of frost has passed.

Where Choose a site in full sun with average, well-drained soil. Annual herbs also grow well in containers.

How Amend the planting area with organic material such as compost before planting. Rake the area smooth and sprinkle on some controlled-release fertilizer. (If planting in containers, use a high-quality commercial potting mix; fertilizer is usually included in the mix.) Sow seeds about ¼ inch deep. Water well and keep the soil moist until plants germinate. Continue to sow seeds at 2-week intervals through the growing season. If planting from six-packs, first water the herbs in their containers, then dig planting holes larger than the plants' root balls, no more than 8 inches apart. Tip the containers on their sides to gently remove the transplants; use your thumb to push the root balls up from the bottom. Loosen the roots, then set each plant in a hole, making sure the top of the root ball is even with the surrounding soil surface. Firm the soil around the roots and water well.

TLC Thin seedlings to 6 to 8 inches apart. Mulch with 2 inches of chopped leaves, grass clippings, or other fine-textured organic material. Water well, especially in dry weather. Fertilize every 2 weeks with a water-soluble fertilizer. Pinch off the growing tips of basil, cilantro, and summer savory to keep plants bushy.

Harvest Snip off leaves with scissors or clippers rather than pulling on the plant. When plants go to seed, allow the seed heads to dry on the plant; then gather and save seeds to sow the following year.

TOP TO BOTTOM: *Slow-bolting cilantro, flat Italian parsley, and sweet basil just starting to flower.*

Herbs, Perennial

We usually think of herbs as members of the kitchen garden, but thanks to their good form, beautiful and fragrant foliage and bountiful flowers, they also make fine additions to ornamental beds and borders.

Most of these herbs evolved to survive drought by producing aromatic oils that seal in moisture; these oils are what give the leaves their distinctive flavors. Some perennial herbs form a shrubby framework over time; others are herbaceous and die down in the winter months, then grow anew in spring. In cold zones, grow these herbs as annuals or as container plants.

PEAK SEASON

Herbs are at their prime during the summer, although some may be harvested year-round in mild climates.

OUR FAVORITES

Chives (*Allium schoenoprasum;* zones 1–7, 17) have clumps of grasslike leaves 8 inches to 1 foot tall, topped with rose-purple or white puffball flowers in spring. Plants may die back in winter. Sprinkle cut leaves on casseroles, potatoes, eggs, and cheese dishes to add a mild onionlike flavor.

Refreshing mint (*Mentha*) can thrive in your garden—or take over if you don't restrain its roots in containers. Varieties include peppermint, spearmint, and orange, apple, ginger, and chocolate mint; heights vary from 6 inches to 1 foot. Most grow in zones 3–7, 17; peppermint and spearmint will grow in all zones. Use mint to flavor iced drinks. salads, or to season stews and lamb dishes. Mint prefers to grow in moist soil.

Oregano (*Origanum;* zones 4–7, 17) is a shrubby plant, growing 2 to 3 feet tall, with 1½-inch-long leaves. The best culinary variety for the Northwest is Greek oregano (*O. vulgare hirtum*), which has mild-tasting, bright green leaves. Use oregano to flavor Italian

Ornamental herbs mingle in and out of the kitchen garden. Shown here are golden oregano, variegated ginger mint, and golden variegated sage.

dishes, stews, sauces, soups, and vegetable dishes.

Rosemary *(Rosmarinus officinalis;* zones 4–7, 17) has woody stems packed with short, needlelike evergreen leaves with grayish white undersides. Old specimens can grow to 5 feet tall. Flowers are blue or light purple. The best varieties for the Northwest are 'Blue Spires', 'Tuscan Blue', and 'Arp' ('Arp' is hardy to −10°F/−23°C). Rosemary adds a strong, pungent flavor to breads, dressings, meat, poultry, stuffing, stews, and vegetables.

Sage *(Salvia officinalis;* zones 2–7, 17) is a 3-foot-tall shrub with velvety, 2- to 3-inch-long gray-green leaves, often variegated; other leaf colors are also sold. The spikelike flower clusters are very showy. The best culinary varieties are 'Berggarten', 'Icterina', and 'Purpurascens'. Sage's strong, savory flavor is good for stuffings, marinades, gravies, breads, and many other dishes.

Thyme *(Thymus;* zones 1–7, 17) has tiny, pungent leaves growing on stems no longer than 1 foot. White, lilac, red, or purple flowers appear in late spring and summer. Varieties include common thyme *(T. vulgaris),* green-leafed lemon thyme *(T. × citriodorus),* and gold-leafed lemon thyme *(T. × c. 'Aureus').* Use in bouquets garnis, breads, eggs, fish, meats, soups, tomato-based sauces, and vegetables.

When Plant herbs from nursery containers in spring, after the last frost.

CLOCKWISE FROM LEFT: *'Tuscan Blue' rosemary, 'Aureum' oregano (Origanum vulgare 'Aureum'), and 'Tricolor' sage.*

Where All herbs enjoy full sun; mint will grow in sun or shade. Most herbs like a poor to average, well-drained soil; mint prefers a moister, richer soil, as do chives. Thyme, sage, and oregano can be tucked into rock gardens; rosemary, sage, dill, and chives can be incorporated into borders. All do well in containers filled with a high-quality potting mix.

How Water the plants in their nursery containers before planting. Dig each planting hole as deep as the plant's root ball and twice as wide. Gently remove the plant from its container, loosen its roots, and place it in the hole. Fill in with soil and press down around the plant. Water and keep the ground moist until plants are established.

TLC Most herbs thrive on neglect. Don't water them too often, but when you do, give them a thorough soaking. Cut back herbs in spring to encourage new growth. Dig up and divide chives when they become overgrown, then replant the divisions.

Harvest Pinch or cut leaves as needed for cooking or bouquets garnis. Regular harvesting will keep plants bushy, as will removing spent flower heads.

255

Peas

There's something about growing peas that is just plain fun. The tender shoots scramble happily up any nearby support—a trellis, bamboo poles, string, or even a row of sticks. Then the shell-shaped white flowers emerge, attracting bees and butterflies. Finally, it's satisfying to hunt amid the foliage for the ripe, juicy pods and nibble them fresh off the vine.

ABOVE: *'Sugar Snap' peas hang from the vine.* RIGHT, OPPOSITE PAGE: *Peas ripening amidst annual poppies.*

A cool-weather crop like lettuce, garden peas will even withstand light frosts. Some are old-fashioned kinds for shelling, some (known as snow peas or sugar peas) have edible pods, and others can be relished either way. This third group, called snap peas, has thick, fleshy pods that stay crisp until the peas inside are developed. Peas may be bush types (rarely more than 2½ feet tall) or vining, and early, midseason, or late ripening.

Peas are at their sugary peak the moment you pick them. Eat them raw, throw them in the salad bowl, or sauté or steam them lightly to preserve their crunchy sweetness.

PEAK SEASON

Peas ripen in late spring.

OUR FAVORITES

Shelling types include 'Alaska', a bush type that matures in less than two months, and 'Maestro' and 'Dual', both bush types with double pods.

Both 'Oregon Giant' and 'Oregon Sugar Pod II' are bush types with flat, edible pods that can be harvested when young.

'Sugar Snap' and 'Super Sugar Snap' are extra-sweet vining snap peas. 'Sugar Ann' and the stringless 'Sugar Sprint' are bush types. 'Mega', also a bush type, handles both colder and hotter weather better than many other snap peas.

When Peas need 3 months of growing time before the first frost. They also need cool soil and air temperatures. In the coastal Northwest, sow peas in August for a fall crop, or plant in spring as soon as the ground can be worked (usually in March or April). In cold areas, sow in spring as soon as the ground can be worked.

Where Like most vegetables, peas need a good 6 hours of sun per day. They also do best in fertile, well-drained soil.

How Amend the planting bed with organic material. Sow seeds 1 to 1½ inches deep, 1 to 2 inches apart. Cover them with soil and water well. The seeds will germinate in a week to 10 days. You may need to help the tendrils of young peas twine around the supports.

ABOVE: *The edible pods of 'Oregon Giant' snow pea are ready to harvest just as the peas inside are starting to swell.*

TLC Water deeply to keep the soil evenly moist. Peas are light feeders. If your soil is good you don't need to fertilize; otherwise use a liquid organic fertilizer or, if your soil is alkaline, a high-phosphorus fertilizer. As the plants grow, mulch with 2 inches of chopped leaves, grass clippings, or other fine-textured organic material. If powdery mildew is a problem in your area, plant resistant varieties. To fend off soilborne diseases, plant peas in a different bed every year.

Harvest Snow peas should be harvested when the peas inside are just starting to swell. Shelling peas should be harvested when the peas make definite, large ridges on the pod but before the bright green color starts to fade. Harvest snap peas anytime. Don't tug on the pod to remove it; grasp the vine in one hand and pinch off the pod with the other.

Salad Greens

In the mild Northwest, you can grow fresh greens for much of the year—and we've come a long way from the flavorless, colorless lettuce balls of old. Now there are varieties of salad greens with flavors that range from mild to spicy, with beautifully ruffled leaves in colors ranging from burgundy to chartreuse.

Many kinds of loose-leaf lettuce are called "cut-and-come-again" crops, because they put out fresh leaves after being snipped for salads. Grow them in baskets for hanging salad bars.

Unlike many other edible plants, lettuces prefer cool, moist conditions (when it gets too hot, they "bolt," or send up flowering stalks). In hot-

This combination of red leaf, romaine, and green leaf lettuces shows how pretty greens can be in the garden. Use them to edge beds or to fill hanging baskets of edibles.

summer areas, look for slow-bolt varieties. When winter weather threatens, you can easily grow lettuce in a glass or plastic cold frame.

Unfortunately, slugs, snails, and earwigs love to hide in the cool damp and nibble on your greens. If these pests are troublesome, plant greens in raised beds edged with copper tape (available at garden-supply stores) or even in half-barrels or window boxes.

PEAK SEASON

Salad greens can be harvested from early spring to first frost.

OUR FAVORITES

Arugula, also called rocket, is an easy-to-grow green with spicy, dark green leaves that can be harvested when young.

Mustard can be grown well into early winter; the aromatic leaves are used in salads and stir-fries. Likewise, the rainbow-colored leaves and stems of 'Bright Lights' Swiss chard.

'Buttercrunch' lettuce has a tightly folded, compact head of tender, buttery green leaves. Romaine-type 'Outredgeous' lettuce has elongated, dark red leaves. 'Red Sails' lettuce has loosely held, crinkly red-and-green leaves. 'Salad Bowl' and 'Red Salad Bowl' are slow-bolting loose-leaf lettuces with deeply lobed leaves.

When Salad greens like the cool, sunny conditions of spring and fall. Start successive sowings every 10 days as soon as the soil can be worked (as early as a month before the last frost date), then again in late summer for a fall crop. Or set out starts from six-packs in early spring and again in fall.

Where Plant in sun to part-shade in fertile, slightly acidic soil that drains well. Lettuce also grows well in containers.

How Prepare the planting bed by adding plenty of organic matter. For containers, use a commercial planting mix formulated for edibles. If planting seeds, smooth the soil, scatter the seeds on the surface, and press them lightly into the soil. If planting from six-packs, first water the plants in their containers. Dig planting holes larger than the plants' root balls, no more than 8 inches apart. Tip the containers on their sides to gently remove the transplants; use your thumb to push the root balls up from the bottom. Loosen the roots, then set each plant in a hole, making sure the top of the root ball is even with the surrounding soil surface. Firm the soil around the roots and water well.

TLC All salad greens require regular, plentiful moisture during their growing season; fortunately, nature often provides it during the spring and fall months. Keep the bed weeded, but be careful not to damage the plants' roots. Feed every 2 weeks with a high-nitrogen liquid fertilizer. Control slugs, snails, and earwigs.

Harvest Begin to harvest leaves as soon as they are large enough for salads or cooking. Once hot summer weather arrives, most lettuces will bolt and can be pulled up and discarded.

ABOVE: 'Red Salad Bowl' lettuce.
LEFT: A raised bed is planted with edible Johnny-jump-ups and butter lettuce.

Squashes and Melons

Growers are developing early-ripening watermelons for the Northwest; this one is 'Rainbow Sherbert', an "icebox" type that ripens in as little as 68 days.

This diverse group includes winter and summer squash, pumpkins, melons, and watermelons—but whether sweet or savory, summer- or fall-harvested, they share certain similarities: sprawling vines that need plenty of room, fruits with juicy flesh and plentiful seeds, and a bountiful harvest for very little effort. Many can be stored for months, canned, or pickled.

These plants' needs are simple: regular water, rich soil, and time to reach maturity. They're great crops to grow organically, by enriching the soil with composted manure or your own homemade compost.

PEAK SEASON

Squashes and melons ripen from midsummer to fall. Seed packets indicate the number of days from planting to harvest.

OUR FAVORITES

Summer Squash

Types include the familiar zucchini; crookneck and straightneck squash; and flat, scallop-edged (pattypan) types. Harvest about 50 days after planting and eat while still tender.

Two longtime favorite zucchinis are 'Black Beauty' (with dark green skin) and 'Gold Rush' (with yellow, waxy fruits and creamy flesh), both of which grow to 8 inches long. For small spaces, try 'Eight Ball' (a bush-type zucchini with dark 3-inch balls) and 'Scallop' (a white pattypan).

Winter Squash

Types include acorn, delicata, butternut, and Hubbard. They are typically harvested late (after about 100 days), and have hard inedible shells.

'Cornell's Bush Delicata' is a compact grower with peanut-shaped, 8-inch-long fruits with cream-and-green-striped skin and light orange flesh. 'Waltham Butternut' has 8-inch-long fruits with beige skin and orange flesh. Both can be eaten young or stored through winter. 'Blue Hubbard', up to 15 inches long, has an unusual bumpy, grayish green shell with bright yellow, sweet flesh. It keeps well.

'Sunny Delight' is a scallop-edged type with bright yellow fruits. It's harvested as a baby vegetable (after 40 days).

Pumpkins

Use pumpkins for jack-o'-lanterns or in pies and other baked goods. They ripen in about 100 days.

Among the best for pies is 'Small Sugar' (a 6- to 8-inch-round heirloom). For decorating and carving, try 'Lumina' (8 to 10 inches round with white skin) or 'Jack-o'-Lantern' (somewhat elongated orange fruit to 8 inches wide and 10 inches tall). Miniature 'Jack Be Little' (2 inches tall by 3 inches wide, with orange skin that stays firm for months after harvest) is used for decoration or carved out as a bowl.

Melons and Watermelons

These fruits enjoy hot summers and are harvested in late summer and fall.

Cantaloupes 'Hale's Best', a longtime favorite, and 'Earligold' are both 6 to 7 inches wide with aromatic sweet, orange flesh. They ripen in 80 days. 'Earlidew' honeydew has 4- to 6-inch fruits with smooth skin and sweet green flesh; it ripens in 75 days.

'Crimson Sweet' watermelon is nearly spherical, 10 by 12 inches around, with crisp flesh; it ripens in 85 days. 'Sugar Baby' is 6 to 8 inches around, with sweet, red, nearly seedless flesh; it ripens in 75 days.

When Plant seedlings or sow seeds directly in the ground after all danger of frost has passed.

Where Squashes and melons need all-day sun, plenty of water, and a rich, moisture-retentive soil. Small-fruited vining types can be grown in large containers. Grow the bigger squashes and melons in a large patch where there's no competition for sun and nutrients.

How Loosen the soil to a depth of 10 to 12 inches and work in compost or other organic matter. Mix in a controlled-release fertilizer before planting. Sow seeds according to package directions or plant seedlings 3 to 5 feet apart, depending on type. Water well. Keep soil moist until seeds germinate.

TLC Squashes and melons need a regular supply of water. Once plants are established, mulch soil with 2 inches of chopped leaves, grass clippings, or other fine-textured organic material. These plants are heavy feeders, so once a month give them a balanced liquid fertilizer formulated for edible plants.

Harvest Cut summer squashes off the stems while they're still young and tender. Winter squashes and pumpkins must be fully mature before harvesting. Cut with an inch of stem and store in a cool place (55°F/13°C). For watermelons, the time-honored test for ripeness is a dull sound when you rap them with your knuckles; the undersides will also have begun to turn yellowish. Harvest watermelons by cutting them from the vine. Other melons are ripe when stems begin to turn yellow and fruits pull easily from vines.

BELOW: *Zucchini bear prodigiously—so heavily that gardeners often end up with too much fruit. Consider picking the blossoms before fruits form, then stuffing and baking them.*

*Squashes and pumpkins grow in all zones; melons in zones 2–7, 17; and watermelons in zones 1–7, 17.

Stone Fruits

The delight of plucking a ripe plum off the tree, beating the birds to the juiciest cherries, or filling a basket with plump peaches is ample reward for planting stone fruits (so called due to their central, single pit). Even small gardens can accommodate stone fruits: peaches are natural semidwarfs, growing only 10 to 15 feet tall, and other types grown on dwarfing rootstocks will stay under 10 feet. The shortest trees are also easier to harvest and to cover with netting if the birds are competing with you for the fruit. For courtyards and other tiny spaces, try a multiple-variety dwarf tree.

Sweet cherries are early-blooming trees that are not suited to the coldest climates; sour cherries are hardier. Peaches and nectarines thrive especially well in warm areas east of the Cascades, and many plums are great choices in most of the Northwest.

Stone fruits are not truly low maintenance plants; you will have to spray appropriately for pests and diseases, thin the fruit as needed, and prune to create a good framework of fruiting branches (especially for newly planted trees). But you'll be well rewarded when you savor the fruits of your labor.

After 3 or 4 years, stone fruit trees start to bear plenty of fruit, sometimes all at once. That's why crops such as these plums are popular for jam making and canning.

PEAK SEASON

Stone fruits ripen in July and August.

OUR FAVORITES

Cherries

Gardeners east of the Cascades can grow the popular 'Bing' and 'Rainier' sweet cherries, but you'll need one of each so they can pollinate each other. 'Bing' has large, dark red, meaty fruit, and 'Rainier' has yellow skin with a pink blush. Both ripen in midseason. Self-fertile varieties that can be grown throughout the Northwest include 'Lapins' (early to midseason, heavy-bearing, crack-resistant, dark red, sweet cherry); 'Surefire' and 'Meteor' are both heavy-bearing sour cherries with fire engine red fruit that can be eaten fresh or baked in pies. They flower late, so the crop isn't harmed by late spring frosts). Sweet cherries grow in zones 2, 6–7; sour types in zones A2, A3; 1–7, 17.

Peaches

West of the Cascades, select a variety that is resistant to peach leaf curl, such as 'Frost' (zones 3–7; mid- to late season, self-fertile, with yellow skin and flesh and tangy flavor) or 'New Haven' (zones 1–7; also mid- to late season and self-fertile, with red-blushed yellow skin). East of the Cascades, try 'Redhaven' (zones 3–5; early, self-fertile, with yellow skin). 'Mericrest' (zones 1–3) is a hardy, midseason nectarine with red skins.

When Plant trees bare-root in winter, or from nursery containers in the fall.

Where Stone fruits need full sun and well-drained soil.

How Water trees in their nursery containers, or soak bare-root plants for an hour. Dig planting holes slightly deeper and wider than the tree's root system. Gently tip the root ball from the container and loosen the roots. Set the plant in the hole, with the top of the root ball (or the graft union of a bare-root plant) slightly higher than the surrounding soil. Re-fill the hole, firming the soil and mounding it slightly. Water thoroughly. Spread 2 inches of mulch around the tree but not directly against the trunk. Keep the soil moist until the tree is well established.

TLC Stone fruits require regular fertilizing. Thin when fruit is small. With cherries, rake your fingers along the of the clusters, taking off roughly half the fruit. With other stone fruits, snip or pull off individual fruits, leaving 2 to 4 inches between the ones that remain. Prune young trees when dormant to create a vase-shaped limb structure. As trees mature, also thin out overlapping branches. Avoid "heading" (cutting branches back partway); this encourages non-productive growth. Spray dormant trees as needed to protect against fungal diseases.

Harvest After three or four years, trees will bear plenty of fruit, all at once. Share the bounty with friends, or try some jam making and canning.

ABOVE: *Sweet 'Redhaven' peach bears heavily over a long period.*

Plums

The two most widely grown types of plums are European and Japanese. European plums bloom later and are better adapted to areas with late spring frosts or cool, rainy spring weather; they also have a moderately high chill need. Many varieties of both types are self-fertile. 'Damson' (zones 2–7, 17) is a late-season, self-fertile European plum with purple skin and tart green flesh; it's good for canning and drying to make prunes. 'Opal' (zones A1, A2; 1–3) is similar but early ripening, with a sweeter flavor. The Japanese plum 'Methley' (zones 2–7), also early and self-fertile, sets a large crop of medium-size fruit with reddish purple skin.

Tomatoes

If you grow no other edible plant, you should grow tomatoes. The reason is simple: taste. The tomatoes you purchase in the supermarket may look pretty, but tomatoes grown at home are the real deal—sweet, tender, juicy, and flavorful.

Of the hundreds of varieties available, which ones should you grow? It depends. Do you want bite-size tomatoes to pluck and eat like berries? Do you live by the foggy coast or in a hot inland valley and need a tomato that can take extreme conditions? Do you plan to try your hand at drying or canning? Whatever your requirements, you can find tried-and-true varieties that score high points for fruit production and taste and are reasonably trouble free. Once you've started growing tomatoes, however, you may venture into more exotic realms, planting tomatoes that are pink, purple, yellow, orange, or even striped.

So-called determinate tomatoes are bushy and compact; they seldom need staking. They produce one large crop, then die. Indeterminate plants are more vine-like, need staking, and bear for longer. Tomatoes won't set fruit unless the temperature is just right, so choose varieties carefully.

'Sun Gold' tomatoes and other small-fruited types are perfect for growing in pots—but the containers must be large enough to accommodate the plants' extensive roots.

PEAK SEASON

Tomatoes ripen from midsummer through fall.

OUR FAVORITES

For coastal areas, it's important to choose quick-ripening tomatoes. Try 'Fourth of July' (indeterminate, with clusters of sweet, small, juicy fruits); 'Oregon Spring' (determinate, with large, fleshy, full-flavored fruits); 'Stupice' (indeterminate, with firm, medium-size red fruits); and mild-flavored 'Willamette' (determinate, with medium-size, meaty fruits).

For hot inland areas, two favorites are 'Beefsteak' (indeterminate, with large, tasty red fruits) and 'Brandywine' (indeterminate heirloom, with big pink fruits perfect for slicing).

In the North, try 'Bush Early Girl' (determinate, with huge yields of sweet-tart fruits on compact plants) or 'Siberia' (determinate; will set fruit when night temperatures are low).

Sweet, small-fruited types such as yellow 'Gold Nugget', 'Yellow Pear', and 'Sun Gold' and red 'Sweet 100' are suitable for any region. All are indeterminate except 'Gold Nugget'.

Paste tomatoes are best for drying and sauce making. Two that will do well throughout the Northwest are sweet-flavored 'San Marzano' (indeterminate) and 'Viva Italia' (determinate).

When Plant tomatoes in late spring to early summer—when soil has warmed and all danger of frost is past. To extend your harvest, plant seedlings at 3-week intervals.

'Oregon Pride' tomatoes (left) and 'Early Girl' (right) are both early-ripening varieties.

Where Tomatoes have deep roots, so plant them in deeply tilled, fast-draining soil that's rich in organic matter. They need full sun and plenty of room to grow.

How Amend planting bed with organic material. Water plants in their nursery containers. Dig planting holes 2 feet apart for determinate varieties and 3 feet apart for indeterminate ones. Place a controlled-release fertilizer in the planting holes according to the package directions. Pinch lower leaves off the tomato stems and bury seedlings halfway in the ground—the stems will send out extra roots. Don't wait for tomatoes to grow before installing your trellis, fence, or wire cages; do it now, so that you can train the plants as they grow.

TLC Fertilize lightly at 2-week intervals after the first blossoms set. Use a low-nitrogen fertilizer such as fish emulsion; too much nitrogen will encourage foliage growth at the expense of fruit. Water consistently and deeply, trying not to splash leaves; damp foliage can encourage late blight. In cool-summer climates, where tomatoes often don't get enough heat for the fruit to ripen, you can prune some foliage off the plants to let some sun in.

Harvest Let tomatoes ripen on the plant, or pick as soon as fruit starts to color, then place on a windowsill to ripen. If you have a bumper crop of unripe fruit and frost threatens, the green fruits are delicious breaded and fried in oil.

Northwest Climate Zones

It can't be said often enough: Successful gardening depends on choosing the right plant for the right place. Our Top 10 plants are among the most reliable performers for Northwest gardens, but that doesn't mean each of them will thrive in every corner of our region. After all, Fairbanks, Alaska, is over 1,800 miles north of Medford, Oregon; Port Angeles, Washington, is located 32 feet above sea level, compared to 2,000 feet for Spokane, Washington; and whereas Kelowna, British Columbia, receives only 11 inches of annual precipitation, Vancouver, British Columbia, gets nearly 50 inches.

We divide the Northwest into 10 broad climate zones (and Alaska into a further three). This book then assigns climate zones to every listed plant. The most important limiting factor for permanent plants (like trees, shrubs, and perennials) is extreme winter cold. For annual vegetables and long-season fruit trees, success depends on heat and the length of the growing season. Zone 5, for instance, has a long growing season, but it's not very warm in summer, so fruit may not ripen. The most favorable climates for growing the widest variety of plants are those that combine a long growing season, warm summers, and mild winters.

Significant differences exist even within single climate zones. The following chart shows some of the variations in temperature, precipitation, and the length of growing season for each zone. You can get more information on your climate from your Cooperative Extension Office and local horticultural societies.

ZONE	SUMMER	WINTER		GROWING SEASON	PRECIPITATION
	Average high	Average low	Ten-year lows	Days between freezes	Inches of rain and snow
1A	80 to 87°F (27 to 31°C)	0 to 20°F (−18 to −7°C)	−18 to −35°F (−28 to −38°C)	50 to 100	9 to 82 (19 average)
2A	82 to 89°F (28 to 32°C)	10 to 20°F (−12 to −7°C)	−20 to −30°F (−29 to −34°C)	100 to 133	10 to 25
2B	84 to 89°F (29 to 32°C)	18 to 23°F (−8 to −5°C)	−10 to −21°F (−23 to −29°C)	135 to 180	9 to 19
3A	81 to 92°F (27 to 33°C)	24 to 27°F (−4 to −3°C)	−5 to −18°F (−21 to −28°C)	151 to 190	9 to 30
3B	85 to 91°F (29 to 33°C)	22 to 28°F (−6 to −2°C)	−5 to −15°F (−21 to −26°C)	92 to 223	8 to 19

chart continues ▶

1A
2A
2B
3A
3B
4
5
6
7
17

Campbell River

4

4

Nanaimo

5

1A

Victoria

5

Forks

Port Angeles

Vancouver

4

Hope

Fraser River

Bellingham

1A

Everett

4

Seattle

5

5

Hoquiam

Tacoma

Olympia

4

Long Beach

5

Longview

Astoria

Portland

4

Lincoln City

5

4

Eugene

Reedsport

Coos Bay

4

Roseburg

Rogue River

Gold Beach

1A

Grants Pass

7

Medford

17

Kelowna

2A

2A

Creston

2B

Sandpoint

Omak

2A

3B

Wenatchee

2B

Spokane

Coeur d'Alene

2A

Moses Lake

Ellensburg

2B

Yakima

3B

3A

Tri-Cities

2B

3B

Lewiston

3A

2A

Walla Walla

2B

Okanogan River

Columbia River

Hood River

3A

The Dalles

3B

Pendleton

3A

2A

2B

La Grande

Snake River

Baker

2A

Salem

6

Bend

2B

Boise

Burns

3A

1A

Willamette River

Klamath Falls

2A

ZONE	SUMMER	WINTER		GROWING SEASON	PRECIPITATION
	Average high	Average low	Ten-year lows	Days between freezes	Inches of rain and snow
4	71 to 79°F (22 to 26°C) (64°F/18°C in Alaska)	30 to 34°F (−1 to 1°C)	8 to 0°F (−13 to −18°C)	165 to 200	32 to 69
5	65 to 77°F (19 to 25°C)	34 to 37°F (1 to 3°C)	17 to 5°F (−8 to −15°C)	200 to 257	21 to 91 (49 average)
6	79 to 83°F (26 to 28°C)	30 to 36°F (−1 to 2°C)	9 to 0°F (−13 to −18°C)	149 to 225	34 to 54
7	86 to 90°F (30 to 32°C)	21 to 32°F (−6 to 0°C)	10 to −2°F (−12 to −19°C)	150 to 175	19 to 61 (34 average)
17	68°F (20°C)	40 to 41°F (4 to 5°C)	24 to 20°F (−4 to −7°C)	278 to 365	78 to 81
A1	68 to 73°F (20 to 23°C)	−28 to −18°F (−33 to −28°C)	−58 to −68°F (−50 to −56°C)	85 to 115 (90 average)	7 to 17
A2	62 to 65°F (17 to 19°C)	3 to 8°F (−16 to −13°C)	−30 to −45°F (−34 to −43°C)	105 to 138	15 to 19
A3	61 to 68°F (16 to 20°C)	15 to 27°F (−9 to −3°C)	−9 to −20°F (−23 to −29°C)	122 to 152	26 to 150 (71 average)

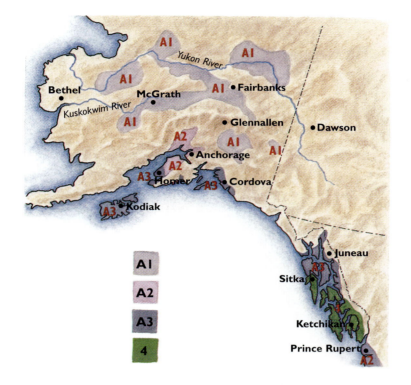

A1

A2

A3

4

Gardening up North

Even in the warmest parts of Alaska, the growing season is short. Nonetheless, the state is famous for vegetables that reach gigantic proportions (cabbages grown in the Matanuska Valley just north of Anchorage can weigh as much as 100 pounds). Why is this? The answer lies in the day length: up to 20 or more hours of light per day coaxes plants into robust growth. The long days have other, unexpected consequences as well. Some annuals and biennials bolt (flower and set seed) before the plant has fully matured, making them good only for the compost pile.

Short day length is not the only challenge. As Patricia Holloway of University of Alaska at Fairbanks has said, "Move to Alaska's Great Interior, and join the ranks of the truly horticulturally challenged!" Extreme summer and winter temperatures, heavy snowfall, and minimal rain (not to mention slugs, moose, and other pests) all conspire to make gardening difficult. However, ingenious northerners have devised strategies to overcome these difficulties.

Choosing the correct planting spot makes a big difference in a northern garden. First of all, find the sunniest location possible. For annuals and edible plants, consider planting on a south-facing slope to maximize the angle of the sun's rays.

Alaskan soils are cold (averaging about 55°F/13°C at a depth of 4 inches), which reduces root growth and limits plants' ability to take up nutrients. You can create warmer growing conditions by planting in raised beds, or you can insulate the soil by mulching it with organic material or covering it with polyethylene. Finally, many northern gardeners start plants in greenhouses or on windowsills in late winter, then gradually move them into outdoor cold frames before planting in the ground in May.

Alaska's many fine Cooperative Extension Offices are constantly discovering new plants for growing in the far North. Take advantage of this expertise by visiting their trial gardens, reading their publications, or viewing the information on their Web sites.

Index Pages listed in *italics* include photographs.